FOURTH EDITION

MW01197005

WORLD LINK 4

DEVELOPING ENGLISH FLUENCY

JOHN HUGHES

NATIONAL
GEOGRAPHIC
LEARNING

Australia · Brazil · Canada · Mexico · Singapore · United Kingdom · United States

National Geographic Learning,
a Cengage Company

**World Link Level 4: Developing English Fluency,
Fourth Edition**

Publisher: Sherrise Roehr

Executive Editor: Sarah Kenney

Senior Development Editor: Margarita Matte

Director of Global Marketing: Ian Martin

Heads of Regional Marketing:

Charlotte Ellis (Europe, Middle East and Africa)

Irina Pereyra (Latin America)

Senior Product Marketing Manager:

Caitlin Thomas

Content Project Manager: Beth Houston

Media Researcher: Stephanie Eenigenburg

Cover/Text Design: Lisa Trager

Art Director: Brenda Carmichael

Operations Support: Hayley Chwazik-Gee,

Avi Mednick, Katie Lee

Manufacturing Planner: Mary Beth Hennebury

Composition: MPS North America LLC

Student's Book
ISBN: 978-0-357-50225-9
Student's Book + My World Link Online
ISBN: 978-0-357-50226-6

National Geographic Learning
200 Pier 4 Boulevard
Boston, MA 02210
USA

Locate your local office at **international.cengage.com/region**

Visit National Geographic Learning online at **ELTNGL.com**
Visit our corporate website at **www.cengage.com**

Printed in China
Print Number: 01 Print Year: 2020

Acknowledgments

Thank you to the educators who provided invaluable feedback throughout the development of the *World Link* series:

Asia

Michael Jake Arcilla, Aii Language Center, Phnom Penh; Fintan Brennan, Meisei University, Tokyo; Tyler Burden, Meisei University, Tokyo; Catherine Cheetham, Tokai University, Tokyo; Will Fan, Xiamen Wanda, Xiamen; Mark Firth, Oberlin University, Machida; Hiroshi Fukuda, Jumonji University, Niiza; Thomas Goetz, Hokusei Gakuen University, Sapporo; Helen Hanae, Reitaku University, Kashiwa; Louis Liu, Meten English, Shenzen; Shaun McLewin, Hanseo University, Seosan; Raymond Monk Jr., Meten English, Dalian; Donald Patterson, Seirei Christopher University, Hamamatsu City; Mongkol Sodachan, Rangsit University, Pathum Thani; Robert Wright, Meten English, Chengdu; Elvira Wu, Meten English, Quanzhou; I-Cheng Wu, Southern Taiwan University of Science and Technology, Tainan City; Xie Yu, SFLEP, Shanghai; Vince Zhang, Thinktown, Hangzhou; Vivi Zhang, Xiamen Wanda, Xiamen

Latin America

Anthony Acevedo, ICPNA, Lima; Jorge Aguilar, Centro de Estudios de Idiomas UAS, Culiacan; Lidia Stella Aja, Centro Cultural Colombo Americano, Cali; Ana Laura Alferez, Instituto Domingo Savio, Mexico City; Lúcia Rodrigues Alves, Seven, Sao Paulo; Alessandra Atarcsay, WOWL Education, Rio de Janeiro; Isabella Campos Alvim, IBEU Copacabana, Rio de Janeiro; Ana Berg, Ana Berg EFL School, Rio de Janeiro; Raul Billini, Santo Domingo; Isabela Villas Boas, Casa Thomas Jefferson, Brasilia; Lourdes Camarillo, Escuela Bancaria Comercial, Mexico City; Cinthia Castañeda, Centro de Idiomas, Coatzacoalcos; Enrique Chapuz, Universidad Veracruzana, Coatzacoalcos; Giseh Cuesta, MESCyT, Mexico City; Carlos Fernández, ICPNA, Lima; Vania Furtado, IBEU Copacabana, Rio de Janeiro; Mariana Garcia, BUAP, Puebla; Jeanette Bravo Garonce, IPA Idiomas, Brasilia; Luiz Henrique Bravo Garonce, IPA Idiomas, Brasilia; Fily Hernandez, Universidad Veracruzana, Coatzacoalcos; Manuel Hidalgo Iglesias, Escuela Bancaria Comercial, Mexico City; Dafna Ilian, ESIME, Azcapotzalco; Rubén Jacome, Universidad Veracruzana, Coatzacoalcos; Beatriz Jorge, Alumni, Sao Paulo; Gledis Libert, ICDA, Santo Domingo; Rocio Liceaga, International House, Mexico City; Elizabeth Palacios, ICPNA, Lima; Emeli Borges Pereira Luz, UNICAMPI, Sao Paulo; Patricia McKay, CELLEP, Sao Paulo; Victor Hugo Medina, Cultura Inglesa Minas Gerais, Belo Horizonte; Maria Helena Meyes, ACBEU, Salvador; Isaias Pacheco, Universidad Veracruzana, Coatzacoalcos; Miguel Rodriguez, BUAP, Puebla; Nelly Romero, ICPNA, Lima; Yesenia Ruvalcaba, Universidad de Guadalajara, Guadalajara; Eva Sanchez, BUAP, Puebla; Marina Sánchez, Instituto Domingo Savio, Mexico City; Thais Scharfenberg, Centro Europeu, Curitiba; Pilar Sotelo, ICPNA, Lima; Rubén Uceta, Centro Cultural Domínico Americano, Santiago De Los Caballeros; Italia Vergara, American English Overseas Center, Panama City; Maria Victoria Guinle Vivacqua, UNICAMP, Sao Paulo

United States and Canada

Bobbi Plante, Manitoba Institute of Trades and Technology, Winnipeg; Richard McDorman, Language On Schools, Miami, FL; Luba Nesteroba, Bilingual Education Institute, Houston, TX; Tracey Partin, Valencia College, Orlando, FL

SCOPE AND SEQUENCE

PRONUNCIATION	SPEAKING	READING	WRITING	ACTIVE ENGLISH	ACADEMIC SKILL	GLOBAL VOICES
Pausing in non-defining relative clauses p. 7	Talking about your weekend; Omitting words p. 6	Can Millennials Unplug in the Parks? p. 10	An opinion paragraph p. 14	Talk about communities p. 8 Describe trends p. 14	Understanding words from context p. 11 Note-taking p. 12	K. David Harrison: Talking Dictionaries p. 15
Stressed syllables p. 23	Ways of agreeing p. 20 Interviewing someone p. 28	Blood, Sweat, and Sequins p. 24	A cover letter p. 28	Talk about work p. 22 Talk about skills and qualities p. 28	Key words p. 26 Open / Closed questions p. 28	Hannah Reyes Morales: Overcoming Challenges p. 29
Stress and pausing in formal speech p. 40	Collaborating p. 34	What Makes You Creative? p. 38	A biography p. 42	Talk about bad habits p. 36 Talk about problem solving p. 42	Using time references p. 42	Jennifer Adler, Sylvia Johnson, Gabby Salazar: Getting Creative p. 43
Contracted forms 1 p. 57	Using fillers p. 50 Asking and explaining how something works p. 50 Describing imaginary situations p. 57	Fact and Fiction in Photos p. 54	A news article p. 58	Talk about online guidelines p. 52 Talk about a newspaper report p. 58	Inferring meaning from context p. 49	Alex Sigrist: Advice to My Younger Self p. 59
Linking (consonant + vowel) p. 67	Hedging p. 64 Giving advice on exam preparation p. 72	Learning the Language of Comedy p. 68	A reflective learning journal p. 72	Talk about memory techniques p. 66 Talk about exam preparation strategies p. 72	Key details p. 70	K. David Harrison, Aziz Abu Sarah, Laurel Chor, Victor Zea Díaz: Language Learning p. 73
Stressing adverbs in sentences p. 79	Repetition in the form of a question; Talking about a film you saw or book you read; Telling a story p. 78	The Journey to Thanjavur (an extract from the novel *The Tyre*) p. 82	A short story p. 86	Talk about a film p. 80 Tell a story p. 86	Improve your vocabulary p. 81 Descriptive language p. 83	Andrés Ruzo: My Grandfather's Stories p. 87

SCOPE AND SEQUENCE

PRONUNCIATION	SPEAKING	READING	WRITING	ACTIVE ENGLISH	ACADEMIC SKILL	GLOBAL VOICES
Intonation in passive reporting p. 101	Being precise; Finding out and getting clarification p. 94	Urban Planning p. 98	A report p. 102	Make guesses about objects p. 96 Present plans p. 102	Writing facts p. 102	T.H. Culhane: Domestic Dragons p. 103
Contracted forms *'ll* and *'ve* p. 109	Pointing something out p. 108	Why Do We Get Annoyed? Does Science Have an Answer? p. 112	A "for and against" essay p. 116	Talk about differences p. 110 Explain reasons p. 116	Supporting evidence p. 106 Referring to evidence p. 108	Robert Wood: The Impact of Miniature Robots p. 117
The schwa sound /ə/ p. 123	Linking words p. 122	Weird Animal Questions p. 126	A summary of data (based on survey results) p. 130	Talk about brags and bluffs p. 124 Talk about survey results p. 130	Understanding connotation p. 120	Ben Mirin: Inspired by Animal Voices and People p 131
Homophones p. 137	Speculating p. 138	When "Happy Birthday" Went to Court p. 142	An announcement p. 146	Talk about punishment p. 140 Talk about rules p. 146	Identifying reference words p. 143	Malaika Vaz: The Impact of Our Actions p. 147
Rising or falling intonation p. 159	Hedging in making a deal p. 152	The Etiquette of Eating p. 156	A letter of complaint p. 160	Talk about selling new products p. 154 Talk about complaints p. 160	Recording vocabulary p. 150	Alex Sigrizt: Small Changes p. 161
Linking sounds p. 172	Showing amazement p. 166	Women in Space p. 170	A speech p. 174	Talk about ads p. 168 Talk about controversial topics p. 174	Determiners p. 167	What's the Most Beautiful Thing You Have Ever Seen? p. 175

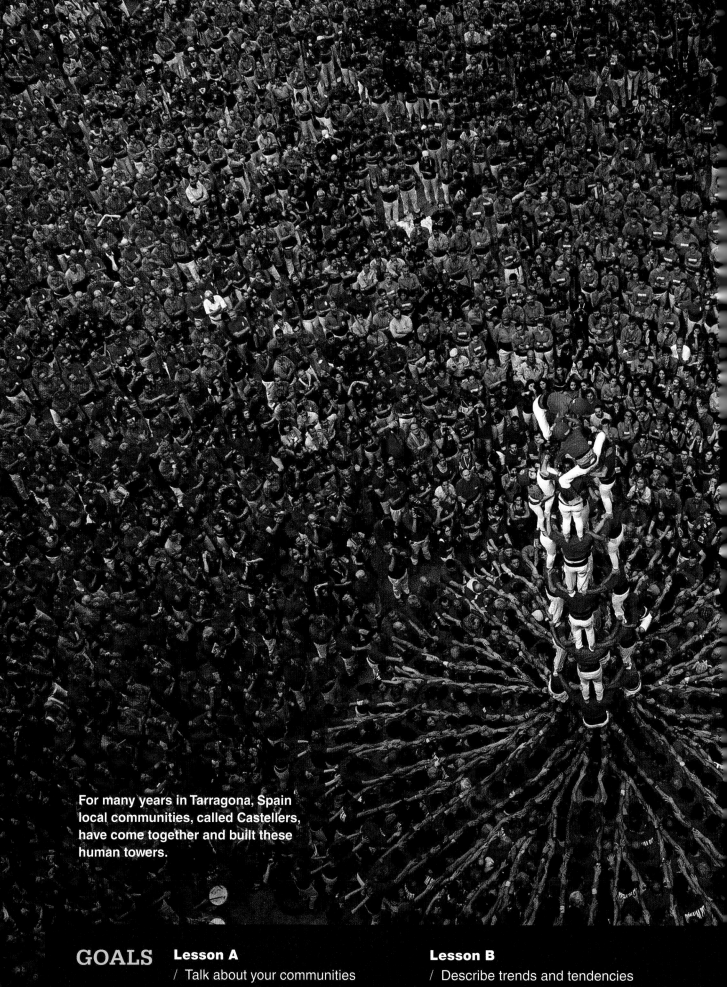

For many years in Tarragona, Spain local communities, called Castellers, have come together and built these human towers.

GOALS

Lesson A

/ Talk about your communities

/ Ask about free-time activities

Lesson B

/ Describe trends and tendencies

/ Argue for and against

1

COMMUNITY

LOOK AT THE PHOTO. ANSWER THE QUESTIONS.

1. Why do you think this type of activity is good for the local community?

2. When does your local community come together for a special event or activity?

WARM-UP VIDEO

A Do you ever play board games? When do you play them? If not, why?

B Watch the video. Check (✓) the reasons the people give for playing checkers.

☐ Making friendships

☐ Winning competitions

☐ Learning to communicate

☐ Taking a break from going online

☐ Carrying on traditions

C Watch the video again and complete these quotes.

1. "We know their family, we know their friends, we know what they do and how they _____ in _____."

2. "Checkers _____ back a camaraderie that you will never find _____ in life again."

3. "I do not have a _____ yet. I like to think that I'm waiting until I get good _____."

4. "He's a friend of mine, but on the _____, he wants to beat me bad. Of course, he gets _____ every now and then."

D Would you like to join the Checkers Club? How important is it to have local communities like this? Discuss as a class.

VOCABULARY

A Read the article and find out what the numbers in the circles mean. In general, do you think the numbers are true for you?

How large is your actual **circle of** friends? 5? 15? More than 150? According to one theory, humans can only **keep in touch** with a maximum **community** of 150 people at any one time. So, while you might have thousands of **so-called** friends from different **walks of life**, you only have something **in common** with around 150 of them. If you were planning a party, that number would be smaller—you'd invite about 50 friends and **acquaintances**. In the evenings and on the weekends, you probably **hang out with** about 15 on a regular basis. As for your **close-knit** family and friends—most of us can count these **meaningful** relationships on one hand.

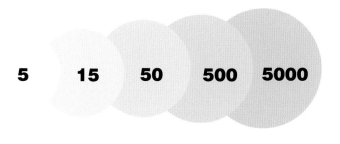

5   15   50   500   5000

B Match the words and phrases in blue with these meanings.

_____ **1.** a group of people

_____ **2.** the meaning is not really true

_____ **3.** different backgrounds

_____ **4.** connected by strong relationships

_____ **5.** shared with other people

_____ **6.** important and deep

_____ **7.** maintain contact

_____ **8.** close friends

_____ **9.** people you know, but not close friends

_____ **10.** spend free time with

C Work in pairs. Ask and answer these questions.

1. How large is your actual circle of friends?

2. Where do you meet acquaintances and people from different walks of life?

3. Do you think you are part of a close-knit community?

4. How do you keep in touch with all your family and friends?

5. Who is one person you have a meaningful relationship with?

D In pairs, discuss these topics and find at least five things you have in common with each other.

- family and friends
- TV, films, books, music
- local community
- sports and games
- use of social media
- work and education

" I have three brothers and two sisters.

Me, too. "

LISTENING

A Look at the photo and read the caption below. Have you ever worn costumes like these? Why do you think people attend events like Comic-Con?

B **Identify a speaker.** Listen to four interviews at a Comic-Con event. Match the speaker (1–4) to the statement. There is one extra statement. 🎧2

_____ a. This person fell in love at Comic-Con.

_____ b. It's a chance to meet up with old friends.

_____ c. You can meet famous people and complete strangers.

_____ d. All the latest computer games are available to try out.

_____ e. It's an opportunity to express yourself once a year.

C Listen again. Answer these questions. Circle _Yes_, _No_, or _Don't know_. 🎧2

1. Does Diego think that people are judged for who they are at Comic-Con?   Yes / No / Don't know

2. Do most of the people at Comic-Con come from similar backgrounds?   Yes / No / Don't know

3. Does Stella always come to the event with her close friends?   Yes / No / Don't know

4. Has someone taken Stella's photo this year?   Yes / No / Don't know

5. Is the computer game voice-over artist at the event?   Yes / No / Don't know

6. Does everyone wear a costume at Comic-Con?   Yes / No / Don't know

7. Did Rachel and Alan start talking in the cafe when they first met?   Yes / No / Don't know

8. Did they wear costumes at their wedding?   Yes / No / Don't know

D Work in pairs. Ask and answer these questions.

1. In your school or place of work, do you think people can be themselves or are they judged?

2. Are you a member of a particular community, club, or group? If so, are its members from similar backgrounds or do they come from different walks of life?

Comic-Con conventions around the world attract hundreds of thousands of people each year. They dress up as characters from their favorite books and movies and have the opportunity to meet some of the actors and authors. Shown below: London.

SPEAKING

A cosplayer dressed as Captain America arrives at New York Comic-Con.

A Shawna and Keith work in the same office. Listen to their conversation. Then answer the questions. 3

Shawna: Hi. How was your weekend? Do anything fun?

Keith: Yeah, I did. Actually, it's a bit embarrassing.

Shawna: Go on. Tell me!

Keith: Promise not to tell anyone who works in the office?

Shawna: I promise.

Keith: Well, a friend invited me to this event where everyone dressed up as comic book characters.

Shawna: Oh, you mean Comic-Con! It's a blast! Who did you go as?

Keith: Well, there was a group of us, so we all went as a superhero. I was Captain America.

Shawna: You're joking! I want to see photos!

Keith: I don't have many. This is a picture that shows us when we arrived.

Shawna: You look amazing. Who are all these other people with you?

Keith: They asked to have their photo taken with us. There were thousands of people there and everyone was so friendly. It was amazing!

Shawna: The next time you go, tell me!

1. Where did Keith go over the weekend?

2. Why do you think he doesn't want Shawna to tell anyone else?

B Practice the conversation with a partner.

C Work in pairs. Imagine you share an office. Choose one of these events and create a new conversation similar to the one in **A**. Include some of the useful expressions from the box.

1. costume party
2. a Carnival or Mardi Gras parade
3. a 70's party

D Get together with another pair.

Pair 1: Perform your conversation for the other pair.

Pair 2: Listen. Which useful expressions did you hear?

GRAMMAR

A Read the Unit 1, Lesson A Grammar Reference in the appendix. Complete the exercises. Then do the exercises below.

DEFINING RELATIVE CLAUSES			
	Main clause	**Relative clause**	
For things	This is a photo	**that**	shows my family.
For people	Don't tell anyone	**who**	works in the office.
For possession	I have a friend	**whose**	family is a group of musicians.
For places	It's an event	**where**	everyone dresses up.
For time	This was at the entrance	**when**	we arrived.
NON-DEFINING RELATIVE CLAUSES			
My brother, **who's an accountant,** loves going to Comic-Con. (I have one brother.)			
The whole performance was canceled, **which was really annoying**!			

B **PRONUNCIATION: Pausing** The commas are missing in these sentences with non-defining relative clauses. Listen to where the speaker pauses and write in the commas. Then listen again and repeat. 🎧6

1. I've invited over 50 people to my party which is probably enough.

2. Miles who is probably my best friend can't come to my wedding!

3. My father's company which he set up thirty years ago is closing down.

4. Independence Day which is on September 7th in my country is so much fun.

5. A so-called friend ate my sandwich which is really annoying!

C Work in pairs. First, individually write the names of an object, a famous person, and an annual event or celebration in your country. Then, write a definition for each one using a defining relative clause. Next, take turns reading your definitions aloud. Can your partner guess the words?

It's a thing that . . .   *It's a person who . . .*   *It's an event where / when . . .*

D Rewrite the description below. Make the description more natural and more interesting by adding new information using relative clauses.

For example: *On the weekend, a man, who had just started a new job, moved into a new apartment, that was . . .*

> *On the weekend, a man moved into a new apartment. He didn't know anyone in the building. His neighbors invited him to their party on the fifth floor. The party started at eight o'clock. He met lots of other people.*

E In groups, take turns reading your new descriptions. How many new relative clauses have your classmates added? Are they defining or non-defining?

ACTIVE ENGLISH Try it out!

A Read the text below and answer the questions.

1. What is the purpose of a Community Service Project? Who benefits?

2. How many relative clauses are there in the text? Underline them.

Developing a Community Service Project

Community service is work done by a person or group of people that benefits others. It is often done near an area where you live, so it's a great way to meet people from different walks of life and help your own community. The people who often benefit most include children and senior citizens—and, of course, you also benefit by helping others and gaining work experience. It's also a great way to make new friends. Here are six ideas for projects you could do:

a. Organize a car wash and donate the profit to a charity

b. Look after a neighbor's pet when they are away

c. Coach a youth sports team

d. Paint over graffiti

e. Go shopping for elderly people

f. Plant trees in your local park

B Work in pairs. Discuss and rank the community service projects in **A** in order of their usefulness (1 = most useful, 6 = least useful). Think of another project that you and your friends could do in your local area.

a. _____

b. _____

c. _____

d. _____

e. _____

f. _____

g. Another project

_____

C Work in groups. Imagine your English class has the opportunity to do a community service project and your school has offered its building for free.

1. Brainstorm ideas for different types of community service that would make good use of the school.

2. Choose the best idea and prepare a list of reasons why it's a useful community project.

D Present each of your ideas in **C** to the class. Vote on which project is the best idea.

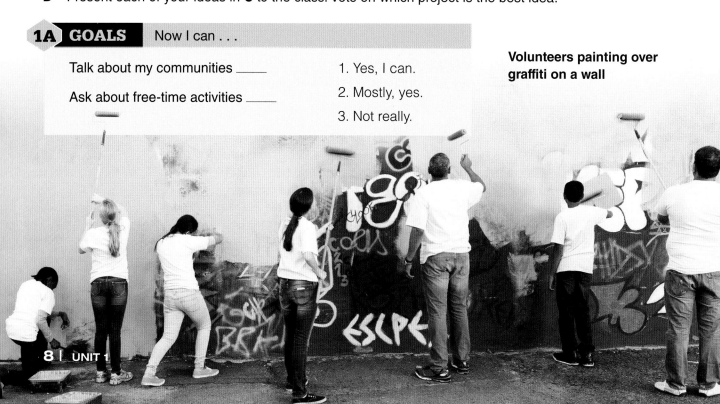

1A GOALS Now I can . . .

Talk about my communities _____

Ask about free-time activities _____

1. Yes, I can.
2. Mostly, yes.
3. Not really.

Volunteers painting over graffiti on a wall

VOCABULARY

A Look at the results of a survey and discuss these questions.

1. Do you think any of the results are surprising? Why?

2. These results are from the US. How different do you think they would be in your country?

3. The chart doesn't show results for Generation Z (people born after 1997). What do you think the percentages would be for that generation?

Connectivity in the United States				
Generations	. . . own a smartphone	. . . own a tablet computer	. . . se social media	. . . think the internet has mostly been good for society
Millennials Born 1981–1996	93%	53%	86%	84%
Generation X Born 1965–1980	90%	55%	76%	74%
The Baby Boomers Born 1946–1964	68%	52%	59%	68%
The Silent Generation Born before 1946	40%	33%	28%	63%

Source: Pew Research Center, Survey in 2019

B Read these sentences about the chart. Write the names of the correct generations.

1. The **overwhelming majority** of ____Millennials____ and ____Generation X____ own a smartphone.

2. **Just over two thirds** of _____ own one.

3. **About three quarters** of _____ use social media and think the internet has been good for society.

4. **Approximately one third** of _____ own a tablet computer, whereas **just over half** of _____ own one.

5. **Nearly two thirds** of _____ think the internet has mostly been good for society.

C Study the pairs of words. Do they have a similar meaning or a different meaning? Write *S* or *D*.

__S__ 1. about / approximately

____ 2. majority / minority

____ 3. huge / overwhelming

____ 4. connected / separated

WORD BANK
generation people born and living at about the same time
tendency when you often behave or do things in a certain way
connectivity the state of being connected to others
fractions one fifth, one quarter, a third, a half

D Carry out a similar survey by asking the four questions from the chart. For example: *Do you own a smartphone? Do you think that the internet has been good . . . ?*

E Report the results of your survey to the class.

❝ The majority of us own . . .   Just over a third of us . . . ❞

CAN THE MILLENNIALS
UNPLUG IN THE PARKS?

As Timothy Egan sets off through the Grand Canyon, how will his millennial son manage without connectivity?

[1]On our journey through the Grand Canyon, me and my son, Casey, will see ancient fossils from a time when the rock was under the ocean. We'll take a boat down the Colorado River and, at night, we'll sleep under the sky and look at the universe. As we get ready to leave, my son complains he has no phone service and can't check the score for a game. I tell him that's a good thing.

[2]Casey is a millennial, in his mid-20s. I'm a baby boomer. My generation loves the national parks to death. His generation will have to save them in the future. The night before, we gorged on social media, sent our final text messages, used the internet to find the best Mexican restaurant, and used our smartphone's GPS to guide us back to our hotel. Now for the diet: a fast from our devices—our overconnectedness. What could be a better antidote to our eight-second attention span than a landscape that is nearly two billion years old?

[3]I sense that Casey is not convinced. And in that, he is not alone. A recent survey reported that the overwhelming majority of millennials—71% —said they would be "very uncomfortable" on a

Young adults hold hands at a campground in Joshua Tree National Park, California.

one-week vacation without connectivity. For baby boomers, the figure was exactly a third, at 33%. For Jonathan Jarvis, director of the National Park Service, this presents a challenge. "Young people are more separated from the natural world than perhaps any generation before them."

4But rather than rage against the times, the National Parks are now attempting to attract more school-aged "Generation Z" visitors by joining the digital age. Visitors to their website can take a virtual tour of every national park, and their social media targets a generation that spends at least 50 hours a week in front of a screen—for children 11 to 14 years old, it's nearly 12 hours a day.

5But even if the National Parks are now embracing technology, that doesn't mean wiring up the parks so you can get a signal on your phone. Even after a sublime first day spent on the river and an evening feast of prime rib cooked over a gas stove, Casey and I experience a bit of internet withdrawal.

6"We should just let it go," I suggested. "Try to be mindful. Stare at the stars. Drift."

7"I get it," replies Casey, "this thing about being disconnected. But everyone I know likes to share—publicly—what we're doing. We are social travelers. If you can't share it now, is it really happening? Just a thought." 🎧7

A Answer the questions in pairs.

1. Look at the photo. How are the people connected? How do they feel about it?

2. Read the title of the article. What do you think millennials are unplugged and disconnected from in the parks?

B Read the article about a father (F) and son (S). Who feels the following? Write F, S, or both.

_____ 1. He is excited about the journey.

_____ 2. He spent the night before online.

_____ 3. He isn't sure about not having the internet for a few days.

_____ 4. After the first day, he wishes he could connect.

C Read the article again and answer these questions in your notebook.

1. What does the father hope to see and do on their journey?

2. Why does his son complain?

3. What two generations do they each belong to?

4. Where do they eat the night before they leave?

5. What do the percentages 71% and 33% refer to?

6. How are the National Parks trying to attract Generation Z?

D Understand words from context. Circle the words and phrases that can replace the underlined words. Use the paragraph numbers to help you find them.

> **ACADEMIC SKILL**
>
> **Understanding words from context**
> When you read a text with new words, try to guess their meaning from context before you look them up in a dictionary. Then try to use the words in your own sentences.

Paragraph 2

1. I like the national parks a lot.

2. I'm not hungry today! I ate so much ice cream last night!

3. Today I'm going to eat very little for a day or so.

Paragraph 4

4. Young people often get angry about the age they are growing up in.

Paragraph 5

5. Wow! The view from our hotel is amazingly beautiful!

Paragraph 6

6. You need to be more aware of other people's feelings.

E Read the last paragraph in the article again. Discuss the question in groups. Does everyone you know like to share—publicly—what they're doing? What are the advantages and disadvantages of sharing online?

LISTENING

A You are going to hear a news report about the community in the photo. What do you think the word *indigenous* means? What other words might describe this community?

B **Listen for the main idea.** Listen to the news report. What do you think is the main message of the report? 🎧 8

1. Modern technology has a negative effect on traditional communities.

2. Traditional communities fail because they don't use technology.

3. Modern technology can be helpful in traditional communities.

C Listen again and answer the questions by writing notes. 🎧 8

Where is the news report from?	
What technology does Rumilda use?	
What does a "forest monitor" do?	
What is changing the community's land?	
What did the forest provide them in the past?	

ACADEMIC SKILL
Note-taking
When you take notes, listen for key words, such as verbs and nouns. The speaker stresses these types of words.

D How do you think digital and modern technology have improved people's lives in your country or local community? Tell the class.

Members of an indigenous community called the Mbya Guaraní in Paraguay

GRAMMAR

A Read the Unit 1, Lesson B Grammar Reference in the appendix. Complete the exercises. Then do the exercises below.

SUBJECT-VERB AGREEMENT
Subject + singular verb
Everyone / Someone / No one has a laptop. **Each / Every** student **speaks** two languages. **One of / None of** our community **uses** a cell phone. **Two hundred kilometers / miles / meters isn't** a long way. (with quantities and amounts) **The United States / The United Nations has** many states / members. (with plural countries / organizations)
Subject + plural verb
None of / Some of my family **use** technology. **Both** my sister **and** my brother **live** with me in this apartment.
Subject + singular verb or plural verb
Our community **lives** in this region. (= the community as a whole) Our community **live** in houses around this region. (= individual members of the community) **The majority of** my friends **spend** time on social media. (*majority of* + plural count noun + plural verb) **The majority of** our time **is** wasted on social media. (*majority of* + noncount noun + singular verb)

B Check (✓) the correct sentences and correct any mistakes.

☐ 1. One of my apps aren't working properly. _____

☐ 2. None of my class know how to answer this question. _____

☐ 3. The whole family is going on vacation. _____

☐ 4. Not everyone speak Spanish in Paraguay. _____

☐ 5. One half of the students own a tablet. _____

☐ 6. The country doesn't agree on this political issue. _____

☐ 7. The country has a public holiday today. _____

☐ 8. The majority of millennials has grown up using a cell phone. _____

C Match the sentences.

_____ 1. My soccer team is ready to start the game.   a. Two players are late.

_____ 2. The team aren't all here yet.   b. Two players forgot theirs.

_____ 3. The team feels optimistic.   c. Everyone is here.

_____ 4. The team don't all have their uniforms.   d. They think they can win.

D Complete these sentences with information that is true for you, using an appropriate verb. Make two sentences true and one sentence false.

1. My family _____.

2. The majority of my friends _____.

3. One of my favorite _____ is _____.

E Work in pairs. Take turns reading your sentences and guess which one is false.

ACTIVE ENGLISH Try it out!

A Look at the photo below and read the caption. Do you think the older fans are enjoying the moment more than the other fans? Why? Tell the class.

B WRITING Read the Unit 1 Writing Model in the appendix and answer the questions below.

   1. Is the writer for or against digital communities?

   2. How many arguments does the writer give for her opinion?

   3. Overall, do you agree or disagree with her views?

C Work in groups. Brainstorm arguments for digital communities in response to the writer of the paragraph in **B**.

D Choose the three best arguments from **C** and write your own paragraph.

E Work in two groups. You are going to have a classroom debate and then vote on this topic: "Digital communities and social media have had a positive impact on humans." One group is for digital communities and social media. The other group is against.

   1. Each group prepares its list of arguments either for or against. You have five minutes to prepare.

   2. Each group takes turns presenting their main arguments. Then they discuss and ask questions about their opinions.

   3. Take a class vote.

1B GOALS Now I can . . .

Describe trends and tendencies _____

Argue for and against _____

1. Yes, I can.
2. Mostly, yes.
3. Not really.

As a movie star arrives, almost everyone is more interested in their phone than the moment.

GLOBAL VOICES

A Watch the video. Number the events described (from 1 to 5) in the order you see them.

   1   a. K. David Harrison introducing his organization and its purpose

_____ b. Young students learning words from their ancestors' language

_____ c. A map of the world showing areas where languages are dying out

_____ d. Someone looking up words on the Talking Dictionaries website

_____ e. A father and son recording words and phrases from their language

B Watch the video again. Circle the correct answer.

1. What is the main aim of the Living Tongues Organization?

   a. To teach disappearing languages

   b. To preserve endangered languages

   c. To save traditional communities

2. What is David Harrison's opinion of technology?

   a. That it is good for teaching language

   b. That it is a very positive thing

   c. That it is a positive thing in his work

3. Who usually records the endangered languages?

   a. Harrison and his colleagues

   b. The people who speak it

   c. Teams of experts

4. How do local communities benefit from the Talking Dictionaries website and app?

   a. They can share local news and information with each other

   b. They learn how to use modern technology

   c. They share their language and culture with the wider world

C Work in pairs. David Harrison's Living Tongues Organization sometimes asks people to donate money so they can save languages. Imagine you are going to advertise the work of Harrison's organization in order to raise money. Which benefits would you emphasize in your advertising? What slogan can you use in your advertisement?

K. David Harrison and Greg Anderson interview Ichiro John, a Mwoakilloan elder.

Work on a ship includes cleaning the deck while ships sail over rolling waves.

GOALS

Lesson A
/ Talk about work-life balance
/ Take part in a meeting

Lesson B
/ Identify skills and personal qualities
/ Ask and answer interview questions

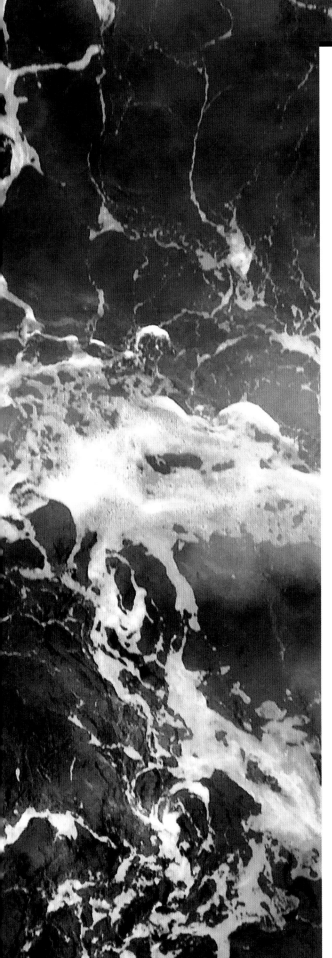

THE WORKING WEEK

LOOK AT THE PHOTO. ANSWER THE QUESTIONS.

1. What type of work is this person doing?

2. What do you think are the pros and cons of this job?

WARM-UP VIDEO

A Many meetings use technology to connect people who are in different locations. What communication problems might occur in these meetings compared to face-to-face meetings?

B Watch a conference call meeting and decide if the statements are true (T) or false (F).

1. Everyone arrives on time. _____

2. Participants introduce themselves. _____

3. One person keeps getting disconnected. _____

4. Paul has difficulty entering. _____

5. People speak at the same time and interrupt each other. _____

6. Everyone is looking at the same image on their screens. _____

7. Everyone leaves at the same time. _____

8. It's easy for everyone to tell who else is in the meeting. _____

9. Everyone agrees the meeting was a good use of time. _____

10. One person does not tell anyone that they are in the meeting. _____

C Work in groups. Write a list of guidelines for people attending conference call meetings in order to avoid the problems in the video.

For example: *Always arrive on time for the conference call.*

VOCABULARY

A Read about a company and a school. Then answer the questions by checking (✓) the correct box(es) with a partner.

Most people **take it for granted** that we need five days for work and school, but do we really? Recently, a financial services company in New Zealand introduced a four-day week. The company's two-month test period showed that the work **performance** of its 240 employees remained the same. And with the same amount of pay and vacation, staff **morale** improved, and cases of staff **burn out** were reduced.

Could schools also learn something about work-life **balance** from this? In 2018, when a school in Colorado cut classes on Mondays from their timetable, teachers and students were healthier and happier. Although some parents complained, teachers felt less **pressure** with more time to plan. **Anxiety** among students went down with no change to student performance—in fact, some exam results were even better with this more **flexible** approach.

	Company	School	Neither
1. A four-day week was introduced.			
2. Performance got worse.			
3. Some people didn't like the idea.			
4. Everyone felt less stress.			

B Match the words in blue to the definitions.

1. when the correct level of importance is given to each thing (e.g., work and free time) _____

2. the feeling of being very worried _____

3. think it's true without checking _____

4. it makes you feel anxious or worried _____

5. when you become sick from too much work _____

6. how successful you are (at work or at school) _____

7. the amount of confidence or hope everyone feels _____

8. able to change _____

WORD BANK
Compound adjectives usually use a hyphen:
four-day week
part-time job
three-day weekend
work-life balance

C Work in pairs. Imagine you want to introduce a four-day week at your school or company. Prepare a list of reasons to present to the head of the school or the company.

D Afterwards, join another pair and compare your list of reasons.

LISTENING

A Listen to a meeting on the system of *flextime*. What do you think are the benefits of flextime? Are there any disadvantages? 🎧9

B Listen again. Take notes on the items below. 🎧9

- any benefits
- any difficulties

C **Listen for details.** Listen again and answer these questions with *Yes*, *No*, or *Don't Know* (because the information is not given). 🎧9

1. Overall, are the staff in favor of having a system of flextime?

   Yes　　No　　Don't know

2. Has someone complained that two departments already have an unofficial system of flextime?

   Yes　　No　　Don't know

3. Is one of the difficulties that staff don't like the idea of working core hours?

   Yes　　No　　Don't know

4. Does Paolo dislike the system because it will affect his work?

   Yes　　No　　Don't know

5. Does Maria check up on where her staff are all the time?

   Yes　　No　　Don't know

6. Does Laura completely agree with Maria?

   Yes　　No　　Don't know

7. Do they come to an agreement on flextime before they discuss working from home?

   Yes　　No　　Don't know

D Work in pairs. Overall, how would you describe the tone of the meeting? Give reasons for your answers.

- formal or informal?
- direct or indirect?
- polite or impolite?

E Work in groups of three. Discuss these questions.

1. Do you think flextime is a good idea?

2. What type of businesses could adopt flextime practices in their offices? What type of businesses would not be able to adopt flextime? Why?

Some companies have a system of **flextime**. This means that employees in a company can start and finish their work day at different times, though they might have to be at work during certain core hours in the middle of the day.

SPEAKING

A group of people is discussing a work agenda during a business meeting.

A Listen and read. Answer the questions. (10)

Chen: OK, let's get started. We need to discuss the idea of working from home so that staff have the option to work from home one day a week. How do we feel about that?

Amelia: I'm not at all convinced, because there's some work you have to do in the office.

Beverley: I don't follow you. What do you mean?

Amelia: Well, if I need a meeting with staff, then they need to be at work.

Beverley: I get your point, but it's a question of planning. You always schedule a staff meeting on a certain day, and so everyone has to come in on that day.

Chen: I tend to go along with you, Beverley. For the system to work, managers also need to be flexible.

1. What is the aim of the meeting?

2. Who disagrees with the new proposal? Why?

3. Why does Chen agree with Beverley?

B Work in groups of three and practice the conversation.

C Complete the chart. Write expressions from the conversation in **A** in the second column. Add your own expression in the third column.

USEFUL EXPRESSIONS (12)		
Start the discussion	Let's get started . . .	Let's begin.
State the aim		
Ask for an opinion		
Disagree		
Say you don't understand		
Ask for an explanation		
Show understanding and then disagree		
Agree		

D Work in groups of three. You all work for the same company, and currently lunch break is from 12 to 1. Some employees would like a more flexible lunch break, so they can spend less time having lunch and end their work day earlier if they want to. Have a meeting to discuss the suggestion.

GRAMMAR

A Read the Unit 2, Lesson A Grammar Reference in the appendix. Complete the exercises. Then do the exercises below.

DYNAMIC AND STATIVE VERBS
Dynamic verbs with the simple present and present continuous

You can use dynamic verbs in the simple present to talk about facts and routines:
   *My company **employs** 250 people. / I **start** work at nine.*
You can also use dynamic verbs in the present continuous to talk about an action happening now, or repeated actions over a period of time:
   *My company **is employing** more staff right now. / This week **I'm starting** early, at eight.*

Stative verbs with the simple present

You use stative verbs to talk about states, such as existence, beliefs, and possession:
   *I **know** what you mean.* (=belief)   *This **belongs** to me.* (=possession)
Some stative verbs are only used with the simple present (not with the present continuous); for example, *agree, believe, belong, know, seem, understand*:
   I understand what you mean. ✓   ~~*I'm understanding what you mean.*~~ ✗

Stative verbs with the simple present and present continuous

You can use some stative verbs with both the simple present and the present continuous, with a change in emphasis or meaning:
   I love my job. = A general comment about your job.
   I'm loving my new job. = So far, my new job is great.
   I think he's five years old. = It's my belief or opinion.
   I'm thinking about leaving my job. = I'm considering it.
   Gill is a nice person. = She's always like this.
   Gill is being nice. = She's behaving like this right now, but it isn't normal.
You can also use *always* with the present continuous to express irritation.
   We're always having meetings! = It's a repeated event and it's very annoying.

B Work in pairs and explain the difference in meaning between the verbs in sentences *a* and *b*.

1. a. I have a meeting at 3.   b. We're always having meetings!

2. a. Eduardo comes from Colombia.   b. Eduardo is coming from Colombia.

3. a. He's very helpful.   b. He's being helpful today.

4. a. What do you think?   b. I'm not sure. I'm thinking about it.

5. a. I like this idea a lot.   b. I'm liking this idea more and more.

C Think of three things that annoy you about your place of work or study; for example, the way things are done, or somebody you work or study with. Then write three sentences using *always* + present continuous.

For example: *I have a colleague who <u>is always talking and keeping me</u> from working.*

1. _____

2. _____

3. _____

D Work in pairs. Take turns telling each other about your annoying problems in **C**. Your partner should listen and then suggest possible solutions.

> 66 Maybe you should explain to your colleague that you need to concentrate while you are working, but that you're happy to talk during a coffee break.

START / **FINISH**	**1.** How many hours a week do you spend in meetings?	**2.** What are you working on right now?	**3.** Explain why you are late for work. Miss your next turn.
17. Are you loving this game? Why?			**4.** always
16. currently			**5.** Move to another player on the board. Tell them about something that really annoys you.
15. You have to work late. Give an excuse why you can't. Miss your next turn.			**6.** Name one thing that is always annoying you at work or school.
14. Name one way to improve staff performance and improve their work-life balance.			**7.** nowadays
13. Move to another player on the board. Ask for their opinion on flextime and then agree or disagree with them.			**8.** Move to another player on the board. Tell them some gossip about someone at work.
12. frequently	**11.** Name one way to reduce pressure on your staff and avoid burn out.	**10.** How many vacation days do you take a year?	**9.** Explain why you are returning late from your lunch break. Miss your next turn.

THE WORKING WEEK GAME

Work in groups of three. You are going to play a game with a lot of different conversations around the office.
Each player places a game piece on START.
Flip a coin to move (Heads = Move two squares. Tails = Move one square)

RED SQUARES
Follow the instructions.

ORANGE SQUARES
Ask the question to the player on your left.

GREEN SQUARES
Move to another player on the board and follow the instructions on the square you are leaving.

BLUE SQUARES
Ask a question to the person on your right using the time expression given.

2A GOALS   Now I can . . .

Talk about work-life balance _____

Take part in a meeting _____

1. Yes, I can.
2. Mostly, yes.
3. Not really.

VOCABULARY

A Read these sentences from job advertisements with words describing personal qualities. How many of the words in **blue** do you know? Check any unknown words in a dictionary.

1. We're looking for **reliable** young people with plenty of self-**motivation** who are able to manage themselves without supervision.

2. You must be **confident** with clients and demonstrate **enthusiasm** for the product.

3. The role of full-time caregiver in the nursing home would suit someone with **maturity** and **patience**.

4. This internship is the ideal opportunity for any **determined** student interested in a future career in the video-gaming industry.

5. To work in our bank, you will have a proven track record of **honesty** and **independence**. Experience with handling money is desirable.

6. We have a position for an **experienced** person who is **willing** to work weekends.

B Complete the chart with the **blue** words in **A**. Then write the missing adjective or noun form of each word.

ADJECTIVES		NOUNS	
reliable (4)	motivated (4)	reliability (6)	motivation (4)

WORD BANK
We often turn adjectives into nouns by using these suffixes:

-ility, -ation, -ence, -ity, -ent, -ty, -ness

C **PRONUNCIATION: Stressed Syllables** Listen and check your answers in **B**. Write the number of syllables in each word and underline the syllable with the main stress. Notice how the stress can change with different word forms (e.g., *reliable* (4) *reliability* (6).) 🎧13

D Work in pairs. You each have a different crossword with adjectives describing personal qualities.

1. Prepare your clues to define your words (without using the word). For example: *willing—always wanting to help and do one's best.*

2. Take turns asking for and giving a definition. When you guess a word, write it in your crossword. For example:

B: What's 1 Down?

A: Able to work alone without much help.

B: Independent?

A: Correct.

Student A: Turn to your crossword on page 214.

Student B: Turn to your crossword on page 215.

BLOOD, SWEAT, AND SEQUINS

**Emily Ainsworth
standing with
circus crew
member**

A Have you ever been to the circus? What types of performers did you see there?

B **Paraphrasing.** Read the article and circle **T** for *true* or **F** for *false*. Underline the parts of the text that tell you the answer.

1. Emily visited Circus Padilla because she wanted to get a job.   T / F

2. She hadn't been a dancer before.   T / F

3. It's a fact that Mexico has the most circuses in the world.   T / F

4. It's impossible for people who are not born in circus families to get a job in the circus.   T / F

5. Fewer people are going to the circus these days.   T / F

6. Emily doesn't think you can see anything else quite like it.   T / F

[1] When Emily Ainsworth—a National Geographic Explorer—showed up at the Circus Padilla in Mexico City one day, she got more than she bargained for. She'd planned to take a series of photographs capturing the lives and work of the performers. Instead, Emily was handed a costume and they got her to dance on the stage. "They offered me a job on my first night there. They turned on the music and I went to perform for the first time." Emily had no prior experience as a dancer. "My main skill was that I looked quite gangly and white, and people thought it would be funny if I had a dancing act." As a result of her willingness and enthusiasm, Emily went on to work with seven different circuses around Mexico City, including the well-known Circo Hermanos Vazquez, Circo Atayde, and the American Circus, to name just a few.

[2] It is claimed that Mexico has more circuses than any other country in the world. Some are tiny, family-run businesses with only four or five performers, most of whom are siblings and relatives. Others are much more grandiose, like traveling villages. These circuses employ about 50 people, and some of the richest, most successful circuses travel the length and breadth of the Americas.

[3] The working life of a Mexican circus performer is notoriously tough. Emily calls it a world of "blood, sweat, and sequins[1]" where most performers have "generations of circus blood pumping through their veins" and many artists "die in the ring, rather than of old age." It's a close-knit community that most of its people are born into, and it's rare for an outsider like Emily to join it. Talents and tricks are passed down through generations. Parents get their children to perform in the ring even before they start to walk.

[4] If a life in the circus has always been challenging, perhaps now the industry is facing its biggest challenge. In the past, circus audiences were always reliable and would come back year after year. But more recently, it has seen a dramatic fall in audience numbers. The traditional circus is competing with new forms of cheaper, more modern entertainment such as online TV and video gaming. On top of that, the use of animals in circuses was banned in 2015, causing some of Mexico's best-known circuses to close down, with many performers losing their jobs.

[5] Those still determined to perform have retrained and reinvented themselves; for example, instead of jumping from horses, now they perform stunts on motorbikes. Emily believes that these performers continue to offer something unique. Circus people "challenge us to think how different our own lives could be if we worked on the basis that they do—that anything is possible for our own selves, we are only limited by our imagination." (14)

[1]**sequins** shiny, decorations that people often put on costumes

C Circle words and phrases in the text with the following meanings.

Paragraph 1:

1. When you receive something unexpected

2. Very tall and thin, and moving awkwardly

Paragraph 2:

3. Very large and impressive in appearance

4. From north to south and east to west

Paragraph 3:

5. Clever acts to deceive the audience

6. The part of the circus where people perform

Paragraph 5:

7. Actions showing great skill and courage

D Work in pairs. Imagine you own a circus and you need some new performers. Write a short description of the job and the type of people you are looking for (e.g., what skills, talents, abilities, and personal qualities should they have?).

LISTENING

A Work in groups of three. Look at this list of job skills and personal qualities.

- knowledge of a particular subject
- ability to solve problems
- communication skills (written and spoken)
- patience and honesty
- ability to persuade other people
- willingness to learn more skills
- ability to manage and motivate teams of people
- ability to work independently

B For each of these jobs, choose the three most important skills and personal qualities from the list in **A**. Then join another group and compare your choices.

artist   data analyst   language teacher   police officer   sales manager

C **Listen for gist.** Listen to the advice of a career counselor. Which is the best title for his talk? 🎧15

1. Comparing jobs in the past, present, and future
2. How to find your perfect job for the future
3. The skills you need to develop for the future

D Listen again and complete these notes. 🎧15

> **Preparing for your future career**
>
> Why do I need to prepare?
>
> - (1.) _____ jobs in the future doesn't exist yet.
> - Technology and (2.) _____ will do 50% of the jobs we do now.
>
> ### Transferable skills
>
> 1. Written and spoken (3.) _____. For example, communicating effectively in emails or presenting (4.) _____. Also, digital literacy as well as analyzing and making use of (5.) _____.
> 2. Collaborating in teams to (6.) _____ and working independently.
> 3. Leadership and persuasive skills: When something needs (7.) _____, you know how to do it or how to get other people (8.) _____ it.
> 4. Have a broad range of (9.)_____. Be open to upskilling and make sure you (10.) _____!

ACADEMIC SKILL
When you take notes, listen for **key words**. Write the main information as headings and list details using **bullets** and **numbers**.

E Work on your own and decide which of the transferable skills in the notes in **D**:

a. you already have.

b. you'd like to develop more.

c. you'd find very hard to do.

GRAMMAR

A Read the Unit 2, Lesson B Grammar Reference in the appendix. Complete the exercises. Then do the exercises below.

GET / HAVE / NEED + SOMEONE / SOMETHING		
Get someone to do / Have someone do		
get	someone	to + infinitive
I got	my assistant	to fix my printer.
have	someone	bare infinitive
I had	my assistant	fix my printer.
Get / have something done		
get / have	object	past participle
I got / I had	my printer	fixed.
Need + *-ing*		
something	needs	-ing
My printer	needs	fixing.

B Complete the sentences using the words in parentheses.

1. (mechanic / repair / car) I got _____

2. (assistant / carry / box) I had _____

3. (my jacket / mend) I got _____

4. (bicycle / paint) _____

5. (invoice / pay) This _____

C What five places around town do the sentences refer to?

1. I get my teeth checked here.   4. I have pizza delivered from here.

2. I have my hair done here.   5. I get my suit cleaned here.

3. I get my car fixed here.

D Think of three more places that provide you services or where you can get something done. Write a sentence about each place and read them to a partner. Can your partner guess the place?

1. _____

2. _____

3. _____

Craftswoman repairing a bicycle in her bike repair workshop

ACTIVE ENGLISH Try it out!

A Work in pairs and look at the three job ads. List three skills or qualities needed for each job.

Au pair wanted this summer!	**Part-time shop assistant**	**Call center operators**
Our two children need looking after this summer. Must be reliable, willing and patient. Free accommodation and meals with weekly pay.	Enthusiastic person needed for evening and weekend work.	Can you get people to buy insurance? Full-time position with flextime. Training will be given.

B **WRITING** Read the Unit 2 Writing Model in the appendix and answer these questions.

1. Which job is the person applying for?
2. What is the person currently doing?
3. What kind of work experience does he have? Is it relevant?
4. How suitable is the person? Would you interview him for the job?

C Choose one of the other two jobs in **A** and write a cover letter for the position.

D Read the Academic Skill box. Then decide which of these questions are closed and which are open. Write *C* or *O*.

_____ 1. Can you come for an interview on Monday?

_____ 2. Where do you see yourself in five years' time?

_____ 3. Are you able to work independently?

_____ 4. Would you describe yourself as reliable?

_____ 5. Are you good at working in teams?

_____ 6. How would your friends or work colleagues describe your personal qualities?

> **ACADEMIC SKILL**
>
> Closed questions need a *yes / no* answer.
>
> Open questions generate more information and are more useful for interviewing people. Prepare for any type of interview by thinking of the questions you will be asked and the answers you can give.

E Work in pairs and take turns interviewing each other for one of the jobs in **A**. Use some of the questions in **D** as well as your own questions.

2B GOALS Now I can . . .

Identify skills and personal qualities _____

Ask and answer interview questions _____

1. Yes, I can.
2. Mostly, yes.
3. Not really.

Chef in commercial kitchen decorating a dish

GLOBAL VOICES

A You are going to watch a video with Hannah Reyes Morales talking about her work as a photographer. Match her quotes (a–e) to 1–5. Then watch the video to check.

_____ 1. Practice

_____ 2. Workshops and mentors

_____ 3. Technical knowledge and creativity

_____ 4. Sacrifices

_____ 5. Advice to younger self

a. "Having someone older and having somebody who's more experienced . . . to ask you the right questions has always been important."

b. "I would say be alright with who you are."

c. "It's important to know your camera, what its limits are, and to work around it."

d. "One of the first things that I was ever told was (that) your photos are just pretty and not doing anything beyond it."

e. "When you are starting out you are just constantly wondering where your next paycheck will come from."

B Watch the video again and answer these questions in your notebook.

1. Although early feedback was negative about her photos, what did she learn from it?

2 How did having advice from mentors help her develop her skills as a photographer?

3. Why can it be bad if technical knowledge becomes the main thing?

4. What did she have to do, to make ends meet?

5. Why isn't photography as glamourous as everyone thinks?

C Work in pairs and ask and answer these questions about your current job or a job you would like to do in the future.

1. How much can you learn from other people for the job? What do you think you can learn from them?

2. How much technical knowledge do you need? How creative do you need to be?

3. What kind of sacrifices do you need to make for the job?

4. What piece of advice do you think is important for this job?

Hannah Reyes Morales is a photojournalist and a National Geographic Explorer.

Brazilian artist Eduardo Kobra working on a huge mural on a building in central Moscow

GOALS   **Lesson A**
/ Brainstorm new ideas
/ Solve problems

Lesson B
/ Describe creativity
/ Talk about past abilities

CREATIVITY

3

LOOK AT THE PHOTO. ANSWER THE QUESTIONS.

1. Is this kind of art important in our daily lives? Why or why not?

2. Do you think everyone can be creative? Or is creativity only for artists?

WARM-UP VIDEO

A Watch a video about the man who created the Rubik's Cube. Number these events in the order you see them.

_____ a. Erno Rubik was starting his career at university.

_____ b. The Rubik's Cube became the best-selling toy.

_____ c. He made a cube to teach students about space and 3-dimensions.

_____ d. He tried to find a method to solve the cube.

_____ e. There are Rubik's Cube competitions all over the world.

B Complete the sentences with the numbers. Then watch the video again to check your answers.

| 30 | 1980 | 43,000,000,000,000,000,000 (quintillion) |
| 1 | 26 | |

1. There are _____ possible combinations.

2. In 1974, Erno was _____ years old.

3. There are _____ small cubes on a Rubik's cube.

4. After _____ month, Erno cracked the code of the cube.

5. Erno started selling the cube around the world in _____.

C Have you ever used a Rubik's Cube? Did you solve it? Why do you think it is so popular?

VOCABULARY

A Work in pairs and answer the questions.

1. When and where do you get your best ideas?

2. Read the text. Do you agree with it?

The Greek scholar Archimedes creatively **solved a problem** while relaxing in his bath. More recently, when asked the question, "When do you **get** your best **ideas**?" 500 top business people answered "on vacation," "in the shower," or "traveling to and from work"—not one of them said "in the office" or "while **doing work**." In fact, when you need to **make up your mind** about something or **reach a difficult decision**, you probably don't **find inspiration** at your place of work or study, or even your home. Instead, like Archimedes, you need a place where you can **clear your head** and **think outside the box**; maybe at a new coffee shop, working out at the gym, or **getting some fresh air** outside.

B Find the verbs in blue in the text that go with these nouns and write them in the infinitive form.

1. _____ an agreement, a decision, a goal, a conclusion

2. _____ the answer, inspiration, help, a solution

3. _____ some work, business, an exercise, nothing

4. _____ a puzzle, a problem, a crime, a mystery

5. _____ your head, your mind, your desk, a space

6. _____ ideas, advice, some fresh air, things done

7. _____ a mistake, money, up your mind, suggestions

8. _____ outside the box, aloud, the same way, the worst

WORD BANK
Certain verbs go with certain nouns as collocations, or are part of an expression:

make up your mind to decide something

think outside the box to think imaginatively

C Complete the questions with a verb from **B**. Then interview a partner.

1. Who do you normally _____ advice from when you have a problem?

2. What is one of your current goals? How will you _____ it?

3. In a team, is it important for everyone to _____ the same way?

4. When you _____ a mistake in English, how do you learn from it?

5. After a busy day, how do you _____ your head and relax?

LISTENING

A Work in groups. You have two minutes to brainstorm as many words and phrases as possible connected with the topic of "Creativity."

new ideas

Creativity

B Answer the questions about your brainstorming. Share your ideas with the class.

1. How many new words and phrases did you brainstorm?

2. Do you think brainstorming is useful? Why or why not?

C Read about three other ways to brainstorm and generate new ideas. Then listen to three brainstorming meetings and match them to the brainstorming technique in the text. 🎧16

1. _____   2. _____   3. _____

Three ways to generate new ideas

a. Starbursting
Draw a six-pointed star on the board. In the middle of the star, write the problem. Then, on each of the six points, write a question word: *what, who, where, why, when,* and *how.* Ask the group to suggest questions for each point about the problem in the middle.

b. A new perspective
Ask the group to imagine they are someone else, such as a famous celebrity, a historical figure, or someone they know well, like their manager. For example, ask the team to brainstorm solutions as if they are Nelson Mandela. It helps to see things from a different viewpoint.

c. One by one
Everyone leaves the room except for two people. They brainstorm their ideas for a minute. Then, one person comes in and gives their ideas. Then, the next person comes in, and so on until everyone is back in the room. This technique means everyone gets to speak—including shyer people.

D **Verify answers.** Listen again and take notes in the table. 🎧16

	What is the purpose of their brainstorming?	What ideas do they think of?
1.		
2.		
3.		

E Discuss the questions in groups.

1. Which of the three ways of generating ideas seem to work well?

2. Are there any difficulties with the three ways?

3. Which would you like to try at work, at school, or at home?

SPEAKING

A Read and listen to people brainstorm ideas for a new product. Why don't they choose a shampoo for children? Why do they think a shampoo for pets is a good idea? 🎧17

Ryan: As you know, our management would like us to come up with a new shampoo product that reaches a new type of customer. So, I think we should begin with a brainstorming session. You know, try to identify a new type of customer.

Leticia: How about creating something for children?

Irina: Hmm, but we already have shampoo for children.

Leticia: Only for girls. Not boys.

Ryan: OK. At this stage, we'd better not get into detail. Can we just think outside the box? Whatever comes into your mind.

Irina: Point taken. We could make a shampoo for pets. People spend loads of money on their pets.

Leticia: That's a good idea, and we could also have accessories. You know, brushes, towels . . .

Ryan: Yes, let's write that down.

Irina: Should we think about which types of pets? A shampoo for dogs?

Leticia: Absolutely, and cats.

Ryan: So, a shampoo for cats and dogs. What else? Rabbits?

A springer spaniel dog being washed in the bathtub with bubbles

B Work in groups of three and read the conversation aloud.

C Complete the Useful Expressions table with words from the conversation in **A**. 🎧19

USEFUL EXPRESSIONS FOR BRAINSTORMING		
Generating ideas		
I think we _____ . . . How _____ . . .? Why don't we . . .?	We'd _____ (not) . . . We could . . . _____ we think about . . .?	
Being positive and encouraging		
Good idea! / Absolutely! Let's write that _____ . What _____? / Any more ideas?		

SPEAKING STRATEGY 🎧18

Positive responses

When working with other people, respond to their ideas in a positive way by adding: *That's a good idea, and we could also . . . / I like it! And how about we also . . . .* This will generate more ideas than being negative.

D Work in groups. Choose one of the products below and brainstorm:

- the type of customer • what it could look like • a name for the product

an umbrella   a cup and straw   an alarm clock

GRAMMAR

A Read the Unit 3, Lesson A Grammar Reference in the appendix. Complete the exercises. Then do the exercises below.

SUGGESTING, EXPRESSING OPINION, AND GIVING ADVICE			
Statement	+ base form	Questions	+ verb + *-ing* + base form
Let's We / You should We / You could I (don't) think we / you should We / You ought to We'd / You'd better	do it another way.	How about . . . What about . . .	doing it another way?
		Why don't we . . . Can we . . . Why not . . . Should we / you . . . Shouldn't we / you . . .	do it another way?

B Rewrite the first sentence using the word in parentheses without changing the meaning.

1. Let's go out for dinner this evening.
   (how) _____ for dinner this evening?

2. You should invite a few other people.
   (ought) _____ a few other people.

3. Should we think of a different name?
   (not) _____ of a different name?

4. What about painting it green?
   (don't) _____ it green?

5. We'd better meet again tomorrow.
   (think) _____ again tomorrow.

6. Why don't we set a time limit?
   (can) _____ a time limit?

C Work in pairs and read about three different problems your friends and colleagues have. Discuss how you could help each person solve the problem.

Problem 1: Your close friend is an artist. She's been trying to paint a picture for weeks, but can't find inspiration. She feels unhappy and unmotivated, but she only has enough money for the next two months. She needs to finish and sell the painting! Make some suggestions.

Problem 2: A friend is a college student. He has his final exams in a month, but he has been sick. He's also spending a lot of time playing video games and watching TV. He needs to study much more. What advice would you give him?

Problem 3: Three friends of yours are sharing a new apartment. Unfortunately, they have started arguing over who is responsible for different weekly chores such as buying food, washing the dishes, and cleaning the house. They all ask you for your opinion.

" She ought to think outside the box.

He should get some fresh air to clear his head! "

ACTIVE ENGLISH Try it out!

A student taps his fingers on the desk.

A Look at this list of bad habits. Which three do you dislike the most? Tell a partner.

People who . . .

- always talk about themselves.
- bite their fingernails.
- eat too fast.
- are always apologizing.
- arrive late for everything.
- hum while they are working.
- procrastinate and leave things to the last minute.

B Do you have any of the bad habits in **A**? What do you think is your worst bad habit? Tell your partner.

C Read the text. Do you think Jurgen Wolff's creative solution sounds like a good idea? Why or why not?

> ### A Creative Solution: Teach your problem
>
> What is one habit or behavior you would like to change about yourself? Maybe you bite your fingernails or drink too much coffee? Or perhaps, with classmates or colleagues, you'd like to become a better listener or arrive on time for meetings? To solve these everyday problems, the creative thinker *Jurgen Wolff* thinks that by describing how to do something, you also learn how to stop doing it. For example, you could give a lesson to a friend on how to be late, how to make sure you never exercise, how to procrastinate, or just about anything else. Your friend listens to your lecture and takes notes. For example, a lesson in how to be late for everything could include these suggestions:
>
> - *You ought to have remove all the clocks from your house so it's easy to forget the time.*
> - *Before you leave the house, you'd better read any new emails or messages.*
> - *You should assume that public transportation will be on time or that there will be less traffic than normal.*
>
> Afterwards, your partner gives you the notes with your advice, and you do the absolute opposite.
> Which of your bad habits will you teach—and change—first?

D Choose your worst bad habit and prepare some notes on how to do it. Then read your notes to a partner and take turns teaching your habits.

3A GOALS Now I can . . .

Brainstorm new ideas _____

Solve problems _____

1. Yes, I can.

2. Mostly, yes.

3. Not yet.

VOCABULARY

A Read these quotes by people who are famous for their creativity.
Which quote do you agree with or like the most? Why?

> "The true sign of **intelligence** is not knowledge but **imagination**."
>
> "True **originality** consists not in a new manner but in a new **vision**."
>
> "Where there is love and **inspiration**, I don't think you can go wrong."

> "**Creativity** comes from a **conflict** of ideas."
>
> "Creativity is inventing, **experimenting**, growing, taking risks, breaking rules, making mistakes, and having fun."
>
> "**Genius** is one percent inspiration, and ninety-nine percent **perspiration**."

B Match the nouns in **blue** in **A** to these groups of synonyms.

creativity **1.** originality, inventiveness, talent

_____ **2.** newness, innovation, individuality

_____ **3.** point of view, concept, perspective

_____ **4.** understanding, brilliance, quickness

_____ **5.** testing, analyzing, examining

_____ **6.** vision, thought, creativity

_____ **7.** ideas, influence, motivation

_____ **8.** struggle, contest, clash

_____ **9.** sweat, hard work, labor

_____ **10.** cleverness, talent, natural ability

WORD BANK
A **synonym** is a word or phrase that means the same or nearly the same as another word. For example:
create make, design
original unique, new
solution answer, explanation
Avoid repeating the same words when you speak or write by using synonyms.

C A *word cloud* is a creative way to remember vocabulary. This one practices words connected to Einstein. Create a similar *word cloud* for a famous person you know. Use words and synonyms in **B**.

A young artist works on a
painting in her apartment.

WHAT MAKES YOU CREATIVE?

Are you a brilliant visionary, a fearless leader, or something else altogether? Take the quiz to find out how your thinking style helps create your best ideas.

1. The inside of my brain probably looks most like . . .
   a. a stage with a microphone.
   b. a subway map.
   c. a complicated invention.
   d. a panoramic landscape.

2. I feel most comfortable . . .
   a. in front of an audience with a message to deliver.
   b. at a networking event with lots of interesting people.
   c. in a workshop with lots of different tools.
   d. in a brainstorming session with a blank sheet of paper.

3. I'm most likely to create . . .
   a. a practical gadget you can use in daily life.
   b. an idea with a community of like-minded creators.
   c. a new and improved version of a household device.
   d. a far-out invention that no one has seen before.

4. My typical approach to cooking is . . .
   a. to assemble the ingredients and inspire someone else to do it.
   b. fusion—I take the best ideas from different cultures.
   c. to tweak and experiment with an existing recipe.
   d. to make something from scratch.

5. When I'm tackling a group project, I'm the one most likely to . . .
   a. keep everybody focused and motivated.
   b. make sure the right people get assigned to the right tasks.
   c. dive into the details and overcome an obstacle.
   d. come up with a grand plan.

A young musician is inspired by nature while playing her violin.

What do your answers mean?

Mostly A's: The leader
You're a doer! You are someone who knows how to motivate a team to get things done. Your best ideas come from figuring out how to inspire change. You have learned that to be successful, you must surround yourself with creative minds.

Mostly B's: The connector
You see possibilities for collaboration and sharing ideas where others might just see boundaries—or nothing at all. You are interested in taking the best from the past and reinventing it in the future.

Mostly C's: The tinkerer
You tend to make changes to existing concepts rather than create something completely new. You're likely to be the person in your home who fixes what's broken. The world needs your practical ideas.

Mostly D's: The visionary
You are a blue-sky thinker*. You see the big picture, looking far ahead when others might get stuck in details. You're a person who always looks for opportunities and never sees barriers. [20]

*blue-sky thinker someone who thinks outside the box

A Think of a situation when you work with a group of people or are part of a team. Write down any words that describe your role in the group (e.g., the leader, the thinker). Tell the class.

B Read and take the quiz. Then read what your answers say about you. Do you think the quiz is true for you? Why or why not?

C **Synonyms.** Circle the words in the quiz that are synonyms of the words in bold.

1. This painting shows a **wide-open and beautiful** view of the countryside.
2. I find it very useful to spend time **meeting and talking to people connected with my work**.
3. This is a useful kitchen **device** for opening tins.
4. My colleagues are **people with similar views**.
5. His opinions can be **a little crazy** sometimes.
6. I like to **slightly change** the recipe from the book sometimes.
7. We haven't found a way to get past the **difficulty**.

8. We've **suggested** a new way of doing things.

D Look at the four types of people. Which type of person would make these comments?

1. "OK, let's have a meeting to come up with some creative ideas!" ___Leader___
2. "I need more time to try out a few more changes to this." _____
3. "How about trying this in a completely different way." _____
4. "I have a good friend who might be able to help us with this." _____
5. "When can you finish this by?" _____
6. "I tried it out without bothering to read the instruction manual." _____
7. "I've added a few modifications, so it'll work better." _____
8. "I'm sure we invented something similar five years ago." _____

E How much do you trust quizzes like this? Have you ever taken other types of personality quizzes? What did you find out?

LISTENING

A   Rank the three inventions in order of importance (1 = most important, 3 = least important). Tell a partner your choices and explain your reasons.

_____ Monopoly   _____ coffee filter   _____ windshield wipers

B   Listen to a documentary about the three inventions. Match the invention to the inventor. 🎧21

_____ **1.** Melitta Bentz

_____ **2.** Elizabeth Magie

_____ **3.** Mary Anderson

C   **Global questions.** Listen again and decide if the answers to the questions are *Yes*, *No*, or *Don't Know* (because the information isn't provided), according to the documentary. 🎧21

1. Are the three women's names in any history books? _____

2. Did Melitta make changes to another object? _____

3. Did Melitta's company make a lot of money? _____

4. Did Monopoly always have the same name? _____

5. When we play Monopoly today, is it to learn about inequality? _____

6. Was Mary Anderson's idea unprofitable because it didn't work? _____

D   Work in two groups. Then work together to compare your two lists and give reasons for your choices. Were any inventions on both lists?

Group A: Brainstorm a list of the five best inventions from the last fifty years.

Group B: Brainstorm a list of the five worst inventions from the last fifty years.

E   **PRONUNCIATION: Stress and pausing in formal speech** Listen to these sentences from the documentary again. Which word does the speaker <u>stress</u>? Where does she pause (/)? 🎧22

Coffee filters. The board game of Monopoly. Windshield wipers.

All very different inventions but they all share one thing in common. They were created by women. Take the everyday coffee filter. In 1908, Melitta Bentz couldn't find coffee . . .

GRAMMAR

A Match the two halves of the sentences from the listening in **B**.

_____ 1. In 1908, Melitta Bentz couldn't

_____ 2. She managed

_____ 3. She'd succeeded in

_____ 4. The device meant drivers

_____ 5. Mary wasn't

a. able to sell her idea in 1903.

b. to find a solution by making holes in the bottom of a metal cup.

c. could see in bad weather.

d. find coffee that didn't taste bitter.

e. creating the first-ever coffee filter.

B Answer the questions about the sentences in **A**.

1. Which two sentences describe failure in the past?

2. Which two sentences describe a difficult task that was completed?

3. Which sentence describes the ability to do something in the past?

C Read the Unit 3, Lesson B Grammar Reference in the appendix. Complete the exercises. Then do the exercises below.

> ### ABILITY IN THE PAST
>
> Use **could** or **was able to** to talk about a general ability or possibility in the past.
> Use **was / were able to** to talk about success in a particular situation.
> Use **couldn't** or **wasn't able to** to describe failure in a specific task in the past.
> Use **managed to** / **succeeded in** to talk about a difficult task that you had the ability to complete.

D Think of a challenge or something you overcame when you were younger (e.g., learning to ride a bicycle or play a musical instrument). Complete the sentences about your experience.

1. I wasn't able to _____
   _____.

2. The hardest part was that I couldn't _____
   _____.

3. Slowly, with practice, I managed to _____
   _____.

4. Until finally, I succeeded in _____
   _____.

E Work in pairs and tell your story from **D**.

A grandfather teaches his grandson to play the guitar.

ACTIVE ENGLISH Try it out!

A Complete a survey. Ask your classmates questions such as *Have you solved one problem today?* or *Are you able to tell a joke in English?* Write six different names by the end.

FIND SOMEONE WHO . . .	
solved a problem today.	was able to whistle when they were ten years old.
is able to tell a joke in English.	makes a common mistake in English.
never learned to play a musical instrument.	managed to run a long distance (e.g., a half-marathon).

B **WRITING** Look at the photo of the artist Yayoi Kusama and one of her installations. Do you think you would like going to an exhibition of her work? Why or why not?

C Read the Unit 3 Writing Model in the appendix and make notes on the following:

- The obstacles she overcame
- The main events and influences
- The moments she succeeded

D Write a similar biography of a famous creative person (e.g., an artist or an inventor).

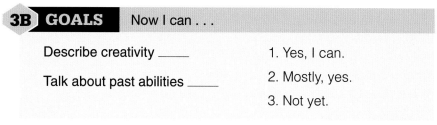

3B GOALS Now I can . . .

Describe creativity ____

Talk about past abilities ____

1. Yes, I can.
2. Mostly, yes.
3. Not yet.

ACADEMIC SKILL
Using time references
When you write a biography or a historical text, use time references such as **at the age of . . .**, **despite this period in her life . . .**, **for many years after . . .**

Japanese artist Yayoi Kusama created this installation, which was displayed at the Infinity art exhibition in the Museum of Modern Art.

GLOBAL VOICES

A   Work in groups of three. Discuss the questions about creativity in the chart in **B**. Then report your opinions back to the rest of the class.

B   In your group, watch a video with three people answering the questions in the chart. Each student watches one person and takes notes in the table.

	Student A: Jennifer Adler (Underwater Photojournalist)	**Student B:** Sylvia Johnson (Documentary Filmmaker)	**Student C:** Gabby Salazar (Nature and Conservation Photographer)
1. How do you get creative?			
2. Is taking risks part of creativity?			
3. Are people born creative?			
4. What can people do to become more creative?			

C   Tell your group what you wrote for each person. As you listen, fill in the rest of the table. Then watch the video again, and check all the information in the table.

D   Write a short summary (100 words) about creativity using the main ideas from the video and in your chart. Then, swap your summary with a partner. Did you both include the same main ideas? If not, discuss your reasons.

Opportunities for inspiration while walking in the Olympic National Park, Washington State

Children enjoying ice slides
at the Annual Snow Festival
In Sapporo, Japan

Fallas Festival

In the spring, the Spanish city of Valencia celebrates a huge street festival. Known as Fallas (in Spanish) or Falles (in the local Valencian dialect), it lasts for five days and nights. The Valencians and thousands of tourists enjoy live music, theater, fireworks, and parades with costumes. Then, on the final night, different local communities bring out huge sculptures that they have created and set fire to them.

Burning Man Festival

Every summer, 70,000 people from different walks of life build a temporary city of tents in the middle of the Nevada desert for the "Burning Man Festival." Everyone is responsible for providing the entertainment and bringing what they need—including food and water. Nothing is for sale, so money is useless. And cell phones don't work because there is no connectivity in the desert.

Sapporo Snow Festival

The very first Sapporo Snow Festival was started in 1950 by a group of high school students. It has since grown into a major international winter festival. For 7 days, around 2 million people from Japan and overseas visit Sapporo to look at hundreds of snow sculptures that might feature a special event or a famous place or person. There are also different types of snow slides and snow mazes, which are popular with children.

A Read about three festivals and complete the notes in the chart.

	Time of year and location?	Who is it for?	What makes it special?	What is the entertainment?
Fallas	Spring in the city of Valencia			
Burning Man			No money, no cell phones	
Snow Festival		People from Japan and overseas		

B Work in groups. Describe a festival or event in your town, city, or region. Talk about:

- the time of year and the location
- who it is for
- what makes it special
- what you can see and do

C Work in groups and plan your own festival. Brainstorm ideas and try to make the following decisions.

- What time of year does it take place?
- Where is it?
- Who is it for?
- What makes it special or different?
- What entertainment is there? (e.g., music, art, yoga)
- Other ideas?

D **You Choose** You need to advertise your new festival. Choose an option and create your advertisement.

Option 1 Write a description of the festival for a website.

Option 2 Record a short video to promote the festival.

Option 3 Make a slideshow with photos and a voice narration.

E Read or watch another group's advertisement for their festival. Answer the questions and tell another group your answers.

1. From the advertisement, did you understand the festival and who it is for?
2. Do you think there is something new or original about the festival?
3. Would you like to go to the festival? Why or why not?

F Work with your group. Discuss the feedback in **E** and decide if you need to change or add something to your festival.

4

THE SECOND SELF

LOOK AT THE PHOTO. ANSWER THE QUESTIONS.

1. Why do people go to this place in Hong Kong?

2. Where do you tend to take selfies? Do you use special backdrops?

WARM-UP VIDEO

A Watch Amber Case describe "The Second Self". What does this term refer to?

B Watch the video and complete these sentences.

1. Amber Case is a cyborg anthropologist. She studies humans and _____, and how the latter affects culture.

2. You are a cyborg anytime you use a tool for the purpose of adapting to a new _____.

3. A computer is an extension of your _____.

4. The ways in which we communicate with each other is very _____ from how it was.

5. Amber uses different online accounts to stay in _____ with people, to keep her followers informed about her work, to share exciting developments, and to conduct _____.

C Do you have more than one online account? If yes, why?

D Do you already follow any of Amber's advice? Which will you follow in the future?

A wedding photoshoot on a bamboo deposit at the "Instagram Pier" in Hong Kong. People use this pier as a backdrop for selfies and portraits.

GOALS

Lesson A
/ Explain how something works
/ Express regret

Lesson B
/ Identify reliable information
/ Describe imaginary situations

VOCABULARY

A Read the article. Which information do you already know? Which advice do you follow?

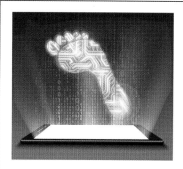

Every time you deliberately post a photo, "like" a comment, or update your online **personal profile**, you are leaving an active **digital footprint**. This means that all your friends can see what you are doing and thinking, but be aware that this type of **data trail** can also be public—it could be as easy for a potential employer to see a photo of you at a party as it is for your best friend.

On the other hand, your "passive" digital footprint is the one you leave behind unintentionally. Websites can collect information on how many times you visit them and at what time of day. This tells advertisers about your online shopping habits. Also, unguarded information left on **social media** or **search engines** can provide criminals with a detailed view of your life, leading to fraud and **identity theft**.

So how can you control your footprint? First of all, don't post anything online you wouldn't be comfortable showing to a room of people (including your boss!). When using social media, check your **privacy settings** so you limit who can read your profile or posts. And finally, use a **secure password** for logging into your **email account**—and make sure it's different than the one you use for **online banking**!

B There are ten collocations in blue in the article. Match six of these to the comments they refer to.

1. "I'm deleting all my information and accounts on social media, so I won't leave one." (2 possible answers) _____

2. "The bank told me someone had tried to use my name and steal my money!" _____

3. "I've changed these, so only my closest friends can access my profile." _____

4. "My grandmother was using her date of birth, so I changed it to something less obvious." _____

5. "I use different ones, so my browser history isn't all in one place." _____

WORD BANK
Collocations with nouns:
noun + noun (compound noun)
data trail, search engine, email account
adjective + noun
online banking, secure password, personal profile

C Work in pairs and practice remembering the compound nouns. One student closes his / her book. The other student reads either the first or second word in the compound noun and says "blank" for the other. Can you guess the missing word?

❝ email *blank*
    email **account** ❞
❝ Correct!

❝ *blank* profile
        personal profile ❞
    ❝ Correct!

LISTENING

A **Use background knowledge.** Think of three reasons why someone might want to disappear completely, so no one could find them. Compare your ideas with the class.

66 Maybe because they won the lottery and didn't want to share the money!

Perhaps they said something embarrassing in public. 99

B Listen to an interview with Miles Thorn about how to disappear. Check (✓) the advice that Miles gives. 🎧23

☑ **1.** If you have a lot of money, go to a country where you are unknown.

☐ **2.** Open a new bank account in a foreign country.

☐ **3.** Work for cash and live in different cities.

☐ **4.** Only contact someone you trust, like a family member.

☐ **5.** Make sure you have deleted all your social media history.

☐ **6.** Create a fake online identity and communicate with fake friends.

ACADEMIC SKILL
Try to infer the meaning of new words or phrases from the context of the listening.

C **Infer meaning.** Listen again and choose the best answers. 🎧23

1. When Miles says *track people down,* he means . . .

a. help them disappear.   b. find them.

2. The phrase *the world is your oyster* means . . .

a. you can take every opportunity.   b. you can do anything and won't get caught.

3. *Work off the books* means to work . . .

a. for a salary and pay taxes.   b. for cash and not pay taxes.

4. People who *couch surf* . . .

a. temporarily stay at different houses.   b. permanently stay at one house.

5. The interviewer is confused about creating a fake identity because he thinks you have to . . .

a. be in Wisconsin.   b. leave Las Vegas.

6. Overall, Miles thinks it's likely that . . .

a. anyone can disappear and never be found.   b. anyone can find you if they can afford to.

D Imagine you want to disappear and create a fake identity. Brainstorm ideas using the categories in the photo at the bottom of the page.

E Work in groups and present your new identity. You can also ask each other questions about your new identities. Which person is the most convincing?

New name? Nickname?   Place you live / home?

Best friend?   Job?

Hobbies? Pets?   Other misinformation?

Chicago

SPEAKING

A Listen and read the conversation between Wang Yu and Gemma. Then, answer the questions. 🎧24

Wang Yu: Gemma, can you give me a hand with something? I downloaded this app, but it isn't working properly.

Gemma: Sure, let me take a look.

Wang Yu: It's a weather app and it's supposed to tell me if it's raining, or if it's going to be hot, or whatever.

Gemma: So, what's the matter with it exactly?

Wang Yu: Well, it keeps asking me for my location. It won't tell me the weather unless I click "allow," so it can access my phone.

Gemma: And?

Wang Yu: Well, I don't want it to know my location. I mean . . . that's private information.

Gemma: Let me see. But it needs to know where you are in order to tell you about the weather.

Wang Yu: Yes, I guess it does.

Gemma: But you don't have to accept it. I mean, if you don't want it to know where you are all the time, click "Don't allow." One second . . . Here you go. Now, write the name of any place in this box.

Wang Yu: Oh, OK. Let's see what the weather's like in . . . er, Chicago?

Gemma: But we don't live in Chicago.

Wang Yu: I know, but that way the app will think I'm in Chicago and it won't know I'm here!

Gemma: Oh, I see.

1. What is Wang Yu's problem with the app?

2. How does Gemma solve the problem?

B Work in pairs and practice the conversation.

C Work in pairs and practice a similar conversation using the useful expressions. Choose one of these problems and ask your partner for help.

1. You were working on a document and saved it. Now you can't find the document on your laptop.

2. You changed the password on your computer. Now when you try to log on, it won't accept the new password.

3. You're looking at a website when the screen of your tablet freezes. It won't respond to your finger.

4. The battery life on your phone is supposed to be nine hours. But it keeps shutting down after only two hours.

SPEAKING STRATEGY 🎧25
Using fillers
Sometimes in a conversation, you want time to think. Use fillers such as Let me see / think, One moment, I mean . . . to show you are thinking.

USEFUL EXPRESSIONS 26
Asking for and offering help
Can you give me a hand with something?
Why isn't this working properly?
It keeps . . . ing
It won't . . . unless I . . .

What's the matter?
Let me take a look.
If you want / don't want it to . . . then . . .
Here you go.

GRAMMAR

A Read the Unit 4, Lesson A Grammar Reference in the appendix. Complete the exercises. Then do the exercises below.

WISH / IF ONLY (present and past)	
PRESENT situation	**Wish statement + past form**
I don't have an internet connection. My laptop won't restart. This password isn't working. I have to go to work.	I *wish* I had an internet connection. (but I don't) *If only* my laptop would restart. (but it won't) I *wish* this password was / were working. (but it isn't) *If only* I didn't have to go to work. (but I do)
PAST situation	**Wish statement + past perfect**
I sent an email to the wrong person. I forgot to back up my data. I bought it online.	I *wish* I hadn't sent the email. (but I did) *If only* I'd backed up my data. (but I forgot) I *wish* I hadn't bought it online. (but I did)
Use *wish* or *If only* . . . to talk about an imaginary situation in the present or past that is the opposite of the real situation. We often use *wish* / *If only* to express regret.	

B Complete the sentence using the verb in bold in the correct past form.

1. I don't **have** my lunch with me. I wish I _____ had _____ my lunch with me.

2. I didn't **have** any breakfast this morning. I wish I _____ had had _____ breakfast this morning.

3. My car **won't** start! If only my car _____ start.

4. We **have** to wear a school uniform. If only we _____ to wear a uniform.

5. They **can't** meet us today. I wish they _____ meet us today.

6. She **lost** her cell phone. If only she _____ her cell phone.

7. I **can't** understand French. I wish I _____ understand French.

8. I never **learned** French at school. If only I _____ French at school.

C Look at this photo. What do you think the people are thinking? Write your ideas using *I wish* and *If only*.

1. _____   3. _____

2. _____   4. _____

A group of people under umbrellas

ACTIVE ENGLISH Try it out!

A Read about a survey below. Then answer the questions.

1. Why do the results show that people want to delete their digital past?

2. Do you have similar feelings to any of the people in the survey? Why?

Six in ten of us post things online we regret, new study finds

"I wish I hadn't posted that selfie!" How many of us have had similar regrets about a photo we shared online or a message we wrote without thinking of the consequences? According to one survey, at least 60% of us. The survey also found that:

- 68% of people worry about the security of their personal data being shared online.
- Over 25% wish they could delete embarrassing online history from when they were a teenager.
- More than half aren't comfortable with shops and businesses storing their data.

B Work in groups and discuss this list of online activities that some people find embarrassing. Rank them from 1 to 5 (1 = most embarrassing, 5 = least embarrassing).

_____ You send an email with a couple of obvious spelling mistakes.

_____ Your parents share embarrassing pictures of you as a baby or child.

_____ You write a private message to a very close friend but post it publicly by mistake.

_____ You take a crazy selfie with friends at a party but mistakenly tag your parents or boss.

_____ You click the *like* button by mistake in response to someone's very bad news.

C Have you, or someone you know, ever made any of the mistakes in **B** (or similar mistakes)? What happened? What do you wish you'd done instead?

D Work in groups. Write six rules or guidelines for people going online and using social media. For example, "Never post pictures from a party until you have checked them the next morning."

1. _____   4. _____

2. _____   5. _____

3. _____   6. _____

E Join another group. Present and compare your sets of rules.

4A GOALS   Now I can . . .

Explain how something works _____

Express regret _____

1. Yes, I can.

2. Mostly, yes.

3. Not really.

VOCABULARY

A Read about the verb *to catfish.*

1. Where does the verb come from?

2. Is it a type of crime?

---

catfish (noun) *a type of river fish*

to catfish (verb) *to set up a* fake *online identity in order to* deceive *someone*

English dictionaries have recently added a new verb: *to catfish.* It comes from a documentary film called *Catfish*, in which a young man starts an online relationship with someone who isn't telling the **truth**. He discovers she has set up a fake online profile with **fictional** family and friends. During the film, we learn that catfish were once put in tanks to keep other fish interested and active, so "*to catfish*" refers to the idea of making other people interested in you. The good news is that, by the end of the movie, the man and the woman do, in fact, become friends.

Since the original film was made, there have been numerous reports in the media of catfishing, including many high-profile celebrity cases. The typical aim of anyone who catfishes is to **steal** money from their **victim** or to gain access to their personal details. The victims also include people whose photos are stolen and reused. Currently, the act of catfishing itself is not **illegal**, though catfishing that results in loss of money is treated as a **crime**.

B Complete these sentences using the words in blue in the text.

1. I don't think you're telling me the _____. I think you are lying.

2. There's a lot of _____ news. I don't know what to believe.

3. Have you ever been a _____ of identity theft?

4. It's _____ to drive faster than the speed limit.

5. The man tried to _____ people into thinking he was their friend.

6. The most common type of _____ is theft.

7. The police arrived before the robbers managed to _____ anything.

8. Superman is a _____ character. He isn't real.

WORD BANK
When you learn a new word, check whether it has other word forms: truth (n), true (adj), truly (adv)

C The word *catfish* has two word forms, a verb and a noun. Write the word forms for the blue words in **A**. Use a dictionary to help you.

D Work in pairs and write five sentences using words you wrote in **C**.

E Join another pair. Take turns reading your sentences from **D** aloud, leaving out the key word. Can the other pair guess the missing word?

> " The police decided the criminal wasn't telling the _____.
>
> Truth? "
>
> " Correct!

Large catfish jumping out of the river

FACT AND FICTION IN PHOTOS

Every year, the Natural History Museum in London runs the **prestigious** Wildlife Photographer of the Year competition. The competition attracts some of the top photographers in the world. However, there was surprise when the museum announced that a photograph called "The Night Raider" was being **disqualified** as a fake. The photo shows an anteater on a termite mound at night. The museum reported that it had evidence to prove the anteater shown in the photo was stuffed*! In fact, it strongly **resembled** an anteater on display to visitors at the Emas National Park, in Brazil, where the photo was taken.

This kind of story is becoming increasingly common as we find ourselves deceived daily into believing photos always show the whole truth. On the contrary, modern software techniques allow magazine covers to show Photoshopped models, and social media shares **manipulated** news images to provoke responses. Look at the example here: Calob Castellon started a project to show how photos that are posted and published can be transformed into something that catches your eye. The use of fake photos is not illegal (as long as they are not used as part of a crime) and neither is it new. As far back as 1917, there was the famous case of two young girls named Frances and Elsie who took photos of fairies by the stream behind Elsie's family's home. At the time, the photos caused a sensation when they were printed in newspapers, with many people believing the fairies were real. It wasn't until sixty years later that Frances and Elsie finally admitted that they had deceived everyone by drawing the fairies themselves.

Unlike the readers of newspapers in 1917, you'd expect twenty-first century consumers of news and media to be much better at separating fact from fiction when it comes to photos. But how good are we? Not good at all, says university researcher Sophie J. Nightingale. In a test designed by Nightingale, more than 700 people were shown ten images. Some were original and some were **altered**. Participants could only tell if an image was altered 60 percent of the time. Only 45 percent could say what had been changed in the image.

"It's a bit worrying," said Nightingale. "Photos are incredibly powerful. They influence how we see the world. They can even influence our memory of things. If we can't tell the fake ones from the real ones, the fakes are going to be powerful, too." She is especially worried about the implications of fake photos being used as evidence in court cases. She is concerned that people will stop believing that *anything* is real: "If you just go around telling people 'don't **trust** anything,' then people will **lose** all **faith** in images, which is equally problematic. At the moment, when it comes to fake photos, we have a lot more problems than solutions, I'm afraid."

So, we all need to be on the lookout for photos that are fake or changed in some way. A badly altered image will have bad or blurred edges where one object is put on another, or the lighting on two objects might be different. Try an image search online to find out if part of the image has been taken from elsewhere. And, as a general rule, if the photo looks too good to be true or gets an emotional reaction, it's probably one that you need to study more closely. 🎧27

*stuffed when a dead animal is preserved so it still looks alive

Which one is real: the young woman floating on clouds or lying in cotton on the floor?

A Look at the photos. How do they make the fake image?

B **Scan for Information.** Read the article and decide if these statements are True or False.

1. The photographer of "The Night Raider" won the competition before being disqualified. T / F

2. Fake photos in the media only began in the twenty-first century. T / F

3. Nowadays, most people are able to spot fake photos. T / F

4. Nightingale is concerned about fake images and also that people believe everything is fake. T / F

5. There are some simple guidelines for identifying images. T / F

C Complete each sentence with the correct word or phrase from the article.

1. If something is prestigious, it is *respected / well-known.*

2. If you are disqualified, you have *broken the rules / lost a competition.*

3. If you resemble someone, you *dress / look* like them.

4. If something is manipulated or altered, it *has / has not* been changed.

5. If you trust someone, you believe they always tell *the truth / lies.*

6. If you lose faith in someone, you stop *meeting / trusting* them.

D Discuss these questions in groups or as a class.

1. Nightingale thinks it will be problematic if we don't trust anything we see or read and if we lose faith in images. Do you agree with her? Why?

> **ACADEMIC SKILL**
> When you see a new word you don't know, try to infer its meaning from the context.

2. Have you ever read or seen something online that you believed was real, but later realized was fake?

LISTENING

A When you read a news headline online, how do you decide:

- whether to click on it and read the story?
- whether the information is real or fake?

Share answers with a partner.

B Read the infographic "How to identify fake news." Categorize the advice in two ways:

✓ Yes, I already do this.　　　　　　　　✗ No, I don't do this.

HOW TO IDENTIFY FAKE NEWS

**What is
the source?**

Research the site,
its mission,
and its contact info.

**Who is
the author?**

Research the author.
Do they exist?
Are they credible?

**What is
the date?**

Check if it is an old story
and if the story is related
to current events.

**What is
the bias?**

Think about whether their
beliefs can affect
their judgment.

**What do
you know?**

Read more about
the topic. Find out the
whole story.

**What are the
supporting sources?**

Check the sources
and see whether they
support the story.

**What is
the objective?**

Check that the story
is not meant
to be a joke.

**What do
experts say?**

Visit a fact-checking
site to make sure that
the information is true.

C Listen to a short lecture and answer the questions. 🎧28

　1. Which advice in the infographic does the lecturer also mention?

　2. What other advice does she give?

D Read these statements from the lecture. Complete the sentences with a missing word from the lecture. Then listen again and check your answers. 🎧28

　1. "Every day, thousands of completely untrue stories go viral because they have an o _____ headline."

　2. "We tend to click on news that confirms our own set of beliefs and b _____."

　3. "How do we decide what is serious journalism and what is a j _____?"

　4. "Ask yourself, 'Who is the s _____?' 'Which newspaper or website publishes it?'"

　5. "If you're going to quote the story, then make sure it's c _____."

　6. "Try visiting fact-checking websites. They're always on the lookout for
　　o _____ news stories."

E Work in groups of three. Discuss which of these news sources you trust 100%, mostly trust, or don't trust at all. Give reasons for your answers.

TV news	national newspapers	news websites	social media sites
radio news	video bloggers	local newspapers	friends

GRAMMAR

A Read the Unit 4, Lesson B Grammar Reference in the appendix. Complete the exercises. Then do the exercises below.

PAST UNREAL CONDITIONALS	
If clause	**Result clause**
1. If I'd known the person was a fake,	I wouldn't have replied.
2. If we hadn't seen it on TV,	we wouldn't have believed it!
Result clause	**If clause**
3. I would have ignored the news	if I'd realized it was untrue.
Past unreal conditionals are used to talk about imaginary situations that did not happen in the past. The situation described is often the opposite of what happened. The result clause presents an imagined result. It can come first (1, 2) or second (3) in the sentence with no change of meaning.	

B **PRONUNCIATION: Contracted forms** Read these sentences with past unreal conditional forms. Underline any words that can be contracted in everyday speech (e.g., *had / would* → *'d, had not / would not* → *hadn't / wouldn't*). Then listen and check your answers. ◁29▷

1. If I had seen the weather forecast, I would have worn more clothes!

2. We would never have known about the virus if we had not had the software.

3. If you had checked other sources, your facts would have been correct!

4. The librarian would have checked if we had asked her.

C Read the affirmative and negative sentences from people talking about their past. Using past unreal conditionals, write the correct form of the verb in parentheses.

1. He studied English in college. If he hadn't studied English, he _____ (become) an English teacher.

2. I didn't play soccer at school. If I _____ (play) at school, I would have enjoyed it.

3. We met on vacation. If we hadn't met on vacation, we _____ (get) married.

4. The source wasn't credible. If she hadn't checked, she _____ (knew) the news story was fake.

D **Transcription.** Write down two true events from your past and one fake event. For example, *I studied science.*

1. _____ 2. _____ 3. _____

Next, write three sentences using past unreal conditionals to talk about the consequences of these past events on your life. For example, *If I hadn't studied science, I wouldn't have become a . . .*

1. If . . . _____ 2. If . . . _____ 3. If . . . _____

E Work in pairs and tell each other about your past using your sentences in **D**. Can you guess which situation is fake?

ACTIVE ENGLISH Try it out!

A Read the following conspiracy theories. Why do you think people believe them? Do you believe any of them? Why?

- Elvis Presley is still alive.

- Humans never landed on the moon.

- The government doesn't want us to know that aliens are on Earth.

Do you know any other famous conspiracy theories? Tell the class.

WORD BANK

conspiracy theory (n) a belief that an organization such as the government is responsible for something unexplained

storm (v) move angrily and forcefully towards a place

B Read the newspaper report and discuss the questions as a class.

1. Why do you think the event "went viral"?

2. What was the conspiracy theory?

3. Why do you think some news goes viral?

ALIEN EVENT ATTRACTS LESS THAN 200

If Matty Roberts had known the trouble he'd cause when he posted a fake Facebook event, maybe he wouldn't have bothered. Within days of inviting people to "Storm Area 51" and see the aliens, his event went viral, with three million people interested in taking part. Area 51 is the US Air Base that is famous for a popular conspiracy theory that says the government is hiding aliens there with spaceships. Reportedly, at least one in five of us believe that aliens are real, but on that day, fewer than 200 people showed up. "I'm a little disappointed because it's a lot less people than they said online." said Nathan Brown, who probably wished he hadn't driven 700 miles to be there.

C Find and underline examples in the text of these techniques often used in news articles:

a. numbers and statistics

b. quotes from real people

c. statements of fact

d. the writer's opinion or interpretation

D WRITING Read the Unit 4 Writing Model in the appendix and write a short news article (100–120 words) about a recent event in your local area, place of work, or place of study. Afterwards, post the articles around your class and read each other's news.

4B GOALS Now I can . . .

Identify reliable information ____

Describe imaginary situations ____

1. Yes, I can.

2. Mostly, yes.

3. Not really.

GLOBAL VOICES

A Watch the video of Alex Sigrist talking about past regrets and wishes. Number these in the order he talks about them.

_____ a. Wishing he hadn't left public messages for a 'crush' (or girl he liked).

_____ b. Wishing he'd bought stocks in social networking and tech companies.

_____ c. Wishing he'd taken more photos and made more videos for his memories.

_____ d. Wishing his mother hadn't seen his embarrasing college photos.

B Watch the video again and answer these questions.

1. What example does Alex give of learning from your mistakes at the beginning?

2. How does he think he probably looked to his classmates, best friend, and little brother?

3. Alex uses the phrase 'beyond cringe-worthy' meaning something causing extreme embarrassment. What is Alex referring to?

4. In 2009, why did Alex start posting videos from South Korea?

5. What is lesson number three?

C Think about your life five years ago, and then complete these sentences with a different idea about you.

If I'd known _____ five years ago, I would have _____.
I wish _____ five years ago.

D Work in groups and take turns reading your sentences from **C**. Who gives some really useful advice?

This photo shows three friends in a haunted house in the Nightmare Fear Factory in Niagara Falls, Canada. The haunted house takes pictures of visitors and posts them online. How do you think the men in the photo feel? Do you think they are happy their photo is online? And in this book?

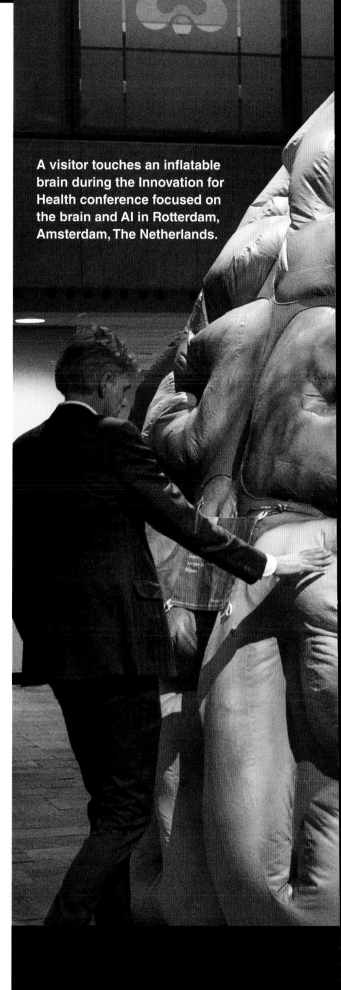

5

BRAINPOWER

LOOK AT THE PHOTO. ANSWER THE QUESTIONS.

1. What type of information are you good at remembering?
2. What do you forget more easily? Why?

WARM-UP VIDEO

A Watch part one of the video. Take the memory tests. How many questions did you get right?

B Watch part two of the video. Answer the questions.

1. What percentage of people couldn't guess the correct answers in the three tests?
2. What similar situation is also stressful for most people?

C Watch the video again. For each statement, select the correct items.

1. The three answers in the three tests:

    soccer ball   headphones   wrench
    glasses   football   hammer

2. The ways they made the tests more stressful:

    flashing lights   time constraints
    person shouting   noise of a clock

3. What happens when we are stressed by speaking in public:

    forgetfulness   increased heart rate
    swollen tongue   lose train of thought

D Do you get stressed and forget things when you have to speak in public? What other types of situations make you feel stressed? Do you have strategies to deal with these situations?

A visitor touches an inflatable brain during the Innovation for Health conference focused on the brain and AI in Rotterdam, Amsterdam, The Netherlands.

GOALS **Lesson A**
/ Describe past objects and habits
/ Help someone make up their mind

Lesson B
/ Tell a joke and a story
/ Give advice on exam preparation

VOCABULARY

A Read the text and write a response starting with one of these phrases:

It's surprising to me because ...   *It isn't surprising to me because ...*

The picture superiority effect is a theory that says that the human brain retains more information as images than as words. If you hear or read a piece of information, then three days later, you'll only recall about 10% of it. With an image added to reinforce the meaning, you'll retrieve 65% more information.

What are some implications of this in our daily lives? Well, a painting on the wall might remind you of a special person, place, or event. Learning new words in a foreign language is easier when you repeat them with a visual stimulus. You're more likely to recollect someone's name if you can recognize him / her from a selfie. Or when you meet old friends, looking at old photos will refresh everyone's memories and help them reminisce.

B Underline any words in the text that start with the letters *re-*. Then work in pairs and try to define each one.

> **WORD BANK**
> The letters *re-* in many English words come from the Latin language. *Re-* means *again* or *once more.*

C Compare the pairs of similar words and match each one to its correct definition.

1. **repeat / remind (someone of)**

   a. say or do something a second time ___*repeat*___

   b. cause someone to think of someone or something they already know ___*remind*___

2. **recall / refresh (your memory)**

   a. remember something _____

   b. be reminded of something you forgot _____

3. **retain / retrieve**

   a. bring or get back something _____

   b. continue to hold or keep something _____

4. **reminisce / reinforce**

   a. enjoy remembering and talking about the past _____

   b. make something stronger _____

5. **recognize / recollect**

   a. remember somebody or something when you see (or hear) them again _____

   b. remember somebody or something by making a special effort to remember _____

LISTENING

A Do you have lots of important family photographs, objects, and mementos in your house? How important are these for remembering the past?

WORD BANK
A **memento** is a small item which reminds someone of somebody or something from the past.

B **Listen for details.** Listen to someone describing their mementos and answer the questions. 🎧30

1. Where does he keep his mementos?

2. What mementos does he have?

C Listen again and answer these questions. 🎧30

1. What didn't he notice as a child?

2. Why doesn't he have many mementos in his apartment?

3. Who gave him the bag? Why?

4. What did he intend to do with the key one day?

5. Where did the broken watch come from?

6. What has he lost touch with?

7. Why did the boy give him the toy cowboy?

8. What does he think people might say about his mojo bag?

D Imagine you have a mojo bag. List three objects you would put in the bag. Then tell a partner about your choices and explain why they are important mementos.

Drawstring pouches are often used to keep mementos.

SPEAKING

A Read and listen to the conversation. Who is being indecisive? Who is trying to be patient? 🎧31

Ines: The plane leaves in three hours, so we need to go to the airport. Are you packed?

Jared: Almost. I'm still of two minds about whether to take this picture of my family or not.

Ines: Maybe you should take a photo of it on your phone.

Jared: Yes, but it brings back happy memories. But never mind. You're right. I'll leave it at home.

Ines: Right. Let's go then.

Jared: One moment. I can't make up my mind about these books. I want something to read on the plane. I have this new book that I haven't read yet, but I also have this old hardback copy of children's stories. I used to read it when I was a child, so it means a lot to me.

Ines: Well, if it means that much to you, don't take it in case you lose it. Keep in mind that you can read the new book and give it away once you've read it.

Jared: OK, I'll take that one and leave this one.

Ines: Great. So, can we go now?

Jared: Just one more thing. It's hard to decide between this old, woolly, red hat and this yellow one. Which do you prefer?

Ines: I don't mind either, but if I had to choose, I'd say the yellow one.

B Practice the conversation with a partner.

C Underline any expressions with *mind* in **A**. Then match the expressions from the reading to the similar expressions below.

  a. I can't decide. (two matches) _____

  b. I don't have a strong objection. _____

  c. It's not important. _____

  d. Don't forget that . . . _____

D Work in pairs. One of you is going traveling for six months around the world. Your bag is packed. There is only room for three extra personal items. Together, choose three items from the list. Explain your reasons.

A framed photo of your family.

A scarf that a friend made for you.

A ball you used to play with as a child.

A notebook to keep a journal.

Your favorite book.

A pack of playing cards.

A stone from your parents' garden.

A letter from your best friend.

SPEAKING STRATEGY 🎧32

Hedging
When people ask for our opinion or preference, we often avoid giving a direct answer by using *hedging language*, which makes our answer less direct. Hedging language includes words and phrases like **maybe /**
perhaps you should . . . /
I don't mind either . . . / if I had
to choose, I'd say . . .

USEFUL EXPRESSIONS 🎧33

Showing indecision Language
I can't decide which . . .
I'm of two minds about . . .
I can't make up my mind about . . .
It's hard to decide between . . .
Which do you prefer?

Helping someone make up his / her mind
Maybe you should . . .
If it means that much to you, perhaps you shouldn't . . .
If I had to choose, I'd say . . .
I think you should . . .

GRAMMAR

A Read the Unit 5, Lesson A Grammar Reference in the appendix. Complete the exercises. Then do the exercises below.

PAST HABITS: *USED TO* AND *WOULD*			
We	used to	live	near the sea.
She didn't	use to	live	here.
Did you	use to	live	in this house?
My family	would / wouldn't	walk	here on weekends.

B Complete the text with the correct form of *use to* or *would*.

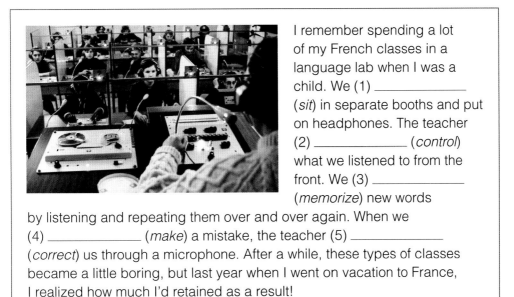

I remember spending a lot of my French classes in a language lab when I was a child. We (1) _____ (*sit*) in separate booths and put on headphones. The teacher (2) _____ (*control*) what we listened to from the front. We (3) _____ (*memorize*) new words by listening and repeating them over and over again. When we (4) _____ (*make*) a mistake, the teacher (5) _____ (*correct*) us through a microphone. After a while, these types of classes became a little boring, but last year when I went on vacation to France, I realized how much I'd retained as a result!

C What do you remember about your past? Write notes in the table about what you used to do as a child and what you do now.

	As a child	Now
In school		
Free-time activities		
Favorite food		
Use of technology		

D Tell a partner about your past and now.

66 As a child I would . . .
but now I . . .

I didn't use to play . . .
but now I . . . 99

66 I used to eat . . .
and I still do!

A Read about four traditional memory techniques. Did you use to memorize words using any of these techniques when you were younger? Do you still use them today?

Creating a "memory palace" in a home, matching facts with locations, helps our brains remember.

Mnemonics

A mnemonic is a technique for remembering facts or spelling difficult words. So, if you can't recall the order of the colors of the rainbow, remember the name Roy G. Biv, which will remind you that the colors are *red*, *orange*, *yellow*, *green*, *blue*, *indigo*, and *violet*. Or, if you often forget the spelling of a difficult word like "rhythm," make up a sentence like "Rock Helps Your Two Hips Move."

Memory Palace

The ancient Greeks and Romans would use memory palaces to store and retrieve facts from their brains. It works by imagining you are walking through your home (or an imaginary palace). In each part of the home, you place a fact or word. For example, place words for anything you can eat in the kitchen. In the yard, place words you associate with being outside. Later, return to these places in your mind to recollect the words.

Chunking

Naturally, the human brain likes to group or "chunk" information into categories. So, with a list of words, three words might all be connected to winter in some way. Perhaps another five words are all things you used to play with as a child.

Storytelling

If you have a list of words or facts, create a short story that includes all of them. The story doesn't have to make sense, but it has to include characters and places. By making a story, you create emotional connections with the information.

B You are going to try to remember 15 words. You have 15 seconds to remember all the words. When your teacher says "GO," turn to page 214. When your teacher says "STOP," close your book and write the 15 words. Use one of the memory techniques in **A** or your own technique.

C Afterward, check your list of words and give yourself a score out of 15. Work in groups and talk about which memory technique you used. Decide which technique seems to be the most effective.

5A GOALS   Now I can . . .

Describe past objects and habits _____

Help someone make up their mind _____

1. Yes, I can.
2. Mostly, yes.
3. Not yet.

VOCABULARY

A Did a teacher or a student say each sentence below? Write T or S.

1. If you don't know a word, **look** the definition **up** in your dictionary. _____

2. I **picked** a few words and phrases **up** in Tokyo. _____

3. I think I need to **drop out** this year. _____

4. Can you **keep up** with the class or are we going too fast? _____

5. I'd like to **sign up** for an English course. _____

6. Before I **hand** this essay **in**, I want to **read** it **over** one more time. _____

7. Let's **go through** the answers to this exercise together. _____

8. Make sure you do your homework or you'll **fall behind** the class. _____

9. Can you **note** the page numbers **down**? _____

B Match the phrasal verbs in **A** to the definitions.

a. enroll in a course _____

b. understand and learn something by doing it _____

c. leave a course before the end _____

d. find a piece of information in a book or on a computer _____

e. check or look at in detail _____

f. read to check for mistakes _____

g. write something so you don't forget _____

h. work at the same speed _____

i. fail to stay at the same level as everyone else _____

j. give to the teacher for grading _____

C **PRONUNCIATION: Linking (consonant + vowel)**
Words ending with a consonant sound and starting with a vowel sound are often linked. Listen and repeat the phrases. 🎧34

look it up   pick up a language   sign up for a course

D Listen and link the phrases. Then listen again and repeat. 🎧35

hand it in   keep up with the class
write it down   drop out of college

E Write a conversation between a teacher and a student. Use phrasal verbs from **A**. Then, in pairs, read the conversations aloud. Count the phrasal verbs the other pair uses.

A toddler plays with building blocks at home.

LEARNING THE LANGUAGE OF COMEDY

For most people, standing up in front of a group of people to give a presentation is stressful enough. So, imagine what it's like for a stand-up comedian trying to make an audience laugh night after night. What could be worse? Well, trying to be funny in a language you are still trying to learn is worse! But for some comics, it's the **ultimate** challenge. You start out by learning a foreign language and then **go on** to understanding what people find funny in other countries and cultures. Here are three comics who signed up for the challenge and discovered that comedy is not **universal**!

Yuriko Kotani

Yuriko had a normal company job in Japan before she moved to England. After ten years living there and picking up the language, she decided to try stand-up. She recollects her first show: "It was absolutely terrifying. I hated it. But then I tried a second time. I got laughs all the way through." Now she writes her comedy in English. Once she performed in Japan and translated her English script into Japanese, but the jokes weren't as funny. One reason people like her in England is because she's **deadpan**. "So many people told me I have a deadpan expression. But I didn't know what deadpan meant! I looked it up in a dictionary. I thought I was smiling! And then I watched the video of myself and thought, yeah, I look deadpan or angry."

Francisco Ramos

Francisco comes from Venezuela and started doing comedy in his **native** language of Spanish. But now he also performs to English-speaking audiences. When he thinks of a new joke, he notes it down in English and then tries translating it into his native Spanish to see if it is still funny. "English is a very short, right-to-the-point language, which is why stand-up works. With stand-up, it's finding the word that could get to your point faster, to get to the joke faster." Also, he naturally speaks fast, so he always

A Answer the questions in pairs.

1. Have you ever watched a stand-up comedian? Was the comedian funny? Why or why not?

2. What makes a good comedian? What do they have to remember?

B **Read for detail.** Read the article about stand-up comedy. Check (✓) the sentences that are *true* for each comedian.

WHICH COMEDIAN . . .	YURIKO	FRANCISCO	BASSEM
1. performed in their native language and then started in English?			
2. had a different job before becoming a comedian?			
3. describes having a bad experience at first?			
4. talks about how they look to a foreign audience?			
5. talks about how they sound to a foreign audience?			
6. has tried translating English jokes back into their native language?			
7. records themselves to analyze performances?			

has to remind himself to slow down when he does stand-up in English, so more people can understand him.

Bassem Youssef

For Bassem, doing comedy is like learning a third language. Born in Egypt, his native language is Arabic, and he studied English. But, as he says, "You can be the best English speaker out there, but comedy is a third language. It's about timing, **delivery**, **pacing**, knowing your audience . . . ." Before becoming a comedian, Bassem was a medical doctor. In his spare time, he set up a YouTube channel with a series of short comedy shows in Arabic. The shows **went viral**, and then he tried performing in English. At first, he learned the hard way, but he started recording himself. "I knew my jokes were funny, but I didn't know why people didn't laugh. I listened to myself, and I was *saying* the jokes, not *telling* the jokes." 🎧36

Comedian Yuriko Kotani performing in English.

C Replace the underlined words in the sentences with words and phrases in bold in the article.

1. English is my <u>first</u> language. *native*

2. Laughing is <u>something that humans do in every country</u>. _____

3. The video was so funny that it <u>spread quickly from one internet user to another</u>. _____

4. His face was <u>without expression</u>, so I couldn't tell if he was being funny or not. _____

5. I'm studying English now and I want to <u>continue</u> to study it in college. _____

6. I would speak a bit faster to improve your <u>speed at which you speak</u>. _____

7. The speaker's <u>manner in which a speech is given</u> was very clear. _____

D **Interpret direct speech.** Read the article again and answer the questions.

1. Why wasn't Yuriko's show as successful in Japanese? _____

2. What surprised her when she watched a video of herself? _____

3. In what way does Francisco think English is a good language for stand-up? _____

4. In what ways does Bassem think comedy is a third language? _____

5. What do you think Bassem means when he says that he was *saying* the jokes, not *telling* them? _____

E Think of a short joke in your language and translate it into English. Then work in groups and take turns telling your jokes. Did your audience find the joke funny?

LISTENING

A Work in groups. Which of the types of tests and exams have you done?
- a driving test
- an English speaking exam
- an eye test at the optician's
- a musical instrument exam
- a qualifying exam for a job
- a spelling test

B Work in groups. Rank the tests and exams in **A** in order from most stressful to least stressful. Give reasons for your choices.

C **Identify a speaker.** Listen to three different people talk about driving tests. Match the person to a–c. 🎧37

_____ a. a student driver

_____ b. a driving instructor

_____ c. a driving test examiner

ACADEMIC SKILL
Key details
If you find it hard to understand someone, just concentrate on the key details.

D **Global inference.** Listen again and circle the correct answer. 🎧37

1. The woman locked herself in *by accident* / *on purpose*.

2. In the end, she *took* / *didn't take* the test.

3. The *student* / *instructor* had put the plastic fruit in the car.

4. The student driver *eventually* / *never* learned the difference between right and left.

5. Most examiners hope to *pass* / *fail* a learner.

6. In the examiner's examples, *one of the learners* / *both learners* failed their test.

E Work in pairs. Take turns remembering and retelling the stories using the words below.

1. day of the test – very stressed – locked the car – examiner tried – unlock the door

2. plastic banana – steering wheel – plastic tomato – a *left turn only* sign – gave up telling

3. not trying to fail – one man – wrong side of the road – strangest test – couldn't remember

A scared driving instructor can't watch as the young man drives.

GRAMMAR

A Read the Unit 5, Lesson B Grammar Reference in the appendix. Complete the exercises. Then do the exercises below.

VERBS + *ING* OR INFINITIVE
No change in meaning Some verbs can be followed by a verb in the infinitive or *-ing* form with little or no change in meaning: *I prefer studying late at night.* = *I prefer to study late at night.*
Change in meaning Some verbs can be followed by either the infinitive form or the *-ing* form, but the meaning changes. These verbs include *remember*, *forget*, *go on*, *mean*, *regret*, and *stop*. *I remember learning to drive.* (= talking about a memory) *Remember to stop at the traffic light when it's red!* (= talking about a necessary action)

B Compare the pairs of sentences. Is there a change in meaning or no real change in meaning? If there is a change in meaning, explain the difference.

1. a. Brent began driving when he was fifty years old.

   b. Brent began to drive when he was fifty years old.

2. a. He went on flying airplanes until he was eighty.

   b. After learning to drive, he went on to fly airplanes.

3. a. I'll never forget teaching one student.

   b. I forgot to teach a student.

4. a. Francisco started doing stand-up comedy.

   b. Francisco started to do stand-up comedy.

5. a. The mistake meant failing him immediately.

   b. I meant to fail him because of a mistake.

C Complete the sentences with the correct form of the verbs in parentheses.

1. As a child, I remember _____ (walk) down this street every day to school.

2. We regret _____ (inform) you that you did not meet the requirements of the course.

3. I'll never forget _____ (meet) you here.

4. Can we stop _____ (buy) some water?

5. The longer I lived in Chile, the more Spanish I went on _____ (pick up) just by talking to people.

6. Did you remember _____ (book) a table at the restaurant?

7. Dropping out of college meant _____ (have) to find a job.

8. I meant _____ (sign up) for yoga classes but missed the enrollment.

D Complete the sentences with your own words. Then tell a partner.

1. This morning, I remembered to . . . but I forgot to . . .

2. As a child, I remember . . . and I'll also never forget . . .

3. On my way home yesterday, I stopped to . . . . Then I went on to . . .

4. Some years ago, I stopped . . . but I went on . . .

ACTIVE ENGLISH Try it out!

A Read some comments by students reflecting on how they prepare for exams. Complete the sentences with the verbs in the infinitive or *-ing* form. There is more than one answer for some sentences.

drink	exercise	take	play	repeat	sleep	study

1. "I enjoy _____ a lot of coffee in the morning to improve my memory."

2. "I like _____ regularly because it helps me remember information."

3. "I prefer studying late into the night and _____ when I feel like it."

4. "I keep _____ key words and facts to myself before exams."

5. "When I'm worried about failing, I try _____ my mind off the exam."

6. "I need to take regular breaks, and I enjoy _____ my piano."

7. "I dislike _____ with others. I prefer _____ alone."

B Work in groups and discuss the comments in **A**. Which do you think are good advice and which are bad advice? What other advice would you give?

C Listen to an expert opinion on the seven comments in **A**. Which does the speaker think are good advice? Did you agree with her in **B**? 🎧38

D **WRITING** Read the Unit 5 Writing Model in the appendix and answer the questions.

1. What language is the person studying? _____

2. How does he structure the journal? _____

3. Does he reflect on both what went well and what didn't? _____

4. Is it clear what he has learned as a result of being reflective? _____

E Write a similar reflective learning journal about one of the topics below.
- Learning English in the last few lessons.
- Another subject you are currently studying.
- An aspect of your working life and professional development.

5B GOALS Now I can . . .

Tell a joke and a story _____

Give advice on exam preparation _____

1. Yes, I can.
2. Mostly, yes.
3. Not yet.

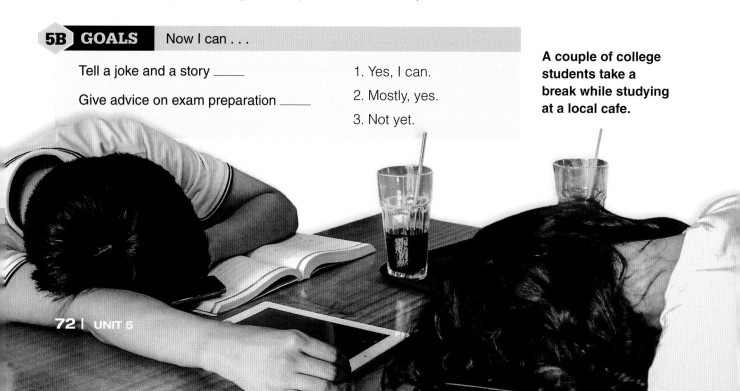

A couple of college students take a break while studying at a local cafe.

GLOBAL VOICES

A Look at the photo. What are the girls trying to learn to do? How difficult to learn does it look? Is learning a language easier or more difficult?

B Work in pairs. You are going to watch a video with people answering these two questions:

1. How did you learn languages?

2. What are your tips for learning a language?

Before you watch, try to predict three different answers you might hear for each question. For example, *I learned languages by watching TV shows in the language. / One tip is to visit the country.*

C Watch the video again with David, Aziz, Laurel, and Victor. Write the name of the correct person to complete each sentence.

1. _____ was mediocre and unsuccessful at learning languages at high school.

2. _____ had to speak the language if he wanted food to eat.

3. _____ grew up learning English from English cowboy movies.

4. _____ learned multiple languages in an immersion setting.

5. _____ thinks that understanding a language is a way to explore a culture.

6. _____ doesn't think people make fun of you when you make mistakes.

7. _____ learned through listening to music.

8. _____ thinks you can learn about a language from books, but you also learn a language through human communication.

D Compare your own experience and views of learning a language with the speakers in the video. Which speaker(s) had similar experiences or has / have views similar to your own? Tell the class.

Learning how to ride a unicycle

6

STORYTELLING

6

LOOK AT THE PHOTO. ANSWER THE QUESTIONS.

1. What story is being represented in the photo?
2. What makes a good story in a movie or a book?

WARM-UP VIDEO

A Watch the video. Make notes about the location, main characters, and important moments in the story. Then work in pairs and compare your comments. Would you recommend it? Why or why not?

B Read the text. Compare this version of the story with the video. Discuss any differences in pairs. Then watch the video again and compare.

A young man was going home on the bus one day when he noticed a young woman. Momentarily, she caught his eye, and he quickly looked away. After she had gotten off at the next stop, he suddenly saw her camera on the seat. Back at his apartment, he looked through her photos. There was the usual stuff—selfies, a birthday cake with her name, friends saying goodbye—until suddenly, he saw himself asleep. He couldn't believe his eyes! He drove back to the stop where she'd gotten off and he figured out where she lived because of a photo of a tall building taken from the entrance of her apartment. He found her name and rang the doorbell. Another woman answered the door and explained that Nasim had moved to Boston. The young man decided to take a photo of himself with his number and he sent the camera to the address. He hoped it would be forwarded to Nasim and that she would call him.

C Work in groups. Imagine you are writing a sequel to the short film. What happens next? Discuss a possible storyline for the new film and then tell the class.

Pan Lingjuan performs a scene from The Legend of Mulan during a dress rehearsal in New York.

GOALS   **Lesson A**

/ Talk about movies and TV series

/ Describe how something happened

Lesson B

/ Use descriptive language

/ Tell a story

VOCABULARY

A Look at this list of types of movies and TV series. Which would you normally choose to watch? What other types of movies or TV series do you like?

_____ science fiction   _____ horror

_____ thriller   _____ period drama

_____ romantic comedy   _____ fantasy

B Match each comment (1–6) to a type of movie or TV series in **A**. Write the number.

1. It's **set** in France during the eighteenth century. I only watch it for the clothes and the **scenery**.

2. The **special effects** with the dragons are great, as well. I binge-watched the whole series over the weekend!

3. In this **episode**, the police are investigating a murder. But don't ask me what's happening. I lost track of the **plot** half an hour ago.

4. The film *2001* is famous for its music and spaceships, but it was **based on** a short story called "The Sentinel," written in 1948.

5. I wish I hadn't read the review before I saw the movie. The article was full of spoilers, so I wasn't surprised when half the **cast** was killed.

6. It's a **remake** about a couple who meet in high school and then fall in love again later in life. The **script** is similar to the **original version**.

> **WORD BANK**
> **binge-watch** to watch a lot of episodes of one TV series in a short period of time
> **original** ≠ remake
> **spoilers** information that tells you what happens in a movie or TV series before you watch it

C Circle the correct word from **B** to complete the sentences.

1. The film is *set* / *based on* an island in the middle of the Pacific Ocean.

2. It's the final *episode* / *cast* tonight!

3. Have you read the *plot* / *script* yet?

4. This one isn't the *original version* / *remake*. It was first made in 1950.

5. I don't like action films with a lot of noise and *special effects* / *scenery*.

D When you try to decide which film or TV series to watch, which of these factors affect your decision the most? Discuss them in groups and rank them in order (from most important to least important).

_____ You like the cast.

_____ It has good special effects.

_____ Your friends also want to see it.

_____ It's based on a famous book.

_____ You like the director's other films / TV series.

_____ It's an original script, not a remake.

_____ It's based on a true story (not fictional).

LISTENING

A **Make predictions.** You are going to listen to a show about film and TV entertainment. Before you listen, look at these phrases from the show and try to predict what it's going to be about.

4,000 words	feel real	knowledge of other languages
fans have tried to learn it	invented languages	Star Trek
fantasy shows		

B Listen to the show and check your predictions in **A**. 🎧39

C Listen again and choose the correct answers. There is often more than one correct answer. 🎧39

WORD BANK
genre a type of film or book (e.g., fantasy, science fiction)

1. What does the presenter think every fantasy show must have these days?

    a. special effects   b. famous actors   c. an invented language

2. How realistic does Doctor Stevens think the invented languages are?

    a. very   b. fairly   c. not very

3. What linguistic features does the invented language of Dothraki have?

    a. pronunciation   b. grammar   c. vocabulary

4. When did the fantasy genre begin?

    a. in the early part of the last century

    b. in the second half of the last century

    c. at the beginning of this century

5. What have people done with the invented language Klingon?

    a. learned to speak it   b. written plays with it   c. written an opera using it

D Answer the questions in pairs.

1. Do you think an invented language improves a book or film? If yes, in what way?

2. Have you ever read any of the books or watched the films or TV series mentioned in the audio? If yes, did you enjoy them?

3. Can you think of any books or films from your country that use invented languages?

Staff members at London's Science Museum dress like extras from the long-running TV series *Star Trek*, and learn to speak Klingon.

quSDaQ balu'a
[KOOSH-dak BA-loo-a]

SPEAKING

A Read and listen to Aiko and Matias's conversation. What does Matias like about the series? What is he afraid of Aiko telling him? 🎧40

Aiko: So? Did you watch the last episode?

Matias: No, I didn't. Don't tell me any spoilers! I binge-watched seasons one, two, and three over the weekend, and I managed to reach episode seven of season four last night.

Aiko: It's amazing, isn't it?

Matias: I'm completely hooked. The characters are so real.

Aiko: Who's your favorite?

Matias: The Queen, I think. She's so evil, but you can't take your eyes off the actress who plays her. And just when you think she's about to die, she always survives! But it's all very different from the books.

Aiko: The books? I didn't know it was adapted.

Matias: Yes, it's all based on a novel set in the same place and time, but the plot is very different.

Aiko: So, how does it end in the book?

Matias: I don't know. I couldn't get into it, and I lost track of the plot, so I never read the end.

Aiko: I wonder if they all die like in the show.

Matias: Spoilers! Don't tell me!

Aiko: Oh, sorry!

B Practice the conversation with a partner.

C Practice a similar conversation in pairs. You both watched the first episode of a new TV series shown in the pictures below. Student A describes the first episode. Student B has also seen the next episode of the series. (Student B turn to page 215.) Start the conversation when you are ready.

(Student B turn to page 215.)

SPEAKING STRATEGY 🎧41

Repetition in the form of a question

In everyday conversations, we sometimes repeat the words at the end of the other person's sentence in the form of a question as a way of showing surprise and asking for more information:

A: It's all very different from **the books**.

B: *The books?* I didn't know it was adapted.

A: I loved **the last episode**.

B: *The last episode?* I didn't know it was finished.

USEFUL EXPRESSIONS 🎧42

Asking about movies and TV series

Are you watching . . . / Have you been watching . . . (a series)?

How was the movie?

Did you watch . . . (the film / the last episode)?

It's amazing / great / fantastic / terrible / boring.

I'm completely hooked!

You can't take your eyes off . . . (an actor / actress)

I couldn't get into it.

I lost track of the plot.

What happens at the end?

How does it end?

Don't tell me what happens!

No spoilers!

GRAMMAR

A Read the Unit 6, Lesson A Grammar Reference in the appendix. Complete the exercises. Then do the exercises below.

ADVERBS
• *-ly* adverbs (adjective + *-ly*) for comment and manner (how): *Fortunately,* she **suddenly** remembered her camera.
• adverbs of time (when) and place (where): *Later,* he was going **back**. . .
• adverbs of focus (to add emphasis): *She was on the bus,* **as well**. / *She'd* **just** *gotten off the bus.* / *She* **even** *left her camera behind.*

B Match the underlined adverb in each sentence (1–7) to the use (a–g).

1. A young man was going <u>back</u> home. __c__

2. <u>Fortunately</u>, she'd left a number. _____

3. He <u>quickly</u> looked away from the young woman. _____

4. <u>Later</u>, the young man took a photo of himself. _____

5. Some fans of the show have <u>even</u> tried to learn Klingon. _____

6. I recognize that movie actor! He's in a TV series, <u>too</u>. _____

7. Most people <u>just</u> know the classic film version. _____

    a. An adverb of manner describing how something is done.

    b. An adverb of comment expressing an opinion on the sentence.

    c. An adverb of place describing where the action happened.

    d. An adverb of time describing when something happened.

    e. An adverb to focus on one thing (and not others).

    f. An adverb to emphasize an additional thing.

    g. An adverb to say something is unusual.

C **PRONUNCIATION: Stressing adverbs in sentences** Listen to the story and underline the stressed adverbs. 🎧43

As usual, Mandy was extremely late.

Fortunately, the bus was, too!

So, we caught it, luckily.

Then suddenly, the bus stopped.

Unbelievably, it had broken down.

We had to run quickly the rest of the way.

Luckily, we were just in time for the start of the movie.

D Work in pairs and take turns retelling the story in **C** with the correct stress.

E Work in pairs. One student reads a sentence and adds an adverb. Your partner repeats the new sentence and adds another adverb. Repeat this and continue adding adverbs until it isn't possible to add anymore.

1. The bus was late.

2. He ran to work.

3. They biked home.

4. I had to stop the car.

5. The child was lost.

6. The film started.

> 66 The bus was extremely late.
>
> Unfortunately, the bus was extremely late. 99

> 66 Unfortunately, even the bus was extremely late.
>
> Unfortunately, even the bus was extremely late, too. 99

Lesson A | **79**

Audience watches movie with special effects.

ACTIVE ENGLISH Try it out!

A Work in pairs.

Student A: Close your book. Student B is going to say the categories and you have to suggest a word for each one. For example, if student B says *verb*, you could say a verb like *run* or *watch*.

Student B: Say the categories to Student A and write down the word(s) they say.

1. a verb: _____

2. a famous male actor: _____

3. a famous female actor: _____

4. an -*ly* adverb before an adjective: _____

5. a location: _____

6. an adjective to describe a woman: _____

7. a synonym for *bad*: _____

8. a plural noun: _____

9. an adverb of comment: _____

10. a focus adverb: _____

B Now repeat the exercise in **A**, but swap roles (Student A reads 1–10).

C Put the ten new words from **B** into this film review and read it to your partner.

My favorite movie in recent months was *Live to* (1) _____ *another day*. It's a new thriller starring the actors (2) _____ and (3) _____. It was a (4) _____ great movie!

The plot was simple. The main character travels to (5) _____ and meets a (6) _____ woman. Together, they fight a / an (7) _____ organization that wants to destroy (8) _____.

The special effects are amazing and the final scene is very exciting. You think the two heroes are going to die but, (9) _____, they survive and they (10) _____ capture the criminals!

D Which of your new words in the review sound natural and correct? Which words would you change?

6A GOALS Now I can . . .

Talk about movies and TV series _____

Describe how something happened _____

1. Yes, I can.

2. Mostly, yes.

3. Not really.

VOCABULARY

A Work in pairs and read the first two sentences of a story in the box. How could you make it more descriptive? What words would you change or add? Then compare your ideas with another pair.

> *It was a nice morning and the sky was blue. Mrs. Jagger felt good and she walked through the nice park, in an old part of town.*

B The chart lists everyday verbs with more descriptive synonyms. Read sentences 1–6 and add the base forms of the words in blue with similar meanings to the chart.

EVERYDAY VERBS	DESCRIPTIVE VERBS	
write	**copy**	scribble
look	**stare**	
shout	**scream**	
walk	**hurry**	
eat	**nibble**	
breathe	**sigh**	
speak	**chat**	

ACADEMIC SKILL

Improve your vocabulary
To make your vocabulary more descriptive, varied, or precise, you can use a thesaurus, which lists words in groups of synonyms and related concepts. However, you still need a dictionary to check the exact meaning of each word.

1. The police officer **scribbled** down the address and started to run.

2. It was a beautiful afternoon and people **strolled** slowly through the park.

3. "Don't **gorge** yourself on those cakes," the children's mother **cried**.

4. He **glanced** at the young woman for a few seconds.

5. Joel fell into the water and started to **gasp** for air.

6. The library was full of people working, so the two teenagers had to **whisper**.

C Work in groups and explain the difference in meaning between the two descriptive verbs (e.g., *copy* and *scribble*).

> 66 *Copy* is when you read something and write it down. *Scribble* is when you write something quickly and carelessly.

D Work in two teams and play a mime game. One student in **Team A** stands up, chooses a descriptive verb, and mimes it. If **Team A** guesses correctly, they get one point. Then a student from **Team B** stands up and mimes a different verb for their team. Continue until each team has mimed eight verbs each.

An empty bench in a green park, bathed in sunlight with a blue sky overhead, invites walkers to stop and enjoy the scenery.

SECOND C

Passengers look out of the windows from the
second class compartment of the Vivek Express.

THE JOURNEY TO
THANJAVUR

आपातकालीन खिड़की
EMERGENCY WINDOW

Santosh had made a huge effort to appear
happy and confident on that **momentous**[1]
day all those months ago when he had waved
goodbye to his family, but in reality it was a
very different story. He was full of **trepidation**[2]
as he climbed aboard the bus. He was leaving
behind his family, his friends, his school, the
place where he grew up—everything he had
ever known. This was a **decisive**[3] break from
his past and he was heading into an uncertain
future. His parents and little sister were standing
on the roadside, waving. Meena, his mother,
was determinedly holding back her tears.

The preparations had started a few weeks earlier
when Meena had decided her son could not
present himself at a job interview in the only
formal clothes he possessed. Although he kept
his trousers exclusively for school, they were
tight everywhere and so short that they barely
reached his ankles. His shirt, too, had faded to

a **nondescript**[4] color and was missing several
buttons. It had been fine for school, but was
definitely not suitable for a job in the big city. So,
taking one of their last remaining banknotes from
the old Pepsi can, Meena took her son to the tailor
in Puttur.

The tailor, an elderly man, was sitting on an old
iron chair, behind a sewing machine. He lifted
his glasses to get a better look at the kind of
customer he was dealing with, while Meena,
anticipating his likely reaction, explained that
Santosh needed a new, but inexpensive, set of
clothes. To assure him of her ability to pay, she
produced the banknote and stood holding it
awkwardly[5] in front of her.

The old man got to his feet with difficulty
and started to take measurements with the
tape measure he had hanging around his neck.
Having scribbled them down on a crumpled
piece of paper, he produced several rolls of textile

from his cheapest range. Finally, after a long negotiation about the price, a delivery time of one week was given, and accepted by Meena.

His mother had also put aside another banknote in the Pepsi can, which she had given to Santosh before he set off. And so, with a hundred rupees in his pocket, he had taken different modes of transport to get to Thanjavur. After the journey to Puttur, another blue and yellow bus took him to Radapakkam, from where a third bus dropped him off at Tiruchirappalli station. There, he **squeezed into**[6] the third class compartment of the train from Chennai, which, after multiple stops, brought him to Thanjavur station, which was just another short bus ride from the very center of the city.

And so, he found himself alone, at seventeen, in a big city for the very first time in his life.

(adapted and abridged from *The Tyre* Chapter 5 by C.J. Dubois & E.C. Huntley, Thistle Publishing, 2018)

A **Staying focused.** Read the story and number the events in the order they happened.

a. Santosh went to a tailor for some new clothes. __1__

b. He left his home town. _____

c. He took three different buses and a train. _____

d. He waved goodbye to his family. _____

e. His mother and the tailor negotiated the price. _____

f. He arrived at Thanjavur station. _____

g. His mother gave Santosh some money for the journey. _____

B Match the descriptive language in bold in the text to its everyday meaning.

1. a. especially important
   b. not very important

2. a. excitement
   b. anxiety

3. a. unhappy
   b. clear

4. a. a dark color you remember
   b. not distinctive or interesting

5. a. in a way that showed some embarrassment
   b. in a way that showed some confidence

6. a. moved into a wide space
   b. moved into a tight space

> **ACADEMIC SKILL**
> **Descriptive language**
> When you read novels and literature in English, notice how the writer uses more descriptive language (e.g., **huge** instead of *big*, **appear** instead of *look*.)

C Work in pairs. Imagine one of these conversations and write it in your notebook. Then join another pair and share your conversations.

1. The conversation between Santosh and his mother on the momentous day he left home.

2. The conversation between Meena and the tailor when they first arrived at the shop.

3. The conversation about the price between Meena and the tailor.

LISTENING

A **Activate prior knowledge.** Which of these stories do you know from books or films? If you know them, tell the class what they are about in two or three sentences.

Cinderella	The Odyssey	One Thousand and One Nights
Frankenstein	One Hundred Years of Solitude	Romeo and Juliet
Mulan		

> 66 It's a story about a . . .   I think it's set in Italy. 99

> 66 In the story, they . . .   It has a happy ending because . . . 99

> 66 The end is sad because . . .   I think the writer was . . . 99

B Listen to a description of the six shapes of stories. Number them in the order the speaker refers to them. 🎧45

a. __1__   b. _____   c. _____   d. _____   e. _____   f. _____

THE SIX SHAPES OF STORIES
In a study of 17,000 novels, researchers found that there are only six "shapes" of stories.

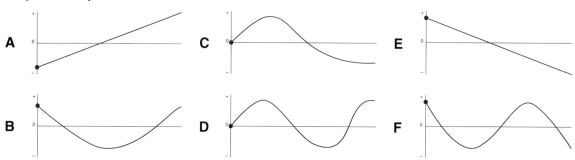

C Listen again and answer the questions. 🎧45

1. In a sentiment analysis, what does the computer decide about a word?
2. What kind of stories often have Shape A?
3. Which two shapes are often used in tragedies?
4. How is the story of Romeo and Juliet different from Shape E?
5. Which part of the story of Frankenstein is more positive?
6. Why is there a "fall" in the middle of Cinderella?

D Work in pairs and think of a story you both know well (either from a movie or a book). Try to retell the story and then decide the shape of your story.

E Switch partners and take turns retelling your stories from **D**. Afterwards, ask your partner to say what they think the shape of your story is. Do you agree? Why or why not?

Antique books from the 19th century have beautifully decorated hard covers.

GRAMMAR

A Read the Unit 6, Lesson B Grammar Reference in the appendix. Complete the exercises. Then do the exercises below.

NARRATIVE TENSES			
The simple past			
Santosh	climbed		aboard the bus.
The past continuous			
He They	was were	leaving standing	his family and friends. on the roadside.
The past perfect			
He	had	made	a huge effort all those months ago.
The past perfect continuous			
He	had been	waiting	for hours.

B Read the opening sentences from five stories. Underline and identify the narrative tenses.

ACADEMIC SKILL
Authentic texts
When you learn a new grammar point, try to find examples of it in authentic texts.

1. The call came in after one a.m. and woke me up. *Haruki Murakami, Men without Women*

2. It was a bright cold day in April, and the clocks were striking thirteen. *George Orwell, Nineteen Eighty-Four*

3. Once upon a time, there was a woman who discovered she had turned into the wrong person. *Anne Tyler, Back When We Were Grownups*

4. The boy's name was Santiago. Dusk was falling as the boy arrived with his herd at the church. The roof had fallen in a long time ago... *Paulo Coelho, The Alchemist*

5. I was lost, it was already dark, I had been driving for hours and was practically out of petrol. *Anna Kavan, Ice*

C Which opening sentence in **B** do you like the most? Tell the class and explain what you think makes a good opening sentence to a story.

D Complete these sentences from short stories using the appropriate form of the verbs in parentheses.

1. That evening, the baby _____ (cry) when she arrived home. Someone else was in the house.

2. My phone rang and the caller whispered, "Where's Bella?" Frightened, Bella _____ (stare) at me as I calmly replied, "I'm afraid she's out. Who's calling?"

3. Everyone _____ (gorge) themselves at the party when a poor-looking man rushed through the door.

4. It had been a long day, so Rohan and Sue _____ (hurry) home.

5. Then one of the guests picked up a scribbled note from the floor. The man _____ (leave) a number.

6. Gradually, the metal object _____ (punch) the clouds and disappeared into the sky.

7. There was a gasp as the police _____ (try) to capture them many times before. Finally, they had them.

8. After everything that _____ (happen), I was happy to go home.

E Work in groups. The sentences in **D** are the opening sentences (1–4) and the final sentences (5–8) from four different short stories. Discuss and decide which pairs of sentences are from the same story. Describe what you think happened in each story to connect the two sentences.

ACTIVE ENGLISH Try it out!

A Work in groups of three or four students and sit in a circle with one dice. You are going to tell some stories using the images below.

1. Roll the dice to see who goes first (highest goes first).

2. The first player rolls the dice and looks at the image that corresponds to the number they rolled on the dice. Use an idea from the image to tell the first sentence of a story.

3. The next player rolls the dice and continues the story with the next sentence.

4. Player three rolls the dice. Continue the story in this way until you have 12 sentences in total (using some images more than once). Try to use some storytelling adverbs.

STORYTELLING ADVERBS
One day . . . Suddenly . . .
Fortunately . . .
Silently . . .
Quickly . . . Luckily . . .

① ② ③
④ ⑤ ⑥

❝ Slowly, they strolled . . .   Fortunately, they had scribbled down . . . ❞   ❝ She suddenly cried . . .

B Tell more stories with new images by turning to the info files on page 216.

C WRITING Read the Unit 6 Writing Model in the appendix and answer the questions below.

1. What traditional story is it based on?

2. How does the writer change the original story?

3. What type of vocabulary and grammar does the writer use?

D Write a short story (120–180 words). Here are some ideas on how to begin:

a. Choose a traditional story, such as a fairytale, and rewrite it in a modern way.

b. Choose an opening and final sentence from **D** on page 85.

c. Reuse the ideas and sentences from your story dice game in **A**.

6B GOALS Now I can . . .

Use descriptive language _____	1. Yes, I can.
Tell a story _____	2. Mostly, yes.
	3. Not really.

GLOBAL VOICES

A Look at the explorer Andrés Ruzo in the photo. Where is he? Why do you think he has gone there?

B Watch a video of Andrés telling three stories. Check (✓) the person who talks about each idea (1–4). You can check more than one person.

	Grandfather	Aunt	Andrés
1. When the Spanish arrived in Peru			
2. Traveling into the Amazon jungle			
3. Going to the Boiling River			
4. Not believing in a boiling river			

C Watch the video again and answer the questions.

1. In the past, what did people believe some cities were made of in the Amazon?
2. Why was the Amazon jungle so dangerous for the early Spanish explorers?
3. Why did Andrés start to believe the boiling river really existed?
4. Why didn't he believe his aunt at first?
5. Why was the canoe called a *peke-peke*?
6. Why does he feel disappointed when he first sees the river?
7. What happened in the end?

D Discuss the questions in groups or as a class.

1. When you were a child, where did you hear, watch, or read stories about the past?
2. Does your country or culture have lots of stories about its past? Which is your favorite?
3. How important is it to keep telling stories about our past?

Andrés Ruzo, geoscientist, conservationist, and National Geographic Explorer, sits on the banks of the Boiling River in Peru.

The Teatro Juarez, located in Guanajuato, Mexico, is thought of as one of Mexico's premier theaters.

If only Hollywood made movies like this every month. I waited until I'd seen it a second time before deciding to review it here in case it wasn't as good as I first thought. In fact, it needs a second viewing. It's a remake, but don't worry about seeing the original first. If the lead actor doesn't win all the movie awards this year, then I don't know who will.

★ ★ ★ ★ ★

I tried to like this exhibition but there wasn't enough that was new or original. The photographer is very skilled at taking us around the world and inside the lives of the people who live in it. There are images from every continent and the scenes of polar bears in the Arctic are particularly emotional. But overall, I felt like I'd seen it before.

★ ★

The best part about this new collection of songs from "The Music Box" are the stories they tell. They avoid singing about the usual subjects and write about imaginary locations and characters. Unfortunately, the quality of the music doesn't match the quality of the lyrics and the tunes just don't stick in your mind.

★ ★ ★

A Read the online reviews. Then answer these questions in pairs.

  1. What is each person reviewing?

  2. Why did they like or dislike it?

B Work in groups and discuss these questions.

  1. Do you trust online reviews? What does your opinion depend on?

  2. Have you ever written an online review? Why or why not?

  3. Which of these do you read online reviews for? How much do they influence you?

  ☐ a book (fiction or non-fiction)

  ☐ music (live or recorded)

  ☐ a movie

  ☐ a performance (e.g., stand-up comedy, theater)

  ☐ an exhibition (e.g., photography, art)

  ☐ a TV series

  ☐ a digital device (e.g., a smartphone)

  ☐ a video game

  ☐ a cafe or restaurant

  ☐ other? _____

C **You Choose** You are going to write a review. Choose something to review from the list in **B**. Then choose an option and follow the steps below.

  Option 1 Write a short review of your choice.

  Option 2 Record a short audio review as a podcast.

  Option 3 Record a video blog of your review.

  In your review:

  • Give general information, such as the name of the event, the location, the author, the director, musicians

  • Give background information, such as the main story, history, features

  • Give an opinion with reasons that help people make a decision

D Work in pairs. Read, listen to, or watch your partner's review. Answer these questions and tell your partner your answers.

  1. What did your partner review?

  2. Was it clear whether they liked or disliked it?

  3. Did the review help you make up your mind? Why or why not?

E Repeat **D** with other classmates. By the end of the lesson, decide which reviewer(s) convinced you and explain why.

Architect Moshe Safdie designed the Jewel Changi Airport, in Singapore. It is a nature-themed complex and includes the world's largest indoor waterfall.

GOALS

Lesson A
/ Investigate and ask difficult questions
/ Ask about everyday objects

Lesson B
/ Discuss urban spaces
/ Describe processes

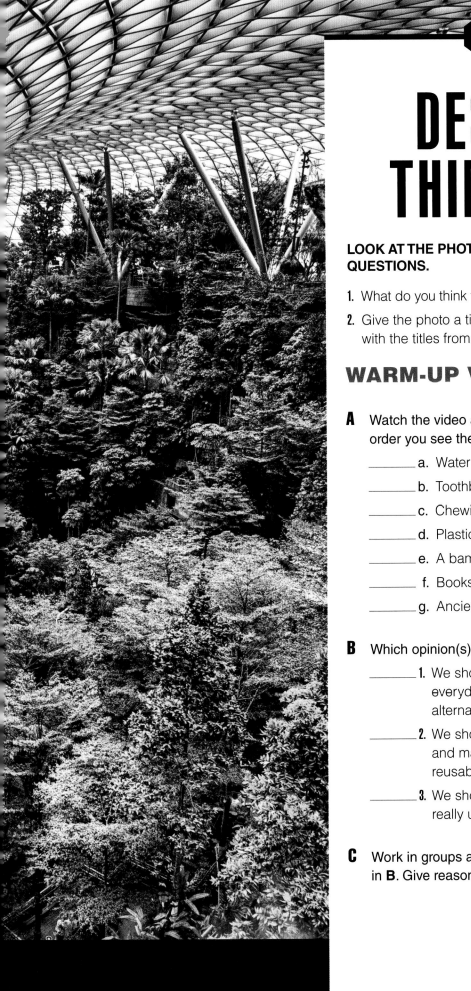

DESIGN THINKING

LOOK AT THE PHOTO. ANSWER THE QUESTIONS.

1. What do you think the message of this photo is?
2. Give the photo a title. Then compare your title with the titles from the rest of the class.

WARM-UP VIDEO

A Watch the video and number the items in the order you see them.

_____ a. Water from a tap

_____ b. Toothbrushes around the world

_____ c. Chewing sticks

_____ d. Plastic toothbrushes

_____ e. A bamboo toothbrush

_____ f. Books about design

_____ g. Ancient teeth

B Which opinion(s) do you agree with?

_____ 1. We should ban plastic in all everyday objects and use alternative materials.

_____ 2. We should ban single-use plastics and make all plastic objects reusable.

_____ 3. We should keep using plastic. It's a really useful material.

C Work in groups and compare your opinions in **B**. Give reasons for your choices.

VOCABULARY

A Do you ever use a straw when you have a drink? What material is it made from?
Read this text and find out about other options.

Straws: The eco-friendly alternatives

More than 100 million single-use straws—most of them plastic and **non-recyclable**—are used each day. They are adding to the global plastic waste problem. What are the **sustainable** alternatives?

1. **Metal:** Popular because they're **durable** and easy to transport and reuse, but the downside is they conduct heat, making them **unsuitable** for really hot drinks!

2. **Paper:** Paper drinking straws have been used since the late 1800s. They fall apart after a while, but they are the most popular **disposable** option.

3. **Glass:** Glass straws are more **breakable** and therefore less **portable** than **reusable** straws made from other materials, but they're easy to wash and can be made in attractive shapes and colors.

Metal straws

4. **Bamboo:** This natural material is a plant-based alternative that is **bendable** and easy to shape. Bamboo straws can be hard to clean, but when it's time to dispose of them, they are easily **compostable**.

B Match the adjectives in blue in **A** to the correct meaning.

_____ 1. can be used for a long time with little or no damage to the environment

_____ 2. fragile, can separate into pieces easily

_____ 3. able to last a long time without being damaged

_____ 4. can be used to grow plants when it decays

_____ 5. easy to carry

_____ 6. not right for someone / something

_____ 7. can be used more than once

_____ 8. designed to be thrown away after use

_____ 9. cannot be used again for a different purpose

_____ 10. flexible, easy to move into different shapes

> **WORD BANK**
> **alternatives** two or more other choices
> **conduct (heat)** allow heat to pass through or along it
> **plant-based** using materials from plants, not animals or man-made materials
> **single-use** can be used only once

C Work in groups. Answer the questions.

1. How many everyday objects can your group think of that are made from plastic?

2. Share your list with other groups. Which group has the longest list?

LISTENING

Bamboo forest in Japan

A Do you use or own anything made of bamboo?

B **Listen for sequence.** Listen to a documentary about the uses of bamboo. Number these uses in the order you hear them. 🎧46

_____ a. In the construction of buildings and bridges

_____ b. In clothing and fashion

_____ c. As fuel in rural communities

_____ d. As an alternative to plastic

_____ e. As food for animals and humans

C Listen again and answer the questions in your notebook. 🎧46

1. Why does the speaker describe bamboo as a "pretty cool plant"?

2. How does the speaker describe pandas?

3. How is bamboo described in Japan?

4. What makes it a popular construction material?

5. What advantages does bamboo have over trees?

6. How does bamboo clothing compare in price to other types of clothing?

7. What warning is given at the end?

D Read these sentences from the listening and match the underlined words to the definitions.

_____ 1. We should consider using one of the most **versatile** plants on the planet.

_____ 2. It **absorbs** large amounts of carbon dioxide and **emits** high levels of oxygen.

_____ 3. Bamboo shoots are known for their health benefits, with lots of **vitamins** and **fiber**.

_____ 4. It's bendable, so it can be **shaped** to suit your needs and will withstand an earthquake.

_____ 5. It's really **taking off** with some of the most famous fashion houses.

_____ 6. The process of **extracting** fibers from bamboo is **time-consuming** and expensive.

_____ 7. Bamboo offers a sustainable answer to our **reliance** on plastic.

a. moved into different forms

b. useful for a lot of different things

c. natural healthy substances

d. take something in gradually

e. send out gas into the air

f. starting to be successful or popular

g. a substance in plants that helps food pass through your body

h. removing or taking something out

i. needing a lot of time

j. dependence on something

E Work in groups and answer the questions.

1. What else absorbs carbon dioxide and emits oxygen?

2. What other types of food contain lots of vitamins and fiber?

3. Our reliance on plastic is excessive. Do we rely too much on any natural resources?

4. What other sustainable and eco-friendly alternatives are taking off these days?

SPEAKING

A Read and listen to a conversation in a clothing store. What does the assistant say makes the socks sustainable? Why does the customer think the socks may not be eco-friendly? 🎧47

Customer: Excuse me, all the labels on all your clothes say they are sustainable. What do you mean by that?

Assistant: Err, well, it means everything in the store is eco-friendly.

Customer: Eco-friendly? In what way is it eco-friendly?

Assistant: Take these socks, for example. They're made from bamboo.

Customer: And?

Assistant: Bamboo grows quicker than cotton.

Customer: How is that better than using cotton?

Assistant: Less water is used in the process of growing bamboo than growing cotton, so it's better for the environment.

Customer: And could you clarify exactly where the bamboo is grown?

Assistant: The bamboo is grown locally and the clothes are made in this country as well.

Customer: That's great. I was worried that everything needed to be transported a long way.

Assistant: As I said, we're a very eco-friendly store!

B Practice the conversation with a partner.

C Work in pairs. You are going to prepare a similar conversation in a clothing store.

Student A: You walk into a shop with a notice that says everything is locally manufactured. Prepare five questions to ask the shop assistant about the clothes, including information about:

- where the clothes are manufactured
- the type of materials used
- the people who make them
- how they are transported
- if they are eco-friendly and sustainable

Student B: You work in the clothing store. Prepare five answers with the information above and try to predict Student A's other questions.

D When you are both ready, start your conversation.

SPEAKING STRATEGY 🎧48

Being precise

Use **exactly** when you want someone to be more precise:

Where **exactly** is it from?

What do you mean by that, **exactly**?

That doesn't sound **exactly** right.

USEFUL EXPRESSIONS 🎧49

Investigating and asking difficult questions

What do you mean by that?

In what way is it . . .?

How is that better than . . .?

Can you clarify exactly where . . .?

Where exactly is it grown / made / transported from?

Are your sure / certain it's . . . ?

GRAMMAR

A Study the sentences from the unit. Match the underlined verbs in the passive to the verb forms in a–g.

_____ **1.** One hundred million straws <u>are used</u> per day.

_____ **2.** Traditionally, houses <u>were built</u> with bamboo.

_____ **3.** Glass straws <u>can be made</u> in attractive shapes and colors.

_____ **4.** Modern bridges <u>are being constructed</u> with it.

_____ **5.** Paper drinking straws <u>have been used</u> since the late 1800s.

_____ **6.** While forests <u>were being cut down</u>, trees <u>were not being replanted</u>.

_____ **7.** Where forests <u>had been replanted</u>, the trees did not grow back fast enough.

a. Simple present

b. Present continuous

c. Present perfect

d. Simple past

e. Past continuous

f. Past perfect

g. Modal verb (*will*, *must*, *can*)

B Read the Unit 7, Lesson A Grammar Reference in the appendix. Complete the exercises. Then do the exercises below.

THE PASSIVE 1 (Tenses and Modals)			
Subject	***be***	**Past participle**	
Bamboo	is	grown	in China.
Recycled plastic	has been	used	in construction.
Toothbrushes	can be	made	from bamboo.

C Complete the text by circling the correct passive or active form of the verb.

Mushrooms: from houses to biofuel

Some mushrooms (1) *pick / are picked* to be eaten. But with over 1.5 million species of mushrooms, many more (2) *leave / are left* in the ground. Now, researchers (3) *are experimenting / are being experimented* with this versatile natural material. In construction, some small structures (4) *have built / have been built* with mushrooms, and in the future, bricks (5) *could make / could be made* from mushrooms, which are portable and durable. In the past, medical doctors (6) *used / were used* mushrooms in parts of Asia. Now, they (7) *are testing / are being tested* mushrooms for the prevention of cancer. And finally, mushrooms (8) *can also convert / can also be converted* into biofuels, so in the future, we might be driving cars that run on mushrooms.

D Work in pairs. Compare your answers in **C**. In each case, explain why:

• you chose the active or passive form.

• a particular tense is used.

 It's the passive form because it's done by someone who we don't know.

It's the simple past because it describes a situation twenty years ago.

ACTIVE ENGLISH Try it out!

Play this game in pairs or a group of four (with two teams of two). One player (or team) chooses an object from the board but does not say what it is. The other player / team has to guess the object by asking five different *yes* / *no* questions. You can use the suggested passive question forms below or make your own questions.

Is it used in / for . . .?	Was it invented in the (seventies) . . . / by . . .?
Is it made in . . .?	Is it often eaten / played / worn . . .?
Is it made of . . .?	Was it built in . . .?

The fewer questions you ask before you guess correctly, the more points you get. So if you guess correctly after your first question, you receive 5 points. After your second question you receive 4 points, your third question 3 points, your fourth 2 points, your fifth 1 point.

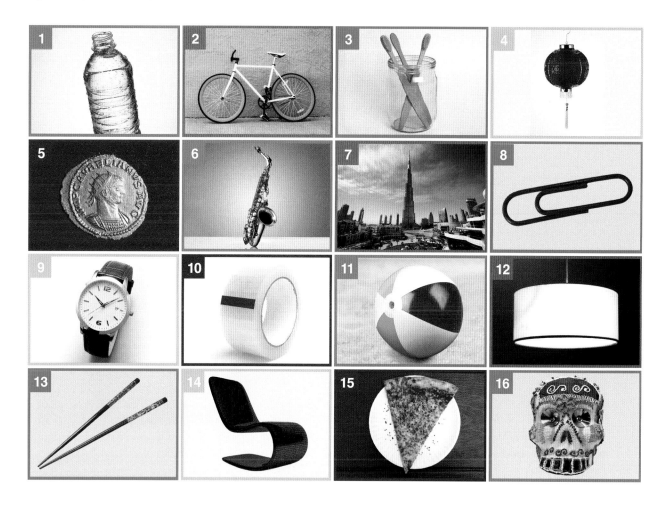

7A GOALS   Now I can . . .

Investigate and ask difficult questions _____

Ask about everyday objects _____

1. Yes, I can.
2. Mostly, yes.
3. Not really.

VOCABULARY

A Read about the city of Medellin. Why is it a good place to live?

Redesigning Medellin

With its warm climate, the Colombian city of Medellin is known as the "City of Eternal Spring." Surrounded by mountains, Medellin has 2.5 million **inhabitants**. Its public transportation system includes a metro and cable cars. Together, these carry tourists and residents from distant **neighborhoods** and **suburbs** to the **vibrant** city center. At the end of the last century, many parts of the city were **run-down** and **overcrowded** and suffered from pollution and poor **air quality**. Nowadays, this same city is winning awards for its sustainable urban redesign. In particular, it's famous for its 30 "green **corridors**." **Garbage dumps** have been turned into gardens, trees were planted on roadsides, and 75 city gardeners were employed to take care of these green **public spaces**.

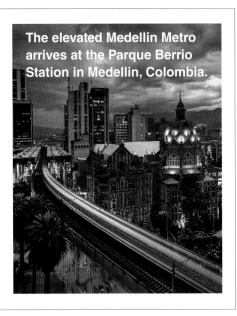

The elevated Medellin Metro arrives at the Parque Berrio Station in Medellin, Colombia.

B Match the words in blue in **A** to the definitions.

1. long passages (usually inside buildings) _____
2. areas of a town or city that people live in _____
3. areas on the edge of a large town or city where people live _____
4. people who live in a particular place _____
5. how good or bad the air is _____
6. areas for trash _____
7. fun and exciting _____
8. areas for people to meet and relax _____
9. in bad condition _____
10. too many people living and working in a small area _____

WORD BANK
awards prizes given for achievements
urban belonging or relating to a town or city
urban redesign new planning of a town or city to make it better
urban space an area in the city

C What do you think about the town or city that you live in? Check (✓) the correct box.

	Great	Needs improvement	Not sure
1. Housing for all its inhabitants	☐	☐	☐
2. Transportation from the suburbs to the center	☐	☐	☐
3. Air quality	☐	☐	☐
4. Green public spaces and sports facilities	☐	☐	☐
5. City center	☐	☐	☐
6. Local food and places to eat	☐	☐	☐

D Work in groups and compare your answers in **C**. Give reasons for your answers.

URBAN PLANNING

The Park Royal Hotel in Singapore was designed to include nature.

A **Prediction.** Before you read the article, which of these do you think are in this sustainable city of the future? Then, read the article and check (✓) the items that it mentions.

☐ oil	☐ trains	☐ plastic bottles	☐ working from home
☐ solar energy	☐ drones	☐ farms and gardens	☐ fast food
☐ wind energy	☐ cars	☐ recycled objects	☐ office space

B Paragraphs 2–8 of the reading are each missing a sentence at the end. Write the letter of the sentence in the correct place in the reading.

a. This encourages the growing and consumption of fresh food.

b. As a result, they are far more versatile.

c. This avoids unnecessary travel.

d. For example, high-speed trains can reach 600 miles an hour.

e. And it's rare to see anything made from plastic these days.

f. Fossil fuels haven't been used for the last ten years.

g. This limited resource is kept for drinking only.

Sustainable cities of the future

[1] By 2050, the world's population is predicted to reach 9.8 billion. Nearly 70% of this **booming** population is expected to live in cities. We asked experts from an urban planning firm how they would design a city of the future. Here's what they came up with.

1. Green roofs

[2] Solar panels and roof gardens are commonly added to buildings. This encourages sustainable energy, roof garden spaces, and small-scale farming. ____

2. Clean energy

[3] The sun's energy is captured by every surface of a building, including the walls and windows. Wind turbines on building rooftops provide additional energy. ____

3. Air quality and transportation

[4] Public transportation continues to be used and electric cars are being driven more and more. For this reason, air quality has been improved, with more trees and plants in public spaces. People also enjoy being transported around the city in **remotely** programmed drones. For out-of-town travel, people use bus lines and rail, which is very fast and efficient. ____

4. Recycling and reuse

[5] Single-use items are a thing of the past. Used items—those that aren't already **biodegradable**—are more easily reused or recycled in crowded communities. ____

5. Self-contained neighborhoods

[6] Homes are reduced in size, but there are more shared spaces for human **interaction**. Most people work fewer hours and either work from home or close to their employer. Neighborhoods are **self-contained** with most daily needs within a 10-minute walk. ____

6. Building design

[7] Low-rise buildings are designed to allow light and air to reach the ground, promoting health and well being. The **interiors** of buildings are designed for different uses, such as office space, homes, or communal areas. ____

7. Growing food

[8] Sustainable agriculture is close to the suburbs and city centers to limit transportation, with some farms moved directly under homes and offices. Plants and **produce** are grown using LED lights, and a new style of gardening has been developed that requires little or no water. ____ 50

C Match the definitions with the words in bold in the article.

1. objects that can disappear naturally with no pollution _biodegradable_
2. from far away _____
3. has everything that is needed _____
4. fruit and vegetables _____
5. time spent talking and doing things with people _____
6. inside of the building _____
7. growing rapidly _____

D Were any of the ideas in the article surprising? Why or why not?

E Work in groups. Make a list of the main problems and disadvantages of your town or city. Then make a list of possible solutions for each problem and redesign your town or city for the future. Afterwards, present your new ideas to the class.

LISTENING

A Work in groups. Imagine you are on the city council and you want to solve the following problems. Try to think of one solution for each problem.

1. The city has a lot of garbage cans, but they are still not being used by everyone. A lot of garbage is often found in the streets and parks.

2. Too many private cars are being driven into the city center and there isn't enough parking. Public transportation isn't being used by enough commuters—even people who live close enough to walk are still driving.

3. The police fine drivers for speeding and there are road signs everywhere. However, the speed limit is still being broken in the city center and near places such as schools and hospitals.

B Take turns presenting your solutions to the class. Listen to each group and vote on the best solution to each problem.

C **Listen for tone and attitude.** Listen to three speakers commenting on solutions for their cities. Write the correct speaker number. 🎧51

a. The solution is criticized by speaker _____.

b. The solution is reported by speaker _____.

c. The solution is supported by speaker _____.

D Listen again and choose the correct answer to each question. 🎧51

1. When different countries and cities have tried to change people's behavior, what were the results?

   a. Always successful   b. Sometimes successful   c. Never successful

2. How much of the trash went into the cans after the changes were made?

   a. All of it   b. More than before   c. Less than before

3. Why does speaker 2 say, "and don't even mention the weekends!"

   a. Because she doesn't drive into the center on weekends
   b. Because commuters only travel in on the weekdays
   c. Because finding a parking spot is worse on the weekends

4. What did the personalized emails include?

   a. A map showing alternative forms of transportation
   b. Alternative places to park your car
   c. Alternative ways to improve your health

5. What do you think "to name and shame" means?

   a. To tell a person when they do something wrong
   b. To call the police when someone does something wrong
   c. To publicize it when a person does something wrong

6. Where are the special signs that the man describes?

   a. In a town he knows about
   b. In a town he has visited
   c. In his home town

E How similar were the solutions in the audio and your solutions in **B**? Would any of the ideas in the audio be useful in your town or city. Why or why not?

GRAMMAR

A Read the Unit 7, Lesson B Grammar Reference in the appendix. Complete the exercises. Then do the exercises below.

THE PASSIVE 2 (Reporting, Infinitive, *-ing*)
Passive reporting **It is said that** they worried about the environment. **It was reported that** there was a 12% drop.
Passive infinitive Private cars **continue to be discouraged** in the city center. The drivers **didn't want to be caught** speeding.
Passive *-ing* forms People **enjoy being transported** around the city by drones. The commuters **are tired of being stuck** in traffic every day.

B Write the words in parentheses in the active or passive form.

It (1) _____ (report) that Costa Rica hopes (2) _____ (become) the first carbon-neutral country in the world. The country (3) _____ (say) that around 80% of its electricity (4) _____ (already / produce) from clean hydropower and other renewable energy. However, one of its biggest challenges is transportation. Fossil fuels such as diesel keep (5) _____ (use) in cars and buses while very few electric vehicles (6) _____ (buy). But, the government plans (7) _____ (cut) taxes on electric vehicles, and it (8) _____ (hope) that this will encourage people to change their vehicles.

C **PRONUNCIATION: Intonation in passive reporting** Listen to these sentences. On which word does the intonation rise? 52

1. It is said that Costa Rica produces clean energy.
2. It is reported that the country hopes to become carbon neutral.
3. It is hoped that people will use electric vehicles.
4. Bamboo is thought to be a sustainable material.

D Listen again and repeat the sentences in **C** with the correct intonation. 52

Due to its many volcanoes, Costa Rica is also exploring geothermal energy as a renewable source.

ACTIVE ENGLISH Try it out!

A Work in pairs. Imagine you are the government of a country and want to make your country more eco-friendly. Give your country a name and write five things you plan to do to achieve this goal (e.g., *We plan to stop single-use plastic bottles from being used by the end of next year. It is also hoped that ...*)

> **Country name:** _____
> 1. _____ .
> 2. _____ .
> 3. _____ .
> 4. _____ .
> 5. _____ .

B Change partners and practice an interview between a journalist and a member of the government. The journalist asks questions about the government's plans in **A** and takes notes. Then switch roles.

> 66 So what are your plans?
>
> The government 99 plans to . . .

C You are the journalist in **B**. Prepare a short TV news report about the government's plans. Then work in groups and take turns reading your reports aloud.

> 66 We hope that . . .
>
> 66 Here is the news . . .
>
> It's reported that 99 the government plans to . . .

D **WRITING** Read the Unit 7 Writing Model in the appendix and answer the questions.

1. What is the main purpose of the report?
2. Why was the report written?
3. How formal or informal is the report? Is it personal or impersonal?
4. Where do you think you might read a report like this?

> 66 It is hoped that . . .

ACADEMIC SKILL

Writing facts

When you write a report, make sure report the facts and what other people said. Avoid giving your opinion unless it's your recommendation at the end.

E Write a report (120–160 words) about how to make your place of study or work more sustainable. Propose three ways to achieve this in your report.

7B GOALS   Now I can . . .

Discuss urban spaces _____

Describe processes _____

1. Yes, I can.
2. Mostly, yes.
3. Not yet.

A village uses solar panels to achieve sustainability.

GLOBAL VOICES

A How easy is it for you to recycle your garbage? What can you recycle? What do you throw away?

B You are going to watch a video about how T.H. Culhane recycles "food waste" in his "domestic dragon." Watch and number these stages in the process.

_____ He cleans and sorts all the plastic, glass, metal, cardboard, and paper from the "food waste."

_____ The heat from the gas can cook food, heat water, and make electricity.

_____ The dragon turns the waste into fuel, fertilizer, and methane gas.

_____ He puts the food waste into the domestic dragon.

_____ He uses solar energy when he doesn't have enough garbage for the dragon.

C Watch the video again and answer these questions in your notebook.

1. What two materials can a biodigester be built from?
2. It is filled with water and microbes. Where do they usually get these from?
3. What are the three pipes for?
4. What does T.H. Culhane ask his friends and students to bring?
5. What does he think one man's trash can be?

D Think of how you practice sustainability, for example, recycling paper, plastics, and cans, being careful with your water consumption, etc.

1. On your own, take notes about which you do and what you find difficult about doing these things.
2. Work in groups and take turns presenting your notes. Talk about the difficulties of doing these things. When you listen to others, take notes about what they say and ask questions afterwards.

T.H. Culhane in a biodigester tank

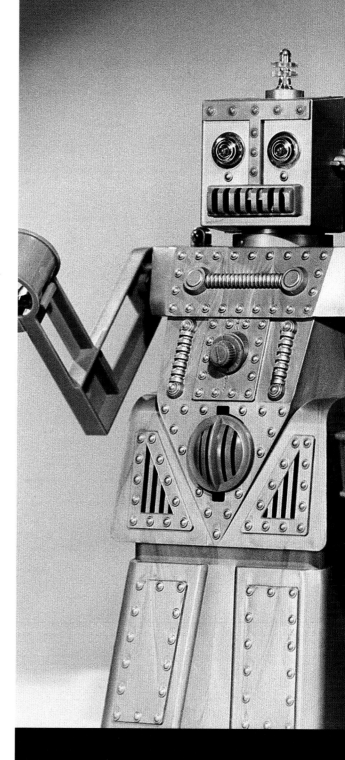

In 1959, toy developers created a futuristic toy robot, space helmet, and goggles with which children could imagine the future.

8

SCIENCE FACT AND FICTION

LOOK AT THE PHOTO. ANSWER THE QUESTIONS.

1. Do children imagine the future while playing? What did you imagine?

2. Make two predictions for the future. Tell a partner.

WARM-UP VIDEO

A Watch the video and check (✓) the scientific discoveries and inventions it shows.

- ☐ Electricity
- ☐ Nuclear energy
- ☐ Space flight
- ☐ Mobile phones
- ☐ Email and text messaging
- ☐ Face-to-face communication devices
- ☐ Robots
- ☐ Microwave ovens
- ☐ Flying cars
- ☐ Self-driving cars

B Watch the video again and answer the questions.

1. In which century did science fiction begin?

2. What were the similarities between Jules Verne's fictional space vehicle in 1865 and NASA's Apollo 11 command module 100 years later?

3. After the invention of cell phones, what type of contact did we want?

4. In what two ways did sci-fi present robots in the past?

5. What does the iRobot Roomba do?

C Answer the questions in groups.

1. Which of the discoveries and inventions in **A** do you already use today?

2. Which do you think you will probably use in the future?

GOALS

Lesson A

/ Present visual information

/ Make predictions

Lesson B

/ Identify causes

/ Explain reasons and results

VOCABULARY

A Read about Achilles the cat. What do his trainers think he is able to do? Why isn't Kristyn Vitale convinced?

Achilles lives in a museum in Russia and some people have a **theory** about him. In the 2018 World Cup, his trainers **experimented** by putting two bowls of food in front of Achilles, each with flags for two competing soccer teams. By eating from one of the bowls, he could **forecast** the **outcome** of a game. Kristyn Vitale, a cat researcher at Oregon State University, has doubts about his trainers' **methods**. "I am not convinced. There's just been no **research** in that kind of thing." However, Vitale also adds that there is scientific **evidence** for cats (like humans) having a side-bias; in other words both humans and animals naturally prefer the right or left, so this could affect which bowl Achilles chooses. Like Achilles, other animals have also predicted sports results; in 2010, Paul the octopus guessed the winner of the World Cup and more recently, a pig called Marcus guessed the winner of the Wimbledon tennis championship. "It's an interesting cultural **phenomenon** that we're going to animals and asking them to predict things," Vitale adds.

B Match the words in blue in **A** to the definitions.

1. predict _____
2. did tests _____
3. ways of doing something systematically _____
4. when someone studies a subject in detail _____
5. the final result _____
6. something that exists or happens that is often unusual _____
7. an idea or set of ideas to explain something _____
8. something that makes you believe that something is true _____

ACADEMIC SKILL

Supporting evidence
When you express an opinion or present information, it's important to use evidence that supports it.

C Complete the sentences using the correct form of the words in **B**.

1. Einstein is famous for his t_____ of relativity.
2. A hurricane is a natural p_____.
3. Isaac Newton watched an apple fall from a tree. It was e_____ of gravity.
4. There's a lot of scientific r_____ to support this theory.
5. Marie Curie carried out e_____ with radioactivity and won two Nobel Prizes.

D Work in pairs and answer the following questions.

1. Can you think of another famous scientist with a theory or discovery?
2. What is the weather forecast this week in your country?
3. What is another example of a natural phenomenon?
4. What is the evidence for climate change?

LISTENING

A Do you ever see people riding horses in your country? What are the advantages of horses as a type of transportation? What are the reasons that people prefer cars?

B **Listen for detail.** Listen to part of a TV show about transportation. 🎧53

1. Where is the TV presenter speaking from?
2. What outcome is being predicted?
3. How quickly did horses disappear as the main type of transportation in the twentieth century?
4. Why aren't some people convinced by the prediction?
5. What question does the presenter suggest we ask any skeptics?

WORD BANK
Skeptics are people who doubt an opinion or view even when there is evidence to support it. If you are **skeptical**, you are not easily convinced and have doubts.

C Guess the missing words in these sentences. Then listen again and check your answers. 🎧53

1. It's estimated that by the year 2040 90% of us will have bought an electric car. That f_____ is based on current evidence in transportation.
2. One t_____ says that most cars on the road will be driven by electric batteries.
3. Doesn't this outcome seem too optimistic? Where is the e_____ to support it?
4. Futurologists' m_____ of forecasting is to study the past.
5. The inevitable o_____ was that there were nearly two million cars on the roads.
6. Some people aren't convinced and remain s_____.
7. Electric cars are not a new p_____ .
8. To any remaining s_____ out there who don't think electric cars will take over anytime soon, just ask yourself . . .

D What do you think about the prediction for electric cars in the future? Circle one of the five responses below and then tell a partner, giving reasons.

I'm totally convinced.	I'm fairly convinced.	I'm not sure.
I'm a bit skeptical.	I'm very skeptical!	

Men riding horses in Jonotla, Mexico

SPEAKING

A Read and listen to a short presentation about this slide. Why do you think the audience member asks about the evidence? 🎧54

Presenter: I'd like to give a short presentation about how people will travel in the future. Let's begin by looking at this slide. As you can see, this graph shows the sales of cars around the world since 2016 and then it predicts sales to 2040. The blue line here represents sales of fossil-fuel cars, which most of us currently drive. In the next few years, this figure won't change very much. This is probably because there isn't an easy alternative, and people won't suddenly change their cars. But take a look at this purple line, which shows the sales of electric cars. It forecasts that by the year 2038, we'll be buying more electric cars than fossil-fuel cars.

Audience member: Excuse me, can I ask a question? Where does this evidence come from?

Presenter: The data is from the research organization, Bloomberg NEF.

100 million units

```
75

50

25

0
   '16   '20   '24   '28   '32   '36   '40
```

B Listen to and read the presentation again. Underline any phrases in **A** that fit into the categories in the Useful Expressions box below. 🎧54

C Look at this slide and prepare a short presentation about it. Then, in pairs, take turns giving your presentations.

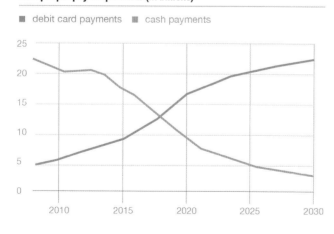

How people pay for products (in billions)

■ debit card payments ■ cash payments

```
25

20

15

10

5

0
   2010   2015   2020   2025   2030
```

SPEAKING STRATEGY 🎧55

Pointing something out

When you present visual information from a slide, it's useful to point at specific parts of the slide and use language to show the audience where to look. For example: *Look at this line **here**. / **This** part shows . . . / And **over there** you can see . . . / **These** numbers represent . . .*

USEFUL EXPRESSIONS 🎧56

Presenting visual information

Starting:
Today I'll talk about . . . / First of all, take a look at this slide.

Explaining the slide:
As it shows you, . . . / The slide shows you . . . / This green line is . . .

Giving reasons:
The reason for this is . . .

Asking questions in a presentation:
I have a question. / I'd like to ask a question. Where . . .?

Referring to evidence:
It's based on research from . . . / The research comes from . . .

GRAMMAR

A Study the three sentences in the chart below. Which future form with *will* talks about:

1. a prediction?

2. a completed action before a given time in the future?

3. a future action in progress over a period of time?

FUTURE FORMS WITH *WILL*			
Future simple	You	will	see more electric cars in the future.
Future continuous	We	will be changing	to electric cars over the next 20 years.
Future perfect	Most of us	will have bought	an electric car by 2040.

B Read the Unit 8, Lesson A Grammar Reference in the appendix. Complete the exercises. Then do the exercises below.

C Complete the article using a future form with *will*. Use the future continuous or future perfect where possible.

In the past, people have tried to predict the future, but they haven't always gotten it right. Here are some predictions from the past that are either partly true or not true yet.

1. In the future, we _____ (eat) food in the shape of bricks and no one _____ (cook). (1950)

2. One day, everyone _____ (have) televisions that produce smells to go with the pictures. (1950)

3. By the beginning of the next century, everyone _____ (stop) listening to live music and will only listen to recorded music. (1906)

4. Using solar energy, tourists _____ (often / travel) into space. (1952)

5. During the twenty-first century, humans ____ _____ (live) in cities on the moon. (1982)

6. The telephone _____ (never / become) as popular as sending written messages. (1876)

7. In 2015, everyone _____ (drive) flying cars. (1985)

8. By 2063, humans _____ (meet) alien life. (1968)

D Do you think any of the predictions in **C** could still come true? Why or why not?

E **PRONUNCIATION: Contracted forms *'ll* and *'ve*** Listen to five sentences. Circle the number of words in each. 🎧57

1. 5 ⑥ 7 8   3. 5 6 7 8   5. 5 6 7 8

2. 5 6 7 8   4. 5 6 7 8

F Write three different sentences about yourself using different years in the future.

1. By the year _____, I will _____.

2. By the year _____, I will _____.

3. By the year _____, I will _____.

G Work in pairs and take turns dictating your three sentences from **F** to each other. Try using the contracted forms *'ll* and *'ve* when you speak.

ACTIVE ENGLISH Try it out!

In pairs, you are going to describe pictures showing the world today and the world in the future. Student A will use the pictures below. Student B will turn to page 217. In both sets of pictures, Picture 1 shows a street and Picture 2 shows a home. As you each describe your pictures, try to find seven differences between the present and the future.

Student A

Picture 1 shows a street today. Describe it to your partner using present forms and find seven differences.

Picture 2 shows a home in the future. Describe it to your partner using future forms and find seven differences.

8A GOALS   Now I can . . .

Present visual information _____

Make predictions _____

1. Yes, I can.
2. Mostly, yes.
3. Not yet.

VOCABULARY

A Read these news and magazine headlines. Underline the cause and decide
if the verbs in blue mean *causes* or *is caused by*.

1. Using cell phones **leads to** an increase in car accidents   causes / is caused by

2. New study: eating chocolate **results in** lower blood pressure   causes / is caused by

3. Coffee **makes** us live longer, say health experts   causes / is caused by

4. Child's intelligence **stems from** mother, not father   causes / is caused by

5. Miracle medicine **brings** new hope to patients   causes / is caused by

6. Frozen water on Mars **gives rise to** belief in life on planet   causes / is caused by

7. Research suggests poor mental health **due to** social media   causes / is caused by

8. Worsening city pollution **because of** 50% traffic increase   causes / is caused by

B Cover up the blue words in **A** and complete this magazine report. Then
look at the words in **A** and check your answers.

Why We Lie

There are lies that (1) s_____ f_____ a desire for
money and riches. The lies of people in power are often
(2) b_____ o_____ their need to stay in power.
And any illegal or bad behavior often (3) g_____
r_____ t_____ a series of ever-worsening lies. But
lying is something most of us do. In a study by the social
pyschologist Bella DePaulo, 147 adults had to write down
everytime they lied. The experiment showed that we lie on
average one or two times a day. Mostly, none of these daily
lies (4) l_____ t_____ anything serious. Some lies are excuses to avoid work,
like pretending to be sick and taking a day off. Others are (5) d_____ t_____ mistakes
we make and trying to cover them up. This is typical for children who start lying between the
ages of two and five, and while this type of behavior often (6) b_____ stress for worried
parents, scientists say it is a normal part of childhood development and doesn't necessarily
(7) r_____ i_____ children growing up into immoral people.

C Complete these sentences in your own words. Then compare your
sentences with a partner.

1. Eating lots of fruit and vegetables results in . . .

2. . . .leads to happiness.

3. . . .causes anger.

4. My level of English is due to . . .

5. Success in life is brought about by . . .

6. . . .stems from hard work.

WORD BANK

Notice the difference in
register between some *cause*
words. In everyday English,
we often use words and
phrases like *because*, *causes*,
and *the reason is* . . . .
In more formal speaking (e.g.,
in a presentation) or in formal
writing (e.g., in a report) we
might also use words such
as *bring about*, *give rise to*,
lead to, and *as a result*.

An umbrella breaking during a storm

WHY DO WE GET ANNOYED?
DOES SCIENCE HAVE AN ANSWER?

A Look at the picture. Why is the person annoyed?

B **Scan for information.** Read the article. Then discuss the questions in pairs.

1. How much can science tell us about why we get annoyed?

2. What are the three essential qualities that make something annoying?

3. What is annoying about the article at the end?

C Check (✓) the annoyances that are listed in the article. Then confirm your answers by reading it again.

☐ When someone eats something that doesn't smell very nice.

☐ When you have to listen to someone else's music.

☐ When someone leaves a train and doesn't take their garbage.

☐ When pop-up ads keep appearing on your screen.

☐ When you keep losing the Wi-Fi signal on your phone.

☐ When your alarm clock isn't loud enough to wake you up.

☐ When you are stuck in traffic on a road that is normally clear.

☐ When you are told that your train is going to be late.

D Underline the words and phrases in the text that match the following definitions.

Picture yourself at a crowded train station or airport. Your train or plane is 20 minutes late even though the sign says it's "On Time." You're surrounded by people talking loudly on their cell phones. The woman on your right is noisily eating something that smells awful. The man on your left is listening to music on his headphones, but you can still hear it. What's worse, he's singing along.

2 Unless you are perfect, a few things in that description—or all of them—will have annoyed you. Surprisingly, science still can't explain what makes certain things especially annoying, and there is very little scientific research or advice on how to prevent life's annoyances. What we do know is that annoyance is a typical human emotion, and there seem to be three essential qualities that drive us crazy.

3 First, anything annoying will be unpleasant but not physically harmful. For example, when searching on the internet, pop-up ads that get in the way of reading or watching something will give rise to extreme annoyance, but they won't kill you.

Second, it must be unpredictable and intermittent. The loud ticking of your alarm clock might annoy you, but over time it ceases to be noticeable, whereas a sudden unpleasant noise or smell will result in annoyance everytime it starts again. Likewise, if you get stuck in traffic every day of the week, then you find ways of dealing with it. But when the traffic jam is unexpected, it will get to you.

5 Finally, to be truly annoying, something might continue for an uncertain period of time; you will put up with your train or plane being late for an hour if someone tells you it's going to be late for an hour. But if it's delayed and delayed and delayed with no explanation, this inevitably ignites anger in most passengers.

6 In the past decade, I've thought a lot about what makes people, things, and situations annoying, and what we could do to keep ourselves from becoming annoyed. The answer is surprisingly simple: All you have to do is . . .

> **Note from editor of this book** We've run out of space on this page and cannot show the rest of the article. We apologize to students for any annoyance this might cause. 58

Paragraph 1: imagine you are *picture yourself*

Paragraph 1: with something all around you

Paragraph 2: make us very angry

Paragraph 3: affecting the human body in a bad way

Paragraph 3: form an obstacle to stop movement or an action

Paragraph 4: now and again, not regular

Paragraph 4: stops

Paragraph 4: annoy or irritate

Paragraph 5: tolerate

Paragraph 5: certain to happen or unavoidable

E Write one thing that annoys you in each of the following categories.

- other people's behavior _____
- sounds or types of music _____
- transportation and travel _____
- eating out and shopping _____
- technology and the internet _____

F Work in groups and present your ideas from **E**. Use some of the words and phrases in **D** in your presentation. After you present, find out if other people in your group are annoyed by the same things as you.

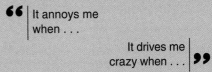

> 66 It annoys me when . . .
>
> It drives me crazy when . . . 99
>
> 66 It also really gets to me when . . .

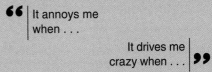

LISTENING

A You are going to listen to a presentation about "Science Citizens." What do they do?

B **Focused listening.** Listen to the presentation and number these photos in the order they are mentioned. 🎧59

C Listen again. Complete the set of notes from the presentation below. 59

What do you think of when you hear the word *science*?

1. A crazy-looking, white-haired gentleman in a _____

2. People with lots of _____ and _____ after their names

   In the past, science was something that anyone could try. Two examples:

3. Benjamin Franklin, who _____ with electricity and invented _____.

4. Hedy Lamarr, who taught herself and developed _____ used in WWII.

   Two examples of Citizen Science projects:

5. NASA has the Globe Observer App to build up a picture of _____. Citizen Scientists have sent NASA more than _____.

6. Projects to test the water in local _____. These are important because water is _____ and it helps _____.

   Two reasons for the growth and popularity of Citizen Science:

7. Smartphones to take images and record data that can be _____.

8. Climate change and the need to monitor _____. For example, the Budburst Project is a way to help scientists and conservationists understand how _____.

D Do you know any citizen scientists? Tell a partner.

GRAMMAR

A Read the Unit 8, Lesson B Grammar Reference in the appendix. Complete the exercises. Then do the exercises below.

CONNECTORS: REASON, RESULT, AND PURPOSE		
The result	**+ connector**	**+ the reason**
Citizen science is popular	due to / because of / as a result of	climate change.
Citizen science is popular	because / seeing as / given that	the climate is changing.
Citizen scientists take photos.	As a result, / Therefore,	we learn about climate change.
The action	**+ connector**	**+ the purpose**
Citizen scientists take photos	in order to / so as to	help other scientists.
Citizen scientists take photos	in order that / so (that)	they can help other scientists.

B Work in pairs and complete these sentences with your own words, giving a reason, result, or purpose.

1. Electric cars are becoming more popular due to . . .

2. People often tell lies because . . .

3. We share selfies in order to . . .

4. The world's population will reach nine billion by 2050. Therefore, . . .

5. We often get annoyed as a result of . . .

6. Countries are using wind and solar energy because of . . .

7. In the future, everyone will have a robot. As a result, . . .

8. Humans will travel to Mars in order to . . .

A man runs by a four-legged robot in the Bishan-Ang Mo Kio Park in Singapore.

C Join another pair and take turns reading your sentences from **B**. How similar or different are your reasons, results, and purposes?

D Work in groups of three or four. You are a town council that wants to make future improvements in your town. You have a list of possible ideas below. but you only have enough money for three of them.

1. Discuss the reasons, results, or purposes for each idea.

2. At the end, choose the three best ideas.

 We can have notice boards in order to tell people about . . .

But due to the cost, we can't afford to build a new . . .

> **Ideas and suggestions for future improvement**
>
> 1. Put up notice boards around town with information about local wildlife.
>
> 2. Provide free bicycles around town for anyone to use.
>
> 3. Put up wind turbines around town to supply clean energy.
>
> 4. Build a lake in the middle of the local park for wildlife.
>
> 5. Put up "No cell phones allowed" signs in some public areas.

A Have you heard of space tourism? Read this article and say if you think space tourism will have a positive or negative impact on our lives in the future.

> ### Space Tourism
>
> We are at the early stages of space tourism, where customers will pay large sums of money in order to orbit the Earth. Some people believe it will lead to new scientific discoveries and the possibility of living in space. Others believe that space tourism will result in faster global warming as a result of the rockets full of rich tourists burning fossil fuels.

B Look at this table about the impacts of space tourism with two ideas from the article. Work in two groups and add more ideas of your own. Group A lists the positive impacts of space tourism and Group B lists negative impacts.

Group A (Positive impacts)	Group B (Negative impacts)
Will lead to new scientific discoveries and the possibility of living in space	Faster global warming as a result of rocket fuel

C Work in pairs with one student from Group A and the other from Group B. Present your ideas and write your partner's ideas in the table.

D **WRITING** Read the Unit 8 Writing Model in the appendix and answer these questions.

1. Which of your ideas in **C** does it include?
2. How many paragraphs are there? Which paragraphs present the arguments for and against?
3. What type of language is important for writing this type of essay?

E Choose one of these titles for a "for and against" essay. Begin by thinking of some positive and negative impacts for your topic. Then write your essay (around 180 words).

1. The impact of self-driving cars in the future
2. The impact of new communication tools on everyday life in the future

8B GOALS Now I can . . .

Identify causes ____	1. Yes, I can.
Explain reasons and results ____	2. Mostly, yes.
	3. Not yet.

GLOBAL VOICES

A How important do you think robots will be in the future? Do you think they will have a positive or negative impact on our lives? Tell the class.

B Watch an interview with Robert Wood and answer the questions.

1. In literature, film, and popular culture, have robots been shown as having a positive or negative impact? In what way?

2. What two examples does Robert give of robots having a positive impact on human knowledge?

3. What advantages does the assembly-line robot have over a human worker?

4. When engineers watch a bee, what kinds of questions do they ask?

5. What three examples of positive impacts does he think his robots could have in the future?

C Work in groups.

1. Imagine you are inventing a robot and make notes:
   • What type of robot is it? Give it a name.
   • What is it able to do? For example, does it clean the house?
   • What are the positive benefits of your robot? How can it change people's lives?

2. Now prepare a one-minute group presentation about your new robot. Imagine you are selling it to everyone else in your class. If possible, draw a picture of it.

3. Take turns giving your presentations to the class. Afterward, vote on which group has the best robot.

The size of this miniature robot is apparent when contrasted with the flower.

9

BODY MATTERS

LOOK AT THE PHOTO. ANSWER THE QUESTIONS.

1. What does the body language of the woman and the horse tell us about their relationship?

2. Which of the five senses do you think the woman and horse are using in this photo?

WARM-UP VIDEO

A Watch a video about people who cannot smell. They have a medical condition called "anosmia." Check (✓) the items that they mention or that you see in the video.

☐ Broccoli   ☐ Popcorn   ☐ Hair
☐ Chocolate   ☐ Butter   ☐ A rose
☐ A new car   ☐ Fresh bread   ☐ A baby
☐ Grass   ☐ Rain   ☐ Barbecues
☐ Perfume   ☐ Exhaust fumes   ☐ Coffee

B Watch the video again and write the missing word(s).

1. Dreaming about broccoli made the woman feel _____.

2. On the train in the morning, the man could smell _____.

3. For the woman, eating faded from color to _____.

4. People say the man's room smells just like _____.

5. "Smell is linked to some of the most important parts of our _____."

C Tell a partner about a smell:

- that you love.

- that you hate.

- that reminds you of a special time or place in your life.

Woman with her horse
in the mountains

GOALS   **Lesson A**
/ Talk about the senses
/ Describe and compare photos

Lesson B
/ Compare people and animals
/ Summarize results

VOCABULARY

A Read some medical myths and the truth about them. Which of the myths have you heard before?

> **Medical Myths**
>
> 1. **Cold weather makes you sick:** Even if you stand around shivering, a winter temperature does not make getting sick more likely.
>
> 2. **Fruit drinks make kids uncontrollable:** Even though sugary drinks aren't recommended, studies show they often actually make children quiet.
>
> 3. **Chewing gum stays in your stomach for seven years:** You may still want to avoid swallowing gum, but this is not true.
>
> 4. **Staring at screens ruins your eyesight:** It might become uncomfortable as your eyes get tired, but it causes no long-term damage.
>
> 5. **Loud, deafening music at concerts causes hearing loss:** It might, but you are at greater risk from everyday, repeated noises, such as trains or machinery.
>
> 6. **Lilacs help you sleep:** These flowers are fragrant, but the smell doesn't necessarily put you to sleep.
>
> 7. **Eating food within 5 seconds of dropping it on the floor is safe:** Quickly grabbing a dropped sandwich in the street is no guarantee, since food attracts bacteria within milliseconds.
>
> 8. **Blushing is due to social anxiety:** It is true that some people go red in social situations, but there are other medical reasons linked to blushing.

B Add the blue words in **A** to the categories of verbs and adjectives.

1. the whole body: sweat, tan, _____
2. the mouth: eat, chew, _____
3. the face: smile, frown, _____
4. taste: salty, spicy, _____

5. sight: see, look, _____
6. smell: perfumed, smelly, _____
7. hearing: noisy, peaceful, _____
8. touch: hold, stroke, _____

C Complete the pieces of advice with the words below. Then discuss with a partner which advice you agree or disagree with.

chew   fragrant   grab   peaceful   spicy   swallow   sweat

1. _____ your food 32 times before you _____ it.
2. At work, don't _____ a sandwich while working. Sit down and take time out for lunch.
3. _____ food is good for your heart, but too much can give you heartburn.
4. When you have a cold, it's good to _____ in a sauna.
5. To relax, burn _____ candles and listen to _____ music in the bath.

ACADEMIC SKILL

Understanding connotation

Some words have a positive (+) or negative (-) meaning, or *connotation*: fragrant (+); smelly (-); smile (+); frown (-).

LISTENING

A Look at the freediver holding his breath underwater for many minutes. How do you think he feels?

B **Identify feelings.** Listen to four conversations. Match each conversation to a person. 🎧60

Conversation 1 _____   Conversation 3 _____

Conversation 2 _____   Conversation 4 _____

a. This person feels angry about something.

b. This person feels unwell with a medical problem.

c. This person feels nervous about doing something.

d. This person feels short of breath.

C Listen again and circle the best answer for each question. 🎧60

1. Why is the first woman worried about Frida?

    a. She is blushing   b. She is out of breath   c. She is doing exercise

2. What does the doctor think might be the cause of the patient's problems?

    a. Sweating and heartburn   b. Spicy meals   c. Large amounts of food

3. What does the person in the third conversation complain about?

    a. The noise   b. The smell   c. The view

4. Where does the couple go?

    a. Into a sauna   b. Into a swimming pool   c. Into the snow

D In the conversations, you heard the expressions below with the word *breath*. Match each expression to its meaning.

1. out of breath _____

2. catch your breath _____

3. take a deep breath _____

4. don't hold your breath _____

5. hold your breath _____

a. return to normal breathing after breathing very hard

b. stop breathing for a moment

c. breathing fast and very hard

d. don't wait for something, because it probably won't happen

e. breathe in and fill your lungs with air

E Work in pairs and write your own short conversation using at least one expression with *breath* from **D**. Then join another pair and take turns reading your conversations aloud.

A group of young women play soccer on a cobbled street in the city of São Paulo, Brazil.

SPEAKING

A Work in pairs. Compare the photo above and the photo on page 118. List three differences between the photos.

B Read and listen to two friends talking about and comparing the two photos.

1. Which photo do they talk about first?

2. What differences do they talk about?

Wang Yu: Hey, did you see that photo with the young women playing soccer?

Marina: Where?

Wang Yu: Here, take a look at this.

Marina: What a great photo! They look a bit out of breath! But really happy.

Wang Yu: I know! You can hear their laughter. And the colors are amazing with their clothes in the foreground and the colors of the murals on the walls in the background. They're all on this website.

Marina: Let's see some more . . . Wow! This one is completely different! Compared to the other photo, it's much more peaceful.

Wang Yu: Yes, you can almost hear the sound of the wind. And the sound of her taking a deep breath.

Marina: I love the way her hand is stroking its neck. She looks quite emotional.

Wang Yu: It reminds me of my own pets . . .

Use of linking words and expressions

When you compare two things (such as two photos), use linking words and expressions to make the comparison clear: *In contrast, / In comparison, / On the other hand, / However, . . .*

C Work in pairs and read the conversation aloud.

D Now describe and compare the following:

- the two photos on page 218
- two photos of people from a website or book that you like
- two photos of people you have taken (e.g., on your phone)

USEFUL EXPRESSIONS

Talking about photos

Introduce the photo

This is a photo I saw on a website / took on my phone / took over the weekend . . .

This photos shows . . . / This is a great photo because . . .

Points of main interest

The colors are amazing because . . .

The people look like . . . / It looks like . . .

They are . . .-*ing* / They seem . . .

Parts of a photo

The foreground shows . . . / In the foreground, . . .

The background . . . / In the background, I can see . . .

At the top / bottom, . . . / On the right / left, . . . / In the middle, . . .

Personal response

I like it because . . .   It reminds me of . . .   It makes me think of . . .

Comparing two photos

It's very similar to / different from the other. / Compared to the other . . .

It's more . . .than . . .

It is / isn't as . . . as . . .

GRAMMAR

A Work in pairs. Underline the comparative, superlative, or *as . . . as* form in each sentence. Is the main word in each form an adjective or an adverb?

1. It's <u>quieter than</u> before. *quieter = adjective*
2. Last night, I didn't sleep as badly as the night before.
3. It's one of the most interesting photos I've ever seen.
4. The people in this photo are more active than in the other one.
5. The background in this photo is as colorful as this one.
6. The app makes you run further everyday.

B Read the Unit 9, Lesson A Grammar Reference in the appendix. Complete the exercises. Then do the exercises below.

COMPARATIVE FORMS (WITH ADJECTIVES AND ADVERBS)		
	With an adjective	**With an adverb**
Comparative	My sandwich looks <u>**better** than</u> yours.	Eat your sandwich <u>more **quickly**</u>!
Superlative	This is the <u>most **beautiful**</u> song I've ever heard.	She plays the piano the <u>most **beautifully**</u>.
as . . . as (*not as . . . as*)	This cake is <u>as **delicious** as</u> my mother's.	I ca<u>n't</u> run <u>as **quickly** as</u> you.

C PRONUNCIATION: the schwa sound /ə/ Listen and notice the schwa sounds. Which words and syllables are normally unstressed in comparative forms? 🎧64

        /ə/ /ə/
1. It's <u>quieter than</u> before.

          /ə/   /ə/
2. My eyesight isn't <u>as good as</u> it used to be.

       /ə/
3. This is <u>the best</u> song I've ever heard.

D Listen and mark the schwa sounds in the comparative forms. Then listen and repeat. 🎧65

1. This color isn't as <u>bright</u> as the other.
2. Which one smells the <u>worst</u>?
3. Your cooking tastes <u>better</u> than ever.
4. I can't swim as <u>far</u> as you.
5. Ron can run <u>quicke</u>r than me.

E Work in groups. Brainstrom three words you know connected with each topic. For each topic, make two or three sentences comparing your three words.

Topic 1: Three senses

Topic 2: Three different smells

Topic 3: Three types of noises

Topic 4: Three flavors or tastes

Topic 5: Three types of physical exercise

> 66 Taste, sight and smell.

> Smell is as important as taste when you eat. 99

> 66 But I think sight is the most important sense because . . .

ACTIVE ENGLISH Try it out!

A You are going to play a game called "Brag or Bluff?" The aim is to win points by bragging about your real achievements in life or by making up false information (bluffing). First of all, work on your own and complete the sentences below. Make some of the sentences true (brag about your achievements) and some of the sentences untrue (bluff about fictional achievements).

B Work in groups of four or five and sit in a circle. One person starts by reading their first sentence aloud. The other players must discuss and decide whether they think the sentence is a brag (and true) or a bluff (and false). If the group guesses correctly, then the person does not win a point. If, however, the group guesses incorrectly, then the person wins one point.

The next person in the circle speaks and the game continues like this. When everyone has read their first sentence, move on to sentence 2, and so on until the last sentence. The person with the most points at the end is the winner.

WORD BANK

brag to show off about something you have done or an ability you have

bluff to try to deceive other people into believing you have experiences or abilities that you do not

Brag or bluff?

1. The most amazing place I ever visited was . . .

2. The most common compliment I get is that I . . .

3. One of my greatest achievements in life is . . .

4. Probably the most delicious meal I ever cooked was . . .

5. The highest score I reached in something was when I . . .

6. I can play different musical instruments, but I'm probably best at . . .

7. In sports, I've been most successful at . . .

9A GOALS Now I can . . .

Talk about the senses _____

Describe and compare photos _____

1. Yes, I can.

2. Mostly, yes.

3. Not yet.

VOCABULARY

A Look at the photo of the dog and the sheep. If animals could speak, what do you think the dog would be saying?

B Match the animals to the sound verbs. Then listen to the sounds and the verbs and check your answers. 🎧66

1. cat _____
2. snake _____
3. lion _____
4. bee _____
5. chicken _____
6. mouse _____
7. small bird _____
8. dog _____

a. tweet
b. purr
c. squeak
d. hiss
e. roar
f. cluck
g. growl
h. buzz

C Read about onomatopoeic words and then match the words in blue in the box to the five categories. (One word matches two categories.)

| buzz | clap | click | groan | grunt | purr | splash | whistle | whizz |

Onomatopoeic words sound like their meaning. Some types of onomatopoeic words use certain letter combinations. Here are five categories:

1. low (negative) sounds with gr-: _____growl_____ _____ _____
2. fast and violent sounds with -ash: _____crash_____ _____
3. short, sudden sounds with cl-: _____cluck_____ _____ _____
4. movement of air sounds with wh-: _____whisper_____ _____ _____
5. long sustained sounds with double letters: _____hiss_____ _____
   _____ _____

D Complete the words from **C** in the sentences.

1. My dog starts to gr_____ when she senses someone is at the front door.
2. My children always gr_____ when I ask them to take the dog for a walk.
3. Everytime I wh_____, everyone's dog comes running except mine!
4. Look out! A _____zzing bee just wh_____ed past your head!
5. There was a loud _____ash when my dog jumped into the lake after the ball.

E Write three more sentences with onomatopoeic words from this page. Then, in pairs, take turns reading your sentences aloud, but leaving out the onomatopoeic words. Can your partner guess the missing word?

A herding dog gets stuck between sheep.

WEIRD ANIMAL QUESTIONS

Here is the latest set of questions from our readers asking if animals' behavior is similar to that of humans.

Do animals flirt?

When humans flirt, they start a conversation and find things in common. Next, they tend to lean towards the other person when speaking and maybe they briefly touch the other person's arm when laughing. So are animals as flirtatious as humans and, if so, how?

Certain species of birds are easily as good as humans—and possibly even better—at flirting by showing off their feathers and colors. Take a type of bird called the Great Argus Pheasant. The male spreads its circle of long feathers while doing a dance around the more plain-looking female; it's almost the same as an evening out at the nightclub.

Male dolphins appear to be much more flirtatious than other types of sea creatures. They will whistle and crash through the surface of the water and make giant leaps in the air to impress female dolphins. And like humans giving gifts, male dolphins will take sea sponges to the females.

Do animals laugh?

Of all animals, chimpanzees are by far the most likely to giggle. The psychologist Marina Davila Ross carried out experiments in which she tickled them and they responded by laughing. She has also concluded that chimpanzees display "laugh faces" with smiling teeth—with or without actual laughter.

While not nearly as giggly as chimpanzees, another type of animal that laughs is the rat. Psychologist Jaak Panskepp found that rats make happy noises when you tickle them. The animals squeak during play, and some rats will even follow the hand that tickles them. Panskepp believes that other animals might also laugh; it is just a question of listening to the sounds they make while they are having fun.

Do animals need sunscreen?

When spending a day at the beach, humans can slap on the sunscreen. But what can animals do when they need protection from the sun? Hippopotamuses and whales are two of the largest species of animals, with more skin to protect than most. Hippos produce a type of "sweat" that combines a red pigment and an orange pigment. The red pigment is an antibiotic and the orange absorbs the sun's harmful UV rays.

With whales, you'd expect them to be protected from the sun's rays due to the fact that they live in the ocean. But they can spend up to six hours a day on the ocean's surface between dives, baking in the sunlight. It turns out that, as with humans, some types of whales have a much darker skin color that protects them from the sun, while other whales with a slightly lighter skin color tend to get a tan. 67

Red-crowned crane courtship dance in snow, Hokkaido, Japan

A You are going to read a page from a website in which readers ask questions about animals and their behavior. Think of one question about animals. Then ask the class.

B Answer the questions with words from the article in your notebook.

1. Are certain species of birds better than humans at flirting?

2. What does the writer compare the Great Argus Pheasant's dance around the female to?

3. What noise do male dolphins make when they flirt?

4. How are chimpanzees' smiling expressions described?

5. Do rats laugh as much as chimpanzees?

6. Why will rats follow someone's hand?

7. What theory does Panskepp have about other species of animals?

8. What is the purpose of a hippo's "red sweat"?

9. What is a misunderstanding about a whale's behavior?

C **Dealing with unknown words.** Underline the words in the text that have the following meanings.

1. playful towards someone they feel attracted to

2. uninteresting and not colorful

3. laughing in a nervous or silly way

4. touch it with your fingers

5. moisture from the skin

6. cooking

7. browner skin

D Work in pairs. Think of a species of animal and compare it to a human:

• Something this animal can do, but a human cannot.

• Something a human can do, but this animal cannot.

• Something this animal and a human can both do.

LISTENING

A Think of an unusual musician that you like. Tell a partner why you like him / her.

B Listen to a radio show about Ben Mirin. Are these statements true or false? 🎧68

1. He leads expeditions around the world, recording animal sounds. _____
2. He tries to photograph animals that he finds in the wild. _____
3. He's probably the world's first "Wildlife DJ." _____
4. He turns animal sounds into music. _____
5. He tries to make sounds like the animals he hears. _____
6. He hopes his music will help animal conservation. _____
7. He records people talking about their local nature. _____
8. He sometimes works with other artists and musicians. _____

C **Listen for specific information.** Listen again and write answers for the following. 🎧68

1. What did Ben use to listen for as a child? _____
2. What phrase is used to mean *something you have always wanted to do or to happen*? _____
3. Which five onomatopoeic animal sounds does the speaker mention?
   _____
4. Which word describes music with a good tune? _____
5. How is music an international language? _____
6. How does he change his music for other countries? _____
7. What does his music make people in New York do? _____

D Work in pairs and answer the questions.

1. Have you ever had a dream come true in your life? In the future, what dream would you like to come true?
2. Can you give some examples of catchy music and musicians that you like listening to? Have you ever created or remixed your own musical recordings?

Orangutan climbs tree in search of fruit in Borneo.

GRAMMAR

A Read the Unit 9, Lesson B Grammar Reference in the appendix. Complete the exercises. Then do the exercises below.

Cheetah

MODIFYING COMPARATIVE FORMS
Comparatives
Small difference: *Other whales have a **slightly lighter** skin color.*
Big difference: *People can listen **far more closely** to animal sounds.*
Add emphasis: *Certain birds are **even better** than humans at flirting.*
Superlatives
*Chimpanzees are **by far the most likely** animal to giggle.* *In my opinion, elephants are **easily the most intelligent** species.*
as . . . as
Small differences: *My dog is **almost as noisy as** the dog next door.*
Big differences: *A shark **isn't nearly as large as** a whale.*

African elephant

B Read the information about the different animals. Then, complete the sentences with modifiers from the box.

	Top speed	Weight	Average lifespan
Cheetah	90 km/h	60–70 kilos	10–15 years
African elephant	40 km/h	5,000 kilos	60–70 years
Chimpanzee	40 km/h	50–60 kilos	50–60 years

All data is approximate and will vary.

Chimpanzee

almost as   by far the   easily   equally   much   nearly   slightly

1. A cheetah is _____ the fastest animal.

2. A chimpanzee can run _____ as fast as an African elephant.

3. An African elephant is _____ heaviest animal.

4. A chimpanzee isn't _____ as heavy as an elephant.

5. A cheetah is _____ heavier than a chimpanzee.

6. A cheetah has a _____ shorter lifespan than the other two animals.

7. A chimpanzee can live _____ long as an African elephant.

C Read the facts and opinions about animals. Add a modifer to each sentence to support your view of the facts or opinions.

a bit   a little   a lot   almost   by far   easily   equally   far   much   not nearly   slightly   twice

1. Dogs are more friendly than cats, and they make better pets.

2. Riding a horse is as dangerous as riding a motorcycle.

3. The ostrich is the largest bird in the world.

4. Elephants are as intelligent as dolphins.

5. Panda bears are cuter than any other species.

D Work in groups and compare your sentences in **C**. Which facts and opinions do you agree or disagree on?

ACTIVE ENGLISH Try it out!

A Study the results from a global survey of pet ownership. Which is the most popular pet in the world? How do the results compare by gender? And by country?

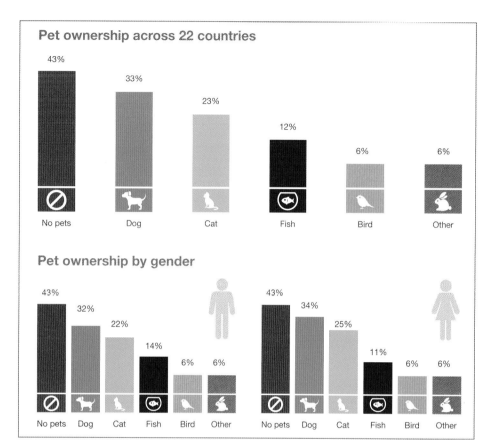

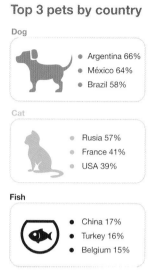

Top 3 pets by country

Dog
- Argentina 66%
- México 64%
- Brazil 58%

Cat
- Rusia 57%
- France 41%
- USA 39%

Fish
- China 17%
- Turkey 16%
- Belgium 15%

B Work together as a class and carry out a similar survey.

1. Ask everyone to raise their hands in answer to the question: Which of the following pets live with you? Dog / Cat / Fish / Bird / Other / No pets

2. For each answer, write the number of hands or a rough estimate of the percentage on the board. (You can also write the results by gender.)

C **WRITING** Read the Unit 9 Writing Model in the appendix and underline any useful phrases you can use in your own writing.

D Write a similar summary about your class, using your survey results in **B**.

9B GOALS Now I can . . .

Compare people and animals _____
Summarize results _____

1. Yes, I can.
2. Mostly, yes.
3. Not yet.

GLOBAL VOICES

A How important are your relationships with animals? What do you most like about them? Tell the class.

B Watch an interview with Ben Mirin and answer the questions.

1. What things inspire Ben Mirin's work? In what way?

2. How does he prepare for his expeditions?

3. Why is preparation important?

4. Where did he go on his latest expedition? What did he learn?

5. What types of things has he created for education and art?

C Work in groups.

1. Imagine you are going on an expedition and make notes:

   • What types of things would you want to observe? Flora or fauna?

   • What would you do with the information you collected?

   • What would be the positive benefits of your information?

2. Now prepare a 1-minute group presentation about your project.

3. Take turns giving your presentations to the class. Afterwards, vote on which group has the best idea for a project.

Ben Mirin working in the field

REAL WORLD LINK BUSINESS IDEAS

Reusable bags
are used around
the world.

A Read three business ideas from a crowdfunding website and answer the questions for each idea.

1. How much is the person trying to raise to start their business?
2. How much does the person want you to pledge?
3. What will you receive if the person achieves his or her goal?
4. If you had the money, which idea would you invest in? Why?

1. Bamboo Shopping Bags

Tired of using plastic bags? I've created a range of shopping bags in four different sizes (S, M, L, XL) that are made from bamboo, so they're durable, reusable, and sustainable. Pledge $30 today and you'll receive our starter pack of high-quality bags in all four sizes in a choice of white, green, or rainbow. Help us achieve our starting goal of $5,000—it's good for us, good for you, and good for the planet.

2. Electrifyurbike

Electric bicycles are a lot faster, far more efficient, and much more fun than your average bicycle, but they are by far the most expensive option. Don't despair—with my conversion kit, you take a standard bicycle and turn it into an electric-powered bike. Anyone can do it because of the easy-to-read manual. In order to help me achieve my start-up goal of $20,000, pledge $200 today and be one of the first to receive a kit.

3. Pet Workout Pal

What will your dog or cat be doing today while you are out? Probably feeling lonely and not getting much exercise. The Pet Workout Pal is a programmable robot that produces up to twenty sounds so that your pet can hear a range of reassuring growls and purrs. Your pet will get the exercise it needs by chasing the unbreakable pal, which moves at different speeds. Pledge $150 and help us make pets around the world much happier and healthier.

B Read the texts in **A** again and match the sentences to the business ideas (1, 2, or 3). There is more than one answer for one sentence.

a. It's added to an existing object. _____

b. It comes in different colors. _____

c. It makes noises. _____

d. It's cheaper to use than an existing product. _____

e. It makes other things move. _____

f. It's environmentally friendly. _____

C Work in pairs and think of a new business you would like to start. Here are some ideas you could use or adapt.

• making clothing from recycled plastic

• inventing and selling a flying car

• making engine fuel from mushrooms

• producing sunscreen for pets

D In pairs, create a crowdfunding description for your new idea in **C**.

Option 1: Write a short text for the website.

Option 2: Create a video presentation of your idea.

Remember to:

• give the business or product a name.

• describe what it does and its key features.

• say what people can pledge and receive in return.

• say how much you need to raise in order to start the business.

E Read or watch another pair's crowdfunding idea and then do the following (still in your pairs):

1. Prepare two or three questions about the idea and ask the other pair your questions.

2. Decide if you will pledge them the money they need. Give reasons for your decision.

10

KEEP IT LEGAL

LOOK AT THE PHOTO. ANSWER THE QUESTIONS.

1. How is the man breaking a rule?

2. Do you think what he is doing is very bad? Why or why not?

WARM-UP VIDEO

A Watch the video. Are these statements true or false?

1. We know why the woman is running from the police. _____

2. The police are making the cattle run towards the woman. _____

3. The police are waiting for her on the other side of the field. _____

B Watch the video again. Complete the missing words.

1. A high-speed c_____ in Florida ended in a field of cattle.

2. The s_____ f_____ her car and ran into the field.

3. Cows are naturally p_____ animals and their first instinct is to f_____ or flee.

4. Female cows become a_____ when they are p_____ their young.

5. It is possible that the fleeing suspect was seen as a t_____ to the cattle.

6. The cattle f_____ her through the fence, where the police a_____ the suspect.

C Work in pairs. Imagine that a police officer is interviewing the woman back at the police station. Write a short conversation using some of the words in **B**. The police officer wants to know why the woman fled from the police and if she is guilty of a crime. Afterward, perform your conversation for another pair or for the class.

A man stands on a cornice of a building in Moscow as his friend takes a photo.

GOALS

Lesson A
/ Talk about crimes and criminals
/ Speculate and make deductions

Lesson B
/ Discuss laws
/ Report back what was said

VOCABULARY

A Work in groups and complete this table. Use a dictionary if necessary.

Type of crime	Verb form	Person	Definition of crime
hacking	hack	hacker	illegally accessing data on a (1) <u>computer system</u>
robbery	(2) _____	robber	stealing something from a person
forgery	forge	(3)_____	copying a signature, banknote, or work of art
mugging	(4) _____	mugger	robbing someone in a public place
shoplifting	shoplift	shoplifter	stealing something from (5) _____
smuggling	(6) _____	smuggler	illegal movement of goods into or out of a country
vandalism	vandalize	(7)_____	damaging public or private property

B Complete these sentences with the correct form of a word in the table.

1. The _____ managed to steal all our customers' personal details.

2. The two _____ must have climbed in through the window at the back of the house.

3. If you hold this dollar bill up to the light, you can see it's a _____.

4. I was walking down the street when someone tried to _____ me and steal my phone.

5. The store owner accused the guilty-looking children of stealing candy and explained that _____ is a crime.

6. The customs officer realized the passenger was trying to _____ her dog into the country when he opened her suitcase.

7. You were seen writing graffiti all over this wall, so you are guilty of _____.

WORD BANK

accuse claim someone has done something wrong or illegal

charge when the police formally accuse someone

crime an illegal action

guilty the opposite of innocent

thief a person who steals

victim the person who suffers because of a crime

C Play the following game in groups of five or six students.

1. Choose one student who is accused of crimes. He or she has to leave the classroom for two minutes.

2. Each of the remaining students (or accusers) writes one imaginary accusation on a piece of paper. (e.g., *I saw you shoplift pet food last week from the supermarket.*)

3. When everyone has written one accusation, the student returns to the classroom.

4. Someone in the group reads out the written accusations. After each accusation is read aloud, the accused student guesses who wrote the accusation. If he or she guesses the identity of the accuser correctly, then that accuser becomes the accused and leaves the classroom. The game begins again.

Is graffiti vandalism or art? Harlem, New York City.

LISTENING

A Where do you normally read or hear the news? What are the main stories in the news this week?

B **Listen for gist.** Listen to four news reports and match them to the crimes below by writing the numbers of the reports. One crime is not mentioned. (69)

a. Murder _____   c. Vandalism _____   e. Shoplifting _____

b. Robbery _____   d. Mugging _____

> **WORD BANK**
> **murder** the crime of killing someone

C Listen again and make notes about the four crimes in the table. (69)

	What mistake did the criminal make?	Did the police catch the criminal? (If so, where?)
1	He sent the police a better photo with a message.	
2		Yes, they did, but we don't know where.
3		No, they didn't.
4	They expected to meet another woman outside in their getaway car.	

D **PRONUNCIATION: Homophones** Some words have different spellings and meanings, but the same pronunciation. Listen to the same pronunciation of the words in bold. (70)

1. He'll spend 25 years in a prison **cell**. / He tried to **sell** stolen goods.

2. The thief wanted to **steal** the violin. / The lock on the door was made of **steel**.

3. The police must have surprised the **pair**. / I'm going to eat this **pear**.

4. The police arrested **two** suspects. / Another woman was in the car, **too**. / They went **to** prison.

5. He left a note for **its** owner. / **It's** suspected they might have carried out a similar theft.

E Listen to more homophones and write them in the sentences with their different spellings. (71)

1. I'm so b_____ today. / Write your name on the b_____.

2. Don't b_____ the law! / Press the b_____ to stop.

3. The color of blood is r_____. / I've r_____ that book so many times.

4. The package is t_____ up with string. / The t_____ is going back out to sea.

5. T_____ are two suspects. T_____ fingerprints are all over the room. / T_____ guilty!

Woman reading a newspaper on a train in Kerela, India

A black bear investigating a cabin. Bears often are drawn to human homes to look for food (often in the trash!).

SPEAKING

A Read and listen to a conversation. As you listen, write the sounds they hear outside. 🎧72

1. _____

Paulo: What was that?

Anders: What was what?

Paulo: Did you hear that noise?

Anders: Yes. It must be the neighbor's cat. It's always coming into our yard.

2. _____

Paulo: There it is again!

Anders: It's probably just the cat in the trash can. It comes looking for food. Don't worry about it.

3. _____

Paulo: What just happened then? It can't be a cat! Maybe it's a burglar. Go and take a look. Take a flashlight with you.

Anders: Why me? Why can't you go?

Paulo: It might be dangerous.

Anders: Exactly!

Paulo: Do you think I should call the police?

B Practice the conversation with a partner.

C Read the Useful Expressions in the box. Under *Making deductions*, which phrases show that the speaker is very certain? Which show the speaker is less certain?

D Work in pairs and practice a similar conversation.

1. Your instructor is going to play some sound effects. Then begin your conversation. 🎧75

2. Your instructor is going to play more sound effects. Start a new conversation. 🎧76

USEFUL EXPRESSIONS 🎧73

Speculating

Noticing something strange
What was that?
Did you hear that noise / something?
What do you think that was?
What just happened (outside)?
There it is again!

Making deductions
It must / can't be . . .
It might be / may / could be . . .
Probably, it's . . . / It's probably . . .
There's definitely something . . .
It's possibly . . .
Maybe / Perhaps it's . . .

Recommending action
Go and take a look.
Take a flashlight with you.
Why me? Why can't you go?
Be careful!
Do you think I should call the police?

SPEAKING STRATEGY 🎧74

Speculating
When you speculate, use modal verbs such as *must / can / could / may / might* to show you are either very certain or less certain:

I think it **must** be a neighbor. (= very certain)

I'm not sure. It **might** be a burglar. (= less certain)

GRAMMAR

A Read the Unit 10, Lesson A Grammar Reference in the appendix. Complete the exercises. Then do the exercises below.

MODAL VERBS FOR CERTAINTY AND POSSIBILITY								
Speculate about present states / actions				**Speculate about present events in progress**				
modal + bare infinitive				modal + *be* + *-ing*				
He	must	be	the thief.	They	might	be	visiting	friends.
Speculate about past events (often based on evidence)								
modal + *have* + past participle								
He	couldn't	have	gotten lost. (The route is easy.)					
She	might	have	broken down. (Her car is very old.)					
They	must	have	stolen the money. (No one else had the key to the safe.)					

WORD BANK
An **inside job** is a crime committed by or with the help of people living or working in the building where it happened.

B Underline the correct verb forms in some of the most dramatic thefts that have taken place in art galleries.

The Louvre, Paris

Nowadays, it (1) *might be / might have been* hard to imagine how anyone (2) *could steal / could be stealing* the Mona Lisa. But in 1911, Vincenzo Peruggia did. He was working in the museum, and he (3) *must hide / must have hidden* the painting under his clothes. Two years later, the police caught him trying to sell it.

Museum of Fine Arts, Montreal

In 1972, armed thieves stole 50 works of art. The police think they (4) *must be climbing / must have climbed* in through the roof and tied up the security guards. The crime was never solved, and you never know—the paintings (5) *might be hanging / might have hung* in someone's house today.

Mohamed Mahmoud Khalil Museum, Cairo

After a painting by Van Gogh was first stolen from this museum, no one (6) *could predict / could have predicted* that it would happen again. But it was stolen again in 2010, and it has not been recovered since. Interestingly, none of the fifty alarms in the museum were working on the night of the theft, so some people believe that it (7) *must be / must have been* an inside job—that is, someone who worked there is the thief.

C Work in pairs. You are police detectives, and you arrive at the art gallery. Make some deductions about what happened last night using the verbs in the box.

climb	cut	smash	steal	wear

ACTIVE ENGLISH Try it out!

A Read about "Banksy." Do you think his work is art or a type of crime? Tell the class.

The artist Banksy is famous for his street art, which has appeared in cities around the world. His work divides opinion. On the one hand, his paintings have sold for millions of dollars to art collectors. On the other hand, it's a crime to illegally paint on walls like this. No one knows who Banksy is, and his paintings often appear overnight. He has never been arrested.

"Graffiti is a Crime" at the exposition called The World of Banksy at Espacio Trafalgar in Barcelona, Spain

B Work in groups. Read about five different situations and discuss the correct punishment. You can choose from the suggestions in the box or make your own. Try to reach an agreement on each case.

ban the person from doing something	name and shame them in the local newspaper
do some unpaid work in the local community	pay a fine
go to prison for a few months	promise not to do it again

1. Two children shoplift some chocolate bars from a local store and try to sell it to friends at school.

2. A group of teenagers paint some street art on a wall in their local park. The police catch them and charge them with vandalism.

3. A hacker accesses the computers of a bank, but he doesn't steal any data. He says he wanted to show the bank how easy it is.

4. A man who recently lost his job is caught stealing money from a house. It's the first time he's committed a crime.

5. A woman is caught breaking the speed limit in her car by 10 miles per hour. It's the third time.

" I think he should go / pay / do . . .

I don't think it's a bad crime because . . . "

" They might have done it because . . .

She's guilty! "

C Each group reports back their five punishments to the class. Which group was the most severe? Which was the most lenient?

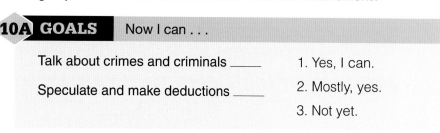

10A GOALS   Now I can . . .

Talk about crimes and criminals _____

Speculate and make deductions _____

1. Yes, I can.

2. Mostly, yes.

3. Not yet.

WORD BANK

fine amount of money you pay for breaking a rule or law

lenient not punishing someone in a strong or severe way

prison a building where criminals go as punishment

punishment what you receive for committing a crime (e.g., prison, a fine)

severe punishing someone in a strong way

VOCABULARY

A Work in pairs. You have two minutes to brainstorm words connected with the topic of "the law." Then join another pair and share your words.

B Match these pairs of words to the correct definition (a or b).

1. **court** _____ / **prison** _____
   a. where it is decided if someone is guilty of a crime
   b. where someone who is guilty might go after a trial

2. **judge** _____ / **jury** _____
   a. a group who listens to a case and decides if a person is guilty
   b. a person who controls a court

3. **law** _____ / **prosecute** _____
   a. the system of official rules in a country
   b. accuse a person of a crime in court

4. **defendant** _____ / **lawyer** _____
   a. someone who gives legal advice and defense
   b. someone who has been accused of a crime

5. **sue** _____ / **case** _____
   a. take legal action against someone
   b. a matter to be decided by a judge in court

C Read about three real court cases. Write in the missing words from **B**.

After getting a ticket for parking in a zone marked "loading only," a woman went to (1) _____. When asked by the (2) _____ why she hadn't parked legally, the woman said that there was a dumpster in her parking spot, so she had parked in the space marked for the dumpster.

A woman brought a (3) _____ against a TV station. She said that its weatherman had incorrectly predicted a sunny day. Instead, it rained, she got wet and caught the flu, and this caused her to miss a week of work. She wanted to (4) _____ the TV company for $1,000.

Charged with speeding, the (5) _____ denied breaking the (6) _____. He told the judge that he hadn't realized he was speeding because he was wearing a brand new pair of shoes and couldn't feel how hard he was pressing the accelerator pedal.

D Discuss each case in pairs. What do you think the judge decided?

WHEN **HAPPY BIRTHDAY** WENT TO COURT

[1]You've probably sung it hundreds of times over cakes and candles, but did you know you were doing something illegal? Until recently, singing the song "Happy Birthday" in public could have resulted in your being sued by a music publisher. (1) _____ However, film and TV companies had to pay every time they used it to avoid being sued (which explains why you rarely hear it sung in movies).

[2]The legal story behind the tune has many twists and turns. It begins back in the state of Kentucky, in the United States, in the late nineteenth century. Two sisters named Patty and Mildred Hill wrote a song called "Good morning." Patty was a kindergarten principal and Mildred was a pianist. Together, the sisters wrote songs that the children would enjoy singing. (2) _____ The tune was simple and the words even simpler: "Good morning to you, Good morning to you, Good morning dear children, Good morning to all."

[3](3) _____ In the early part of the twentieth century, the words were rewritten as "Happy Birthday to you," and the song started to appear in print. Eventually, the copyright to the music expired in 1949, so it was legal to hum the tune as long as you didn't sing the actual words. (4) _____ Someone else owned the words until Warner Chappell bought the copyright to them for around $15 million in 1988.

[4]Owning the copyright meant that Warner Chappell made about $2 million a year from the song. That was until a documentary filmmaker decided to make a film about the song and realized she'd have to pay Warner Chappell $1,500. Along with other artists, she took the case to court and won. A judge ruled that "Happy Birthday To You" should be in the public domain and free for all to use. (5) _____ . 🎧77

A Do you normally sing a particular song at birthdays? Do you know where the song comes from or who wrote it?

B **Prediction.** Look at the title of the article. Try to predict what the article is about and tell the class. Then read it and check your ideas.

C Read the text again and add in these missing sentences.

a. So as a result, you are now legally free to sing it aloud!

b. You won't recognize those words, but you know the tune.

c. In reality, no such case ever went to court.

d. That's because ownership of the lyrics was sold separately from the music.

e. One song in particular proved popular.

D Find and circle words in the article with the following meanings.

1. complicated details and sudden changes (paragraph 2)

2. the legal right of the owner of a work (e.g., a book, movie, photo, or song) to say how other people can use it (paragraph 3)

3. sing a tune without opening your mouth (paragraph 3)

4. belonging and being available to anyone with no legal restrictions (paragraph 4)

E How much do you know about copyright? Test yourself with this true / false quiz.

1. Copyright is only something for famous people like writers, artists, and musicians. _____

2. It's legal to reuse any photo you find online. _____

3. It's legal to download a photo if you have paid the photographer an agreed fee. _____

4. Including a short quote or sentence from a book in your own essay is legal. _____

5. Photocopying a chapter from your favorite book and giving it to friends is legal. _____

6. You write a book and send it to a publisher. But you forget to say you own the copyright, so the book isn't protected. _____

The elephant Trompita gets a birthday cake made of vegetables and fruit for her 56th birthday celebration at the Aurora Zoo in Guatemala.

ACADEMIC SKILL

Identifying reference words
Effective reading includes the ability to identify reference words that refer forward and backward in a text. For example, in the phrase, "You won't recognize **those** words." the word *those* refers back to the previous sentence.

LISTENING

A **Prediction.** Look at the headline from a news report about a river in New Zealand. Why do you think a river might need legal rights?

River given the legal rights of a human by government

Whanganui River, New Zealand

North Island

Whanganui River

South Island

NEW ZEALAND

B Listen and number the items in the order they are described. 🎧78

_____ a. The decision of parliament   _____ c. The real importance of the new law

_____ b. The history of the river

C Read these incomplete notes by a journalist. Predict the words or types of words which are missing. Then listen again and complete the notes. 🎧78

> **Location of river**
> New Zealand: Starts at three volcanoes on the northern (1) _____.
>
> **Reasons for protest**
> - For the local Maori people, it is a (2) _____ river that they have cared for and depended upon for more than (3) _____ years.
> - Modern tourism and industry have had a (4) _____ impact on the river, including a hydroelectric power scheme.
>
> **The new law**
> - Parliament passed new legislation on the 20th of (5) _____, 2017. The new law said that the river had all the (6) _____, powers, and duties of a person.
> - No one knows yet if this means that nature could take humans to (7) _____ and (8) _____ them for the damage they cause.
> - For the Maori people, what really matters is that the new (9) _____ will make humans think about their (10) _____ to the natural world.

D Choose one of these reactions to the law and give reasons for your choice.

- It's an interesting idea. I wonder if it will work.

- It's a silly idea because it limits progress.

- It's a fantastic idea. We should try it in my country.

GRAMMAR

A Study these sentences. Which is direct speech? Which are reported speech? What differences do you notice?

1. It is said that the river started from a teardrop falling from the eye of the Sky Father. _____

2. The new legislation says that the river has all the rights, powers, and duties of a legal person. _____

3. Gerrard Albert said that, "Rather than us being masters of the natural world, we are part of it." _____

B Read the Unit 10, Lesson B Grammar Reference in the appendix. Complete the exercises. Then do the exercises below.

REPORTED SPEECH	
Use reported speech to report someone's words from the past. You often move the tenses "backwards" from direct speech (unless the information is still true).	
Direct speech	**Reported speech**
The judge said, "He's guilty." They said, "The river **has** rights."	The judge said he **was** guilty. (= in the past) They said (that) the river **has** rights. (= still true)

C Interview a partner with these questions. Write down his or her actual words using direct speech.

1. What was the first thing you said when you woke up this morning? Who did you say it to?

   _____

2. What is one question your teacher asked you today?

   _____

3. What are your favorite words from a song? Who sang them?

   _____

4. Think of the best present you ever received. What did you say to the person who gave it to you?

   _____

5. Remember something you heard in a film or TV show last night. What was it? Who said it?

   _____

6. What is the best piece of advice about life you have ever been given? Who gave it to you?

   _____

D Now write complete sentences from your notes in **C** using reported speech. Afterward, swap your sentences with your partner and check that they are correct.

ACTIVE ENGLISH Try it out!

A Work in groups of three and look at the list of different types of security. For each one, say:

- where you might see or use it.
- if you ever use it or if it has been used on you.

Burglar alarm	Fingerprint recognition	Key pad	Pin number	X-ray machines
Facial recognition	Identity badge	Motion detectors	Security camera	
Fencing	Key lock	Password	Security guard	

B Work in the same group and imagine the following. Recently there have been a number of thefts at your place of work or study. Your group has been asked to think of ways and rules to improve security in the building.

> 66 I think we should install security cameras in every corridor . . .

1. You have five minutes to make a list of action points.
2. Join another group and compare your lists.

C **WRITING** Read the Unit 10 Writing Model in the appendix and answer the questions.

1. How many of your ideas from **B** appear in this announcement?
2. Who is the announcement for? Is it for a particular group of people?
3. How would you describe the tone of the announcement? Is it formal? Polite? Direct? Chatty and friendly?
4. How clear is the announcement? By the end, does the reader have all the information needed?

D Write your own announcement (180–200 words) using your ideas for an action plan in **B**. Afterward, swap your writing with a partner and answer these questions:

- Is it clear who the announcement is for?
- Is the tone formal and direct?
- Is it clear and does it include all the important information?

10B GOALS Now I can . . .

Discuss laws _____	1. Yes, I can.
Report back what was said _____	2. Mostly, yes.
	3. Not yet.

Facial recognition system concept

GLOBAL VOICES

A Watch a video with the wildlife filmmaker, Malaika Vaz. Answer the questions in your notebook.

1. What is the main part of her job?
2. What type of illegal crime does she investigate?
3. How does she hope she can help Manta Rays in the future?
4. At the end, what does she say we all need to do?

B Watch the video again and decide if these sentences are true (T), false (F), or we don't know (DK) (because the information isn't given).

1. As well as being a filmmaker, Malaika is a diver and windsurfer. _____
2. Criminals who illegally trade in wildlife can make a lot of money. _____
3. Malaika has interviewed many of the criminals. _____
4. The Manta Rays are killed and sold for food. _____
5. Illegal trafficking is 100% responsible for the loss of Manta Rays. _____
6. You can read the results from India's scientific survey to understand the species. _____
7. Manta Rays are now protected under India's wildlife trade laws. _____
8. She believes COVID-19 has changed many people's attitudes to eating or using wildlife. _____

C Imagine you are a journalist and you are going to interview Malaika about her work. In pairs, write five questions for her, based on the information from the video.

D Change partners and take turns role-playing the interview between the journalist and Malaika.

Malaika Vaz swimming with a Manta Ray during Baa Atoll Expedition in the Maldives

GOALS
Lesson A
/ Get a good deal
/ Ask questions about products

Lesson B
/ Talk about ways of eating
/ Make a complaint

Yiwu market in China has more than 70,000 stalls.

HUNGRY CONSUMERS

LOOK AT THE PHOTO. ANSWER THE QUESTIONS.

1. Imagine you are walking into this stall. What do you think the stall owner says to you?

2. In pairs, discuss how you would respond.

WARM-UP VIDEO

A Watch a video about the market in Yiwu. Number the items in the order you see them.

_____ A trader of door handles

_____ Christmas decorations

_____ Toys

_____ Circular saw blades

_____ Fake flowers

_____ An electric vehicle vendor

B Watch the video again and write the missing numbers.

1. The market is _____ square meters.

2. It's _____ kilometers long.

3. The hoverbike is _____ RMB (about 100 dollars).

4. The door-handle trader from Dubai has _____ shops in _____ countries.

5. The bottom floor of district _____ has toys.

C How do they say their visit to the market changed their worldview at the end of the video?

D If you visited the market in Yiwu, which types of shops would you visit? Why?

VOCABULARY

A Read more about the market in Yiwu. Then write the words in blue in the word web.

When you go shopping, where do you go to **get a bargain**? For the best bargains, possibly the best city in the world is Yiwu, in China. About 60% of the world's cheapest **consumable goods** come from Yiwu. Every day, its vast market of **vendors make deals** on hundreds of **brands**. Factories in Yiwu **manufacture** many of the items; they **mass-produce** everything from toys to zippers to Christmas decorations. An estimated 1,000 containers are **shipped** daily from Yiwu to **retailers** on every continent.

WORD BANK
The words **customer** and **consumer** have a similar meaning. **Customer** refers to buying and **consumer** to using, but we often use them in the same way.

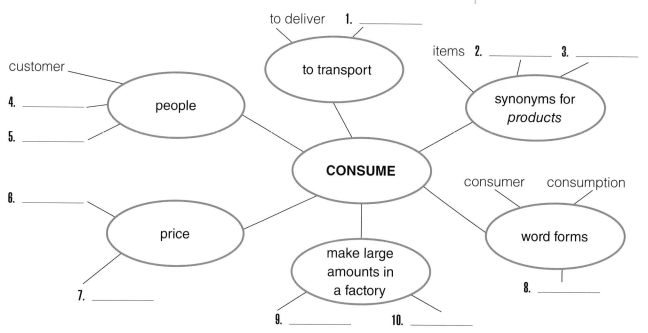

to deliver   1. _____

items 2. _____   3. _____

synonyms for *products*

customer

4. _____   people

5. _____

to transport

CONSUME

consumer   consumption

word forms

8. _____

6. _____   price

make large amounts in a factory

7. _____

9. _____   10. _____

B Complete each sentence with a word in blue from **A**.

1. You can get a _____ when you shop at this market.

2. The goods are _____ from a port.

3. Most customers or _____ try to get a bargain when they buy something.

4. The wholesaler sells the goods from the factory to the _____, who sells to the customer.

5. Let's make a _____. If you buy a thousand today, I'll give you a 25% discount.

6. You recognize a _____ like Nike because of its famous logo.

ACADEMIC SKILL
Recording vocabulary
A word web is a useful way to show groups of words connected to a topic. Include words you already know, and then add new words when you find them in texts.

C In pairs, talk about where you go to get a bargain when you go shopping. Decide what is the best place.

LISTENING

A In your country, is it normal in stores to pay the price shown, or can you ask for a lower price? What does it depend on?

B Listen to an interview and choose the correct answers. 🎧79

1. The advice is for _____

   a. tourists.   b. local customers.   c. vendors.

2. People often avoid markets because they think they'll _____

   a. be deceived into paying too much.   b. have their money stolen.   c. never find their way out.

3. When haggling, Shona says you should _____

   a. take it seriously.   b. have fun.   c. avoid being cheated.

4. When you start, _____

   a. accept the first price you are given.   b. say the exact price you will pay.   c. say a price below what you are willing to pay.

5. Shona thinks tourists should not worry about paying _____

   a. a lot more than a local would pay.   b. a little more than a local would pay.   c. a little less than a local would pay.

C **Match definitions.** Read the questions and match the definitions in the box to the words in bold. Then listen again and answer the questions. 🎧79

| best part | cost more than you can afford | offer in response to another |
| complication | excessively persistent | |

1. For the presenter, what is a **highlight** of any summer vacation? _____

2. What is the **catch** with shopping in a traditional market? _____

3. Who can be really **pushy** in a market? _____

4. What should your **counter-offer** be below? __ _____

5. What won't **break the bank**? _____

D Work in pairs and make a list of tips for tourists for shopping in your country. Use your own ideas and ideas from the listening. Afterward, compare your list with another pair.

❝ Buy your souvenirs from a local market, not from a shopping mall.

A vendor selling fabric at a neighborhood festival in Barcelona, Spain

SPEAKING

A Read and listen to a conversation at a market. How much does the customer pay in the end? Who do you think got the better deal? 🎧80

A customer examines a jacket at a street fair in Berlin's Kreuzberg district.

VENDOR: Hello. Can I help you?

CUSTOMER: Hi, can you tell me how much this jacket costs?

VENDOR: Why don't you try it on? It's my last one.

CUSTOMER: OK. I'll try it, but how much is it?

VENDOR: There. It fits you. And the color looks good, too.

CUSTOMER: Yes, I like it, but what's the price?

VENDOR: Fifty dollars.

CUSTOMER: Wow! Fifty? Isn't there a discount?

VENDOR: That's with a discount.

CUSTOMER: That's too much for me.

VENDOR: I might be able to take forty-five.

CUSTOMER: What about if I pay you thirty?

VENDOR: But it costs me thirty to make them! I can't do it for that.

CUSTOMER: I can probably afford thirty-five.

VENDOR: No, that's too low. I might be able to go down to forty. Doesn't that sound reasonable?

CUSTOMER: Look! This is all my cash. Thirty-five is the most I can pay.

VENDOR: I can take a card.

CUSTOMER: I don't have a card. Only cash.

VENDOR: OK, agreed. I'll take it.

CUSTOMER: Great. That's a deal.

USEFUL EXPRESSIONS 🎧81
Getting a good deal

Making an offer	*Making a counter-offer*	*Making the final deal*
Can / Could you tell me how much this costs?	But it cost me . . .	I'll give you . . .
	No, that's too high / low.	. . . is the most I can pay.
Isn't there a discount?	I can't do it for that.	Agreed. / That's a deal. / OK, I'll take it.

SPEAKING STRATEGY 🎧82
Hedging

When discussing prices and trying to get a bargain, we often **hedge** in English. We avoid answering a question, and use vague language:

It's **around** fifty dollars.   That **seems a bit** high.

I can **probably** pay . . .   **What if I** pay you . . .

B Practice the conversation with a partner.

C Work in pairs and imagine an object in your classroom is for sale. Practice the conversation in the flowchart about your item.

Customer	Vendor	Customer	Vendor	Customer
Ask about the price	Offer a special price	Make a counter-offer	Make a final offer	Make a deal

GRAMMAR

A Read the Unit 11, Lesson A Grammar Reference in the appendix. Complete the exercises. Then do the exercises below.

NEGATIVE AND EMBEDDED QUESTIONS	
Direct questions	**Negative questions**
Is there a discount? Does that sound reasonable?	→ Isn't there a discount? (checking information) → Doesn't that sound reasonable? (showing surprise)
Direct questions	**Embedded questions**
How much does this cost? What's the discount on this? Do you take credit cards?	→ Can / Could you tell me how much this costs? → I'd like to know what the discount is on this. → I was wondering if you take credit cards.

B Rewrite the direct questions as embedded questions.

1. How much does it cost?

   Can I ask _how much it costs?_____

2. Is this available in a larger size?

   I was wondering _____

3. How quickly do they deliver it?

   Do you know _____

4. Why is the blue one more expensive?

   I'd like to know _____   _____

5. Do they offer any guarantee?

   Do you have any idea _____

6. Can you wrap it? It's a present.

   Could I ask _____

C Match the two halves of the questions.

1. Isn't there ____   a. you had this in a larger size.
2. I was wondering if ____   b. give me a discount?
3. Can't you ____   c. the same model in blue?
4. I'd like to know ____   d. how much this costs to ship.
5. Could you tell ____   e. sent it yet?
6. Shouldn't you ____   f. pay by cash?
7. Do you have any ____   g. me what the discount is?
8. Haven't you ____   h. idea where this was made?

Smiling baker at the counter

D Prepare five questions for a partner using the first parts of the questions (1–8) in **C**. Then take turns asking and answering the questions.

66 | Isn't there any homework today?   No, I don't think so. 99

66 | I was wondering if you'd like to have a coffee after class.   Sure, I'd love to! 99

A Work in pairs. Look at the questions about the watch. Say the same questions as negative or embedded questions.

- How much does it cost? Is it on sale?
- Does it come with a warranty? How long is it?
- Where is it manufactured?
- What is it made of? Is it made from sustainable materials?
- Does it come in any other colors?
- Can I buy it in a different size?

B Work alone and prepare to sell a new product (e.g., a bicycle, a children's toy). Write information in the table below about your choice of product.

	You	Your partner
Product?		
Price? Discount?		
Different colors or sizes? Materials?		
Country of manufacture?		
Warranty?		

C Work in pairs and take turns interviewing your partner using negative or embedded questions. Write down their answers in the table in **B**.

11A GOALS   Now I can . . .

Get a good deal _____

Ask questions about products _____

1. Yes, I can.

2. Mostly, yes.

3. Not yet

VOCABULARY

A Work in pairs and study the food idioms in blue. What do you think each expression means? Do you have a similar idiom in your language?

1. These new T-shirts are **selling like hot cakes**, aren't they?

2. He says he wants to order a thousand, but I'd **take that with a grain of salt**.

3. **You can't have your cake and eat it, too**—to get anything you have to work hard.

4. You'd probably get a promotion if you were prepared **to butter** the manager **up** more often.

5. She's a **smart cookie** who set up her own business by the time she was twenty.

6. On weekends, I tend to be a **couch potato** and binge-watch TV series.

7. New customers are always important, but regular weekly customers are our **bread and butter**.

8. **There's no use crying over spilled milk**. If you made a mistake, don't worry. Just start again.

9. Ordering from the supermarket's website was a **piece of cake**, wasn't it?

10. The issue of climate change is a real **hot potato**, isn't it?

> **WORD BANK**
> English has many idioms using food words:
> A topic that gives food for thought is something to think about.

B Work in pairs and play this memory game. One student closes his or her book and the other student reads out the five idioms on the left, leaving a gap or making a noise where a food word is missing. The other student guesses the missing food word. Then switch roles and use the five idioms on the right.

- They're selling like hot . . .
- I'd take it with a grain of . . .
- You can't have your . . . and eat it, too.
- You should try to . . . . someone up.
- My best friend is a smart . . .

- I'm a bit of a couch . . .
- This job is my bread and . . .
- There's no use crying over spilled . . .
- It was easy—a real piece of . . .
- This issue is a real hot . . .

> 66 They're selling like hot BEEP!
>
> Cakes? 99
>
> 66 Correct!

C Work in groups and discuss the answers to the questions.

1. Who do you think is the smartest cookie in your class? Why?

2. On weekends, do you often go out, or are you a complete couch potato?

3. Why is it a good idea to butter up your teacher? How can you do it?

4. What have you all seen online recently that you took with a grain of salt?

5. What grammar point in English was a piece of cake to learn? Why?

THE ETIQUETTE OF EATING

A ferry travels on the Amazon River, between Manaus and Benjamin Constant, Brazil.

A Take this quiz on food etiquette in different countries. Match the country to the rule.

Italy	Japan	Mexico	South Korea	Thailand	United States

1. If an older person offers you a drink, lift your glass with both hands to receive it. _____

2. Never eat your tacos with a knife and fork. Be polite and eat with your hands. _____

3. Cut up food with your fork in your left hand and your knife in your right hand. Then put the knife down and switch the fork to the right hand in order to pick up the food. _____

4. Only drink a cappuccino before lunch. Order one afterwards and you'll be branded a tourist! _____

5. Never stick your chopsticks upright in your rice. _____

6. Don't put food in your mouth with a fork, use a spoon. Forks are used to push the food onto the spoon. _____

> **Word Bank**
> **etiquette** the correct or polite way of doing something with a particular group of people (e.g., eating with chopsticks politely)

B Discuss the questions as a class.

1. Have you heard any of these rules before?

¹ **When visiting new countries, knowing *how* to eat is just as important as knowing what to eat and how to ask for it. But even for experienced travelers, understanding food etiquette is not a piece of cake. It's very easy to get wrong—as travel writer Daisann McLane found out on a river boat in Brazil.**

² "Everyone in the dining hall of the Amazon riverboat is staring at me. Actually, not staring, glaring. At first, I take it with a grain of salt. After all, I'm the lone non-Brazilian among the hundred or so passengers riding the slow wooden boat down the Amazon River. I've been trying my best to blend in. I even pitched my hammock on the crowded deck with everyone else to later sleep, shoulder to shoulder, under the equatorial stars.

³ But still I stick out like a sore thumb. So I smile and nod as I seat myself at the communal dining table in front of my meal of rice and beans, which is included in the boat ticket for the thousand-mile journey. I figure if I acknowledge, in a good-natured way, that all eyes are on me, everybody will stop looking at me and go back to the more important business of eating lunch. Right?

⁴ Wrong. "*Senhora, senhora!*" A wiry man wearing an undershirt is angrily shouting at me. I can't understand what he is trying to say. Another woman takes up the "Senhora!" chorus, and another, and they are all making the same odd gesture—pretending to pat their heads. My face is red with embarrassment; what have I done to upset my fellow passengers?

⁵ Suddenly, I feel a breeze whoosh over my head as the baseball cap I'd been wearing for protection from the harsh Amazonian sun lifts. I turn around, startled, to find it in the hand of the first mate. In his torrent of words, I understand three: *comer não chapéu*—eat no hat.

⁶ Then I get it. On a rickety slow boat on the Amazon, it's okay to eat lunch in your undershirt. And without shoes, even. But under no circumstances can you sit down to eat your beans in Brazil without taking off your hat. Oh well, no use crying over spilled milk. I make a mental note of this important rule and add it to my ever-lengthening list of travel mistakes. 🎧083

2. If you are from one of these countries, do you think it is always true? Does it vary?

C **Skim for gist.** Read the article. What mistake did Daisann McLane make?

D Read the article again and match each subtitle to one of the six paragraphs.
  a. Taken by surprise. _____
  b. I try a new strategy. _____
  c. Trying to look like everyone else. _____
  d. I learn my lesson. _____
  e. What am I still doing wrong? _____
  f. A how-to of eating. Paragraph 1

E Circle words and expressions with these meanings in the text.

Paragraph 2
1. look the same as everyone else
2. very close to the people next to me

Paragraph 3
3. clearly look very different and noticeable
4. with a friendly manner

Paragraph 5
5. surprised

F Work in pairs and list some tips for visitors to your country so they can "blend in." Include advice on:
  • ways of eating food.
  • what types of food to order.
  • greeting people in social situations.
  • dressing for formal meals.

LISTENING

A **Focused listening.** Listen to four different conversations and match them to the pictures. 🎧84

B Listen again and answer the questions. 🎧84

Conversation 1

1. Which of the two people has eaten at the restaurant before?

_____

2. What doesn't one of the people eat? _____

Conversation 2

3. What is the online customer complaining about? _____

4. How satisfied is the customer with the suggested solution? _____

Conversation 3

5. What doesn't Emily pay much attention to? _____

6. Why does Ken sometimes throw food away? _____

Conversation 4

7. How does Chia suggest her friend hold the first chopstick? _____

8. How easy does Chia think it is to use chopsticks? _____

C As a class, discuss how common it is for people in your country:

• to be vegetarian or vegan.

• to order food online instead of going to a store or restaurant.

• to look at or pay attention to expiration dates on food packaging.

• to try food from different cultures and to eat it traditionally (e.g., with chopsticks, with knife and fork, with hands).

GRAMMAR

A Read the sentences with question tags from the listening. Check (✓) the correct meaning.

1. This is a lovely restaurant, isn't it?

   ☐ a. I think it is lovely.   ☐ b. I'm not sure if it's lovely.

2. We shouldn't eat it, should we?

   ☐ a. I'm sure we should eat it.   ☐ b. I'm not sure that we should eat it.

B Read the Unit 11, Lesson B Grammar Reference in the appendix. Complete the exercises. Then do the exercises below.

QUESTION TAGS			
Positive	Negative	Negative	Positive
This is a lovely restaurant,	isn't it?	We shouldn't eat it,	should we?

C Complete the sentences with the missing question tags. Then listen and check. 🎧85

1. You've been here a few times, _____ ?
2. But pizza can't go bad, _____ ?
3. That sounds nice, _____ ?
4. I'll have to order everything again, _____ ?
5. It won't go bad like milk, _____ '?
6. You don't need any help, _____ ?
7. That was a piece of cake, _____ ?

D **PRONUNCIATION: Rising or falling intonation** Listen and compare the intonation of the question tags. In which sentence . . . 🎧86

a. does the intonation rise (∧)?

b. does the intonation fall (∨)?

1. This is a lovely restaurant, isn't it?

2. We shouldn't eat it, should we?

> " You're twenty-two years old, aren't you?
>
> No, I'm twenty-three. "
>
> " You don't like meat, do you?
>
> That's right. I'm a vegetarian. "

E Listen to the sentences in **C** again. Write (∨) when the speaker is sure and the intonation falls or (∧) when the speaker is unsure and the intonation rises. 🎧87

F Work in pairs and prepare six question tag sentences for your partner. Then take turns asking and answering.

- Write three sentences checking information about your partner— you are sure.
- Write three sentences asking for information—you are unsure.

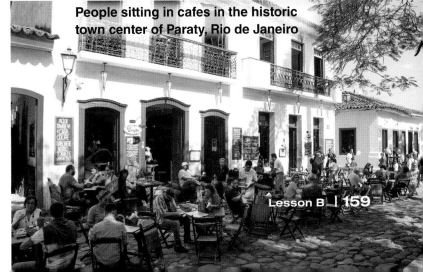

People sitting in cafes in the historic town center of Paraty, Rio de Janeiro

ACTIVE ENGLISH Try it out!

A Take this survey and then compare your answers in groups. Who is the biggest complainer in your class?

Are you the world's biggest complainer? Take this survey by choosing actions a, b, or c for each situation.

1. You receive two books from an online store. One book has a damaged cover.

   a. Do nothing. After all, it would take too long to send it back, wouldn't it?

   b. Ship the book back to them and get a replacement.

   c. Call the company and demand your money back (but keep the books).

2. You ordered a taxi to arrive at 8:00. It is 8:05 and it hasn't arrived yet.

   a. Wait a bit longer. It'll be here soon, won't it?

   b. Call to find out where the taxi is.

   c. Call and go bananas! Demand a discount because the driver is late.

3. You overdrew your bank account for two days and received a penalty charge.

   a. It's easier to pay it, isn't it?

   b. Complain that you think it's unfair because this is the first time it has happened.

   c. Complain and tell them you are moving your money to a new bank.

4. You are a vegetarian and bought a sandwich. You find a piece of chicken in it.

   a. Throw it away.

   b. Never go back to the store again and tell friends not to go.

   c. Take the sandwich back to the store and shout at the chef!

5. It's a very hot day and the air conditioning has broken down in your office.

   a. Buy yourself a fan and some water.

   b. Complain to work colleagues and wait to see if it gets fixed.

   c. Complain to your boss and refuse to work until it is fixed.

> **What do your answers mean?**
>
> Answers mostly (a): You prefer an easy life and don't like to complain.
>
> Answers mostly (b): You like to complain but tend to avoid face-to-face confrontation.
>
> Answers mostly (c): You are a big complainer and enjoy telling people what you think!

B WRITING Read the Unit 11 Writing Model in the appendix and answer the questions.

1. When and why did the person visit the restaurant?

2. What four problems did they have with the service and the food?

3. What two pieces of action does he want the manager to take?

4. How formal is the letter? Does the writer use direct or indirect questions?

C Choose from situations 1, 2, or 4 in the survey and write a similar letter of complaint to the owner of the business.

11B GOALS Now I can . . .

Talk about ways of eating _____   1. Yes, I can.

Make a complaint _____   2. Mostly, yes.

3. Not yet.

GLOBAL VOICES

A How much do you agree or disagree with the opinion in the statement below? Tell the class.

"Your diet is the single biggest thing you can control to help slow down climate change."

B Read these sentences about diet and climate change and match the figures. Then watch the video to check.

| 15 | 60 | ¼ | 330 |

1. As much as _____ of greenhouse gas emissions come directly from agriculture related to farming food, and in particular, livestock.

2. Eating one serving of beef emits about _____ grams of carbon emissions, the same as a five-minute car ride.

3. One serving of chicken is closer to _____ grams of carbon emissions.

4. If we all switched to a Mediterranean diet, we would reduce greenhouse gas emissions by _____ % by 2050.

C Watch the video again and answer the questions in your notebook.

1. What two things does the speaker love?

2. Why is the carbon footprint of a cow so much larger than for other animals?

3. What is one way to address the problem, which the speaker is not going to do?

4. As a result of the information, what changes does the speaker plan to make about his meat and dairy consumption?

5. What does he think is a good compromise?

D How much has the information in this video made you think about changing your diet because of climate change? Choose one response and then explain the reasons behind your response in small groups.

1. I'm going to change my diet immediately.

2. I might start to change my diet a bit.

3. I won't change what I eat.

POINTS OF VIEW

LOOK AT THE PHOTO. ANSWER THE QUESTIONS.

1. How often do you look at the moon? Is it easy or difficult to see from where you live?

2. When you see the moon and stars at night, how does it make you feel?

WARM-UP VIDEO

A These planets orbit the sun. Try to order them from nearest (to the sun) to the furthest away.
Mercury   Neptune   Jupiter   Venus
Saturn   Uranus   Earth   Mars

B Watch the video and check your answers in **A**.

C Watch the video again and answer the questions.

1. What did astronaut James Irwin see that changed him?

2. What is the only way to see a scale model of the solar system?

3. How much space do they need in Black Rock Desert?

4. What will using a time-lapse camera and lights tell us?

5. If the real sun and the model sun are the same size, what does it tell us?

6. In space, what can you hide behind your thumb?

7. What does Wiley think is "staggering"?

D Have you ever seen something that you thought was "staggering"? Tell the class.

View of the moon from Tuam,
County Galway, Ireland

GOALS

Lesson A

/ Describe wonderful, unbelievable places
/ Show amazement

Lesson B

/ Express your opinion
/ Give a speech

VOCABULARY

A Read these sentences from tourist websites about different vacation and travel destinations. According to the descriptions, which places:

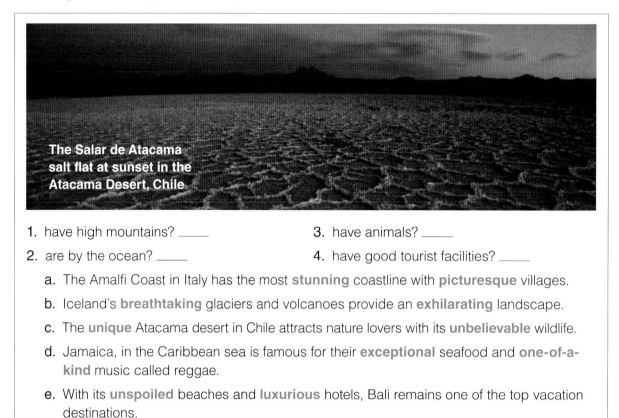

The Salar de Atacama salt flat at sunset in the Atacama Desert, Chile

1. have high mountains? _____
2. are by the ocean? _____
3. have animals? _____
4. have good tourist facilities? _____

   a. The Amalfi Coast in Italy has the most **stunning** coastline with **picturesque** villages.

   b. Iceland's **breathtaking** glaciers and volcanoes provide an **exhilarating** landscape.

   c. The **unique** Atacama desert in Chile attracts nature lovers with its **unbelievable** wildlife.

   d. Jamaica, in the Caribbean sea is famous for their **exceptional** seafood and **one-of-a-kind** music called reggae.

   e. With its **unspoiled** beaches and **luxurious** hotels, Bali remains one of the top vacation destinations.

B Match each word in the pair to the correct definition (a or b).

1. stunning _____
2. unbelievable _____
   a. impressive or attractive
   b. surprising

3. picturesque _____
4. breathtaking _____
   a. something that is amazing (usually about a landscape)
   b. visually attractive (usually about buildings)

5. unique _____
6. unspoiled _____
   a. unlike anything else
   b. unchanged or undamaged

7. exceptional _____
8. one-of-a-kind _____
   a. unusually impressive
   b. very special because of its uniqueness

9. luxurious _____
10. exhilarating _____
   a. making you feel very happy
   b. extremely comfortable

> **WORD BANK**
>
> Emotive adjectives such as **stunning** and **breathtaking** are often used to describe geographical features and places of extreme beauty.
>
> **Unbelievable** can have a positive or negative meaning: an unbelievable view! (+); an unbelievable liar! (-).

C Look at the five places in **A** and decide which you would like to visit. Rank them in order of preference from 1 to 5.

D Work in groups and present your answers in **C** with reasons. Then imagine you are all going on a vacation together. Try to agree on one place you'd all like to visit.

LISTENING

A Do many tourists come to your town or city? Is it a popular tourist destination? Why or why not?

WORD BANK

Use **so** and **such** to add emphasis:

so + adjective: It can be **so rewarding**.

such + adjective + noun: It can be **such an amazing experience**.

B Listen to a travel writer describe five ways to be a tourist in your own hometown. Number these tips in the order she mentions them. 🎧88

_____ a. Take a tour

_____ b. Make a date

_____ c. Get a room

_____ d. Act like a tourist

_____ e. Make the usual unusual

C **Transcription.** Listen again for these sentences and replace the words in bold with the expressions used. 🎧88

1. See your hometown from the **perspective** of a tourist. (3 words) _____

2. I've watched visitors' faces **smile with happiness**. (2 words) _____

3. More often than not, I **run away**. (4 words) _____

4. There's **extra excitement** to waking up in a hotel bed. (3 words) _____

5. Go **in a new, unexplored direction** and head over to a new neighborhood. (4 words) _____

6. Look out for new activities to take you out of **a familiar situation**. (3 words) _____

D Work in groups and imagine you run a tour company. Plan a two-day itinerary for a group of tourists with a list of places, activities, and times of day. When your itinerary is ready, present it to the class. Make sure your itinerary . . .

- shows the town or city from different points of view.
- takes tourists off the beaten track and out of their comfort zone.
- makes tourists' faces light up with an added thrill!

> On Day One in the morning, they'll get a stunning view from . . .

> After lunch, we will take them off the beaten track to . . .

A view of the Miraflores skyline, the steep cliff, and the Circuito de Playas road in Lima, Peru

SPEAKING

A Read and listen to the conversation. How does Midori get Alfie's interest in her news? How does Alfie react? (89)

Midori: You'll never guess what I just did.

Alfie: What?

Midori: Guess!

Alfie: I don't know. What happened?

Midori: This is going to blow your mind! I just gave my notice at work today.

Alfie: No way! You're joking!

Midori: I'm not joking at all. And, I bought myself an around-the-world ticket. I'm finally going on that trip I've always talked about!

Alfie: Oh my gosh! That is unbelievable! So, when are you going? *Where* are you going?

Midori: In three weeks. I'm starting in New Zealand.

Alfie: Oh, wow! I've heard the scenery there is breathtaking.

Midori: So, I have a month in New Zealand and then I plan to fly to Australia . . .

Alfie: I am so jealous! You'll have such a good time.

B Practice the conversation with a partner.

C Work in pairs and take turns telling your partner surprising news. Use some of the ideas below or create your own news.

- you've been offered a new job overseas
- you won money in the lottery
- you're dating a famous celebrity
- you're going on a hiking tour of the Himalayas
- you're going to be on a TV quiz show

GRAMMAR

A With a partner, study these pairs of sentences with determiners. Which is the correct sentence in each pair? Can you explain the rule about the determiner?

1. **a.** Heather Davis is a travel writer. _✓_
   Rule: We use the indefinite article with jobs.
   b. Heather Davis is travel writer. _____

2. **a.** My town is best place in world. _____
   b. My town is the best place in the world. _____

3. **a.** That's your bus over there. _____
   b. That's your bus over here. _____

4. **a.** I've been to some other countries. _____
   b. I've never been to some other countries. _____

5. **a.** Pack less books in your suitcase. _____
   b. Pack fewer books in your suitcase. _____

6. **a.** You have a little time, so leave now! _____
   b. You have very little time, so leave now! _____

B Read the Unit 12, Lesson A Grammar Reference in the appendix. Check your answers in **A**. Complete the exercises. Then do the exercises below.

DETERMINERS	
Determiners are words that come before nouns. They identify the noun or express the quantity.	
Articles	You'll have **a** great time in New Zealand. It's **an** amazing country, and it has **the** most beautiful scenery.
Demonstratives	Can you put **that** bag over there with **these** bags over here?
Possessive adjectives	I'm from Chile. **Its** capital is Santiago, but **my** home is in Temuco.
Quantifiers	We only have **a few** sandwiches, so give one to **each** person in the group and then see if there are **any** left at the end.

ACADEMIC SKILL
Determiners
It's easy to make mistakes with determiners. Make a list of your common mistakes in English to help you correct them.

C Complete the text with the determiners from the box.

a	an	any	each	~~every~~	few	the	X

(1) _Every_ tourist has a bucket list of a
(2) _____ places they'd like to visit one day.
Are (3) _____ of these places on yours?

- Visit the Arctic and the continent of
  (4) _____ Antarctica.
- Dive in (5) _____ Great Barrier Reef.
- Go on (6) _____ hike through the Alps.
- Take (7) _____ adventure tour of Africa.
- Sail to (8) _____ of the Hawaiian islands.

WORD BANK
A person's **bucket list** is a list of places they'd like to visit and things they'd like to do.

D Work in pairs and write a bucket list of five places you'd both like to visit. Then join another pair and compare your lists.

ACTIVE ENGLISH Try it out!

A   Work in pairs and read the TV commercial for a vacation destination. What is
wrong with the text? How could you make the hotel sound more exciting?

"Welcome to your next vacation!"
Are you looking for a nice place to go on vacation this summer? We have a good place for you. This is the Sunny Hotel. Each room has a nice balcony with good views and our restaurant has lots of dishes to choose from, including some seafood. The Sunny Hotel is on a nice beach with a lot of good shops, cafes, and nightclubs, so you can have a good time! Call 465 6345 now to make a reservation.

B   Work in pairs and rewrite the commercial with more exciting words and language.
Use the ideas for words and expressions below if appropriate.

breathtaking view	so unspoiled
exceptional food	such a unique restaurant
It's THE place to stay.	the most stunning . . .
one-of-a-kind destination	

C   When your commercial is ready, join another pair and take turns reading aloud.
Does the hotel sound more exciting now?

D   Work in pairs and write a similar TV commercial for a vacation destination you
know well. (It could be your hometown or a place you have visited on vacation
in the past.) Use exciting words and language. Afterwards, take turns presenting
your new TV commercial to the class.

12A GOALS   Now I can . . .

Describe wonderful, unbelievable places _____
Show amazement _____

1. Yes, I can.
2. Mostly, yes.
3. Not yet.

VOCABULARY

A Complete the sentences with the missing prepositions.

about	behind	for	in	of	to	with	with

1. I'm **in favor** _____ banning private cars from the downtown area.

2. My parents **have doubts** _____ me becoming vegan.

3. The protesters **object** _____ building a new road through the park.

4. I **sympathize** _____ people who want to stop using plastic in packaging.

5. The government **makes a strong case** _____ raising taxes this year.

6. If you go and complain to the manager, I'**m right** _____ **you**.

7. What I **believe** _____ is the right to free health care.

8. I tend to **side** _____ people who hate cell phones at meal times.

B Categorize the words in blue in **A** in the table.

For the argument	Against the argument	Support someone else's view
agree with **approve of**	disagree with (be) opposed to (be) critical of	(You're) right about . . .

C Work in groups and take turns giving your point of view on each of these topics. Use expressions from the table.

- eating a plant-based diet instead of meat
- only allowing electric vehicles downtown

- banning single-use plastics
- working a four-day week
- giving vandals a severe punishment

> I'm in favor of everyone eating a plant-based diet.

> Me, too. I'm right behind you on that!

Plant-based meals are a healthy option.

WOMEN in SPACE

Since the first manned flight into space in 1961, only 11% of the 63 astronauts that followed have been female. But with even more space travel planned in the next decades—and to distant places such as Mars—there's a case for sending all-female space crews. Here's why.

The weight advantage

In general, women are smaller and don't weigh as much as men. Sending lighter humans into space is just plain smart because rocketing into space requires fuel, which costs money. Wayne Hale, an ex-NASA engineer, sympathizes with this view: "Having an all-female crew—or at least a crew of smaller individuals—would be advantageous from the total-weight-mission standpoint." Having a lower body weight is only one part of the argument. On average, women consume less food and need less oxygen. For a short space trip, the differences are negligible, but if you're aiming for Mars or even further, transporting less food and other resources is significant.

Physical effects of spaceflight

Over the last 50 years, NASA has been gathering medical data on the impact of spaceflight on its astronauts. When it comes to gender differences, men seem to be less affected by space motion sickness than women. On the other hand, it's also men who suffer more from the negative effects of zero gravity, including loss of hearing and poor eyesight. NASA astronaut Scott Kelly, who has spent

520 days in space and has the eye problems to prove it, wrote that if scientists can't figure out what's causing eye issues, then "we just might have to send an all-women crew to Mars."

Personality traits

The third reason why women might be a better choice is that future space journeys will require the astronauts to live in a cramped spaceship for months or even years. Unlike space travel in the past, which was fast and needed astronauts with physical endurance, NASA scientists now emphasize the need for astronauts with interpersonal sensitivity who can get along with each other. In tests, men tend to excel in shorter-term, goal-oriented situations, while women do better in longer-term, habitation-type circumstances.

So, let's review. In terms of weight, ability to cope physically, and psychological skills, the arguments are in favor of women. Does this mean that men need not apply for such journeys? Not quite. The data on group dynamics supports the belief that mixed-gender teams are the most successful overall, both in terms of completing tasks and socializing over long periods of time. So, based on the research, we cannot conclude that an all-female crew would do any better than an all-male crew on a long spaceflight. 🎧92

A Read the article about women in space. Which two statements reflect the writer's point about long space journeys?

a. It's doubtful that any type of crew can cope with long space journeys.

b. There is no reason for having an all-male crew, as opposed to an all-female crew.

c. All-female space crews are more effective than all-male crews.

d. Mixed-gender crews are probably the most effective type of team.

B Evaluate evidence. Read the article again and answer each question with *Yes*, *No*, or *Don't know* (because the information isn't given).

1. Is it cheaper to send lighter astronauts into space? _____

2. Does space travel take longer with heavier astronauts? _____

3. Is it only women who are affected by space motion sickness? _____

4. Have scientists discovered the reason for problems with hearing and eyesight?

_____

5. In modern space travel, is physical endurance the most important factor? _____

6. Has NASA selected a male and female team for the journey to Mars? _____

C Identify opinion. Study the sentences from the article. Which sentences are factual (write *F*) and which sentences express the writer's opinion (write *O*). How do you know?

1. Since the first manned flight into space in 1961, only 11% of the 63 astronauts that followed have been female. _____

_____

2. There's a case for sending all-female space crews. _____

_____

3. On average, women consume less food and need less oxygen. _____

_____

4. We just might have to send an all-women crew to Mars.

_____

5. Future space journeys will require the astronauts to live in a cramped spaceship for months or even years.

_____

D Work in groups. Brainstorm three arguments for and three arguments against sending humans into space. Think about issues such as cost, safety, knowledge, and technology. Then discuss the different arguments and reach a final conclusion on your group's point of view, for or against. Then explain your decision to the class.

LISTENING

A Listen to four conversations. Match each conversation (1–4) to the people (a–d). 🎧93

_____ a. A professor and students

_____ b. A husband and wife

_____ c. Two work colleagues

_____ d. A mother and daughter

B **Listen for specific information.** Listen again and answer the questions. 🎧93

Conversation 1

1. Why does the woman have doubts? _____

2. What had they already agreed to do? _____

Conversation 2

3. What is it that they both agree on? _____

4. Why wasn't the woman's manager happy? _____

Conversation 3

5. Why is Rebecca convinced by the author of the text? _____

6. Why does Frank think that the author's opinion is one-sided? _____

Conversation 4

7. How opposed is the mother to her daughter's decision? _____

8. How is the daughter stepping out of her comfort zone? _____

C Work in pairs and discuss. How similar or different are your opinions from the following people? When you disagree, what happens?

• members of your family

• close friends

• colleagues or classmates

D **PRONUNCIATION: Linking sounds** Listen to these groups of words. When a word begins with a vowel, it is often linked with the consonant at the end of the previous word. Sometimes, when a word ends with a vowel, an extra sound is added to link it to the next word. In groups of words the *r*, *w*, and *y* sounds in English are often heard between them. 🎧94

in favor /r/ of

Are you /w/ angry?

any /y/ other countries

E Decide which sound is between these words. Then listen and check. 🎧95

1. any /_/ animals

2. go /_/ off

3. your /_/ opinion

4. the /_/ Amazon

5. fewer /_/ airports

6. you /_/ are

GRAMMAR

A Read the Unit 12, Lesson B Grammar Reference in the appendix. Complete the exercises. Then do the exercises below.

CLEFT SENTENCES	
What I like is . . . What I hate is . . .	eating out in restaurants. other people on their phones.
It's the one thing that . . . It's her opinion that . . .	I find so irritating. I don't agree with.
The thing (that) I don't agree with is . . . The reason (why) I disagree is . . .	smoking in public places. because you have no evidence!

B Write B's responses to A using the words in parentheses as a cleft sentence. Then listen and check your answers. 🎧96

1. **A:** Do you disagree with me?

   B: No, *it's him that I disagree with* _____! (it / him / disagree with)

2. **A:** Did they buy enough food?

   B: No, _____. (what happened / bought / too much)

3. **A:** Did you agree with her view on recycling plastic?

   B: Yes, I did. _____. (it / one thing / we both agree on)

4. **A:** Are you angry because of the students' opinion?

   B: No, _____!
   (the reason / angry / they didn't have any opinions)

5. **A:** Are you a vegetarian?

   B: No, _____. (the person / is / Ania)

6. **A:** Is Machu Picchu in Peru on your bucket list?

   B: No, _____.
   (the one place / my bucket list / Angkor Wat in Cambodia)

C Complete these cleft sentences with your own ideas. Then tell a partner.

1. What I really like about the weekend is . . .

2. . . . . is the one thing I hate doing!

3. One place that I often visit is . . .

4. . . . is a person who I always agree with.

5. What more people need to do is . . .

A tower of the Angkor Wat temple in Cambodia

ACTIVE ENGLISH Try it out!

A A *hot topic* is a controversial topic in the news at the moment. What are some hot topics in your country?

B Look at the list of hot topics below. For each topic, think about your opinion and give it a score from 1 to 5:

1 = I strongly disagree with this view.

2 = I partly disagree with this view.

3 = I neither agree nor disagree.

4 = I partly agree with this view.

5 = I strongly agree with this view.

Contrails left by air traffic in Germany

HOT TOPICS

	You	Person 2	Person 3
1. Space travel is very expensive, and the money should be spent on something more useful on Earth.			
2. Cell phones should be banned in restaurants and at meal times because they make people anti-social.			
3. People should stop flying to other countries because airplanes cause climate change.			
4. Teachers shouldn't assign homework because it's unnecessary and stressful for students.			
5. Health care should be free for everyone and people shouldn't have to pay for it.			

C Work in groups of three and spend about two minutes discussing each hot topic. Do NOT share the numbers you wrote in **B**. Make sure everyone has a chance to speak. As you listen, try to guess what the two other people's opinion is and which number they wrote down for that topic. At the end, when you have discussed all five hot topics, compare the numbers you wrote down and see how correct your guesses were.

D **WRITING** Read the Unit 12 Writing Model in the appendix and answer the questions.

1. What is the topic of the student's speech?

2. What three arguments does she make for her case?

3. Do you support her view? Why or why not?

E Write a similar speech about one of the hot topics in **B** or about a topic of your own choice. Afterward, read your speech to the class and try to convince everyone.

12B GOALS   Now I can . . .

Express my opinion _____
Give a speech _____

1. Yes, I can.
2. Mostly, yes.
3. Not yet.

GLOBAL VOICES

A Watch National Geographic Explorers talk about the most beautiful things they have ever seen. Match the explorer to his or her answer.

1. Bradley Russell, an archaeologist _____
2. Catherine Workman, a conservation biologist _____
3. Tom Cope, a filmmaker _____
4. Fred Hiebert, an archaeologist _____
5. Lee Berger, a paleoanthropologist _____
6. Emily Ainsworth, an anthropologist _____
7. David Gruber, a marine biologist _____
8. Amy Dickman, a zoologist _____
9. Chris Thornton, an archaeologist _____

a. The Congo
b. A skull that is millions of years old
c. A tiny circus with five people
d. The Altai Mountains, Western Mongolia
e. Sunsets in Arabia
f. A life-size statue of Buddha
g. Lake Atitlan, Guatemala
h. Animals in the deep ocean that lit up
i. A pack of African wild dogs

B Some of the explorers show their amazement with these phrases. Watch the video again and match these words to five of the explorers (1–9) from **A**.

a. "I've never been any place as beautiful as that in my life." _____
b. "There's nothing like being the first human being to . . . " _____
c. "It was magical. It was wonderful." _____
d. "It was a really wondrous sort of experience." _____
e. "It's just magic and we get that every single night." _____

C What is the most beautiful thing you have ever seen? Take notes on the following points and then write your answer. Then, in groups, tell the others about your answer.

- where you saw it
- when it happened
- who was with you
- any words to describe your amazement

Jellyfish are one creature with bioluminescence: the ability to produce light, even in dark places.

Jack the chimp interviewing
the writer Jennifer Ackerman

A Have you ever been interviewed by someone or have you been an interviewer? Describe the
experience to the class.

  • What questions were asked?

  • Was the interviewer effective? Why or why not?

B Read three pieces of advice on interviewing and match the person (1–3) to the advice in the text (A–C).

  1. An employer _____   **2.** A journalist _____   **3.** A market researcher _____

THE ART OF INTERVIEWING

Interviewing is a key life skill that we use in many jobs and occupations. It's an ability that takes
time to develop and learn. We asked three experienced interviewers for their advice.

A. "All my interviews take place over the phone. A lot of consumers hang up right away when I call, but you have to take it with a grain of salt—it isn't personal. Part of interviewing involves being an effective listener and gauging people's moods. I usually start off with a friendly introduction like, "I was wondering if you could spare a few minutes to answer some questions . . ." and that indirect approach can work well. Even though I'm asking the same questions about the same consumable goods all day, it's important to sound friendly, whether it's nine o'clock in the morning or four o'clock in the afternoon."

B. "What I like to do before any interview is to spend time finding out about the people involved. If it's a politician, that's easy to do because you can read what they have said in other news reports. If it's for something like a court case, then you also need to understand the legal issue before talking to the lawyers or the accused. Preparation is key, and I like to rehearse how I'm going to ask the questions—especially if I think the person might try to avoid answering them!"

C. "People often think of interviews as a battle between two sides, so it's my job to immediately put them at ease. Shake hands, look the other person in the eye, and establish rapport. Yes, I have planned questions, but the interview needs to feel like a normal conversation; that way, you find out more about a person, such as what they believe in or what they are critical of—it's the best way to distinguish the exceptional candidate from the ones you have doubts about."

C Look at the list of interviewing skills. Which text mentions each skill (A, B, or C)?

1. Research the person you are going to interview. _____

2. Use positive body language to greet the other person. _____

3. Use a polite and friendly tone all the time. _____

4. Make the interviewee feel relaxed. _____

5. Practice asking the question before you meet the person. _____

6. Make the interview more like a natural chat. _____

7. Develop the ability to listen carefully. _____

D Can you think of any more interviewing skills to add to the list in **C**? Tell the class.

E **You Choose** In pairs, choose one of the three options and prepare ten questions.

Option 1: You are a travel journalist who wants to write an article about local vacation destinations. Prepare interview questions for some local people about their region and why it's a good vacation destination.

Option 2: You work for a supermarket and you need to employ students for part-time positions over the summer months. Prepare interview questions for the job candidates.

Option 3: You work for a market research company that is finding out how people shop online and what they think makes a good shopping website. Prepare interview questions.

F Switch partners and take turns asking and answering your questions. Then give the interviewer feedback on his or her performance as an interviewer, using the list of skills in **C**.

> " You really made me feel relaxed.

> " Your body language showed you were listening.

LANGUAGE SUMMARIES

UNIT 1: COMMUNITY

LESSON A	LESSON B
Vocabulary	**Vocabulary**
circle of	generation
keep in touch	tendency
community	connectivity
so-called	fractions
walks of life	overwhelming majority
in common	just over . . .
acquaintances	about . . .
hang out with	approximately . . .
close-knit	nearly . . .
meaningful	millennial
camaraderie	baby boomer

Speaking Strategy
Omitting words
In everyday conversations with friends and colleagues, we often omit words and shorten sentences:
~~Did you~~ have a good weekend?
~~Did you~~ do anything fun?
~~Do you~~ promise not to tell anyone?

UNIT 2: THE WORKING WEEK

LESSON A	LESSON B
Vocabulary	**Vocabulary**
take it for granted	reliable
performance	motivation
morale	confident
burn out	enthusiasm
balance	maturity
pressure	patience
anxiety	determined
flexible	honesty
flextime	independence
four-day week	experienced
part-time job	willing
three-day weekend	
work-life balance	

Speaking Strategy
Ways of agreeing
When we express opinions, we can agree or disagree strongly or partially.
Strongly: I **totally** agree. I **strongly** disagree. You're **absolutely** right. I'm **not at all** convinced.
Partially: I **tend to** agree. I agree **to some extent**. **On the whole**, I agree with you. **I get your point, but** I don't agree on everything . . .

UNIT 3: CREATIVITY

LESSON A	LESSON B
Vocabulary	Vocabulary
solved a problem	intelligence
get ideas	imagination
doing work	originality
make up your mind	vision
reach a difficult decision	inspiration
find inspiration	creativity
clear your head	conflict
think outside the box	experimenting
getting some fresh air	genius
	perspiration

Speaking Strategy
Positive responses
When working with other people, respond to their ideas in a positive way by adding: *That's a good idea* **and** *we could* **also** . . . / *I like it!* **And** *how about we* **also** . . . This will generate more ideas than being negative.

UNIT 4: THE SECOND SELF

LESSON A	LESSON B
Vocabulary	Vocabulary
personal profile	fake
digital footprint	deceive
data trail	truth
social media	fictional
search engines	steal
identity theft	victim
privacy settings	illegal
secure password	crime
email account	
online banking	

Speaking Strategy
Using fillers
Sometimes in a conversation, you want time to think. Use fillers such as *Let me see / think, One moment, I mean . . .* to show you are thinking.

UNIT 5: BRAINPOWER

LESSON A	LESSON B
Vocabulary	Vocabulary
repeat	look up
remind (someone of)	picked up
recall	drop out
refresh (your memory)	keep up
retain	sign up
retrieve	hand in
reminisce	read over
reinforce	go through
recognize	fall behind
recollect	note down
memento	

Speaking Strategy
Hedging language
When people ask for our opinion or preference, we often avoid giving a direct answer by using "hedging" language, which makes our answer less direct. Hedging language includes words and phrases like *Maybe / Perhaps you should ...*, *I don't mind either ...*, *If I had to choose, I'd say ...*

UNIT 6: STORYTELLING

LESSON A	LESSON B
Vocabulary	Vocabulary
set	copy
scenery	stare
special effects	scream
episode	hurry
plot	nibble
based on	sigh
cast	chat
remake	scribbled
script	strolled
original version	gorge
binge-watch	cried
spoilers	glanced
	gasp
	whisper

Speaking Strategy
Repetition in the form of a question
In everyday conversations, we sometimes repeat the words at the end of the other person's sentence in the form of a question, as a way of showing surprise and asking for more information:

It's all very different from **the books**.	I loved **the last episode**.
The books? I didn't know it was adapted.	**The last episode**? I didn't know it was finished.

UNIT 7: DESIGN THINKING

LESSON A	LESSON B
Vocabulary	Vocabulary
non-recyclable	inhabitants
sustainable	neighborhoods
durable	suburbs
unsuitable	vibrant
disposable	run-down
breakable	overcrowded
portable	air quality
reusable	corridors
bendable	garbage dumps
compostable	public spaces
alternatives	awards
conduct (heat)	urban
plant-based	urban redesign
single-use	urban space

Speaking Strategy
Being precise
Use **exactly** when you want someone to be more precise:
Where **exactly** is it from?
What do you mean by that, **exactly**?
That doesn't sound **exactly** right.

UNIT 8: SCIENCE FACT AND FICTION

LESSON A	LESSON B
Vocabulary	Vocabulary
theory	leads to
experimented	results in
forecast	makes
outcome	stems from
methods	brings
research	gives rise to
evidence	due to
phenomenon	because of
skeptics	
skeptical	

Speaking Strategy
Pointing something out
When you present visual information from a slide, it's useful to point at specific parts of the slide and use language to show the audience where to look. For example: Look at this line **here**. / **This** part shows . . . / And **over there** you can see . . . / **These** numbers represent . . .

UNIT 9: BODY MATTERS

LESSON A		LESSON B
Vocabulary		Vocabulary
shivering		click buzz
sugary		groan clap
swallowing		grunt splash
staring		purr whizz
deafening		whistle
fragrant		
grabbing		
blushing		
brag		
bluff		

Speaking Strategy
Use of linking words and expressions
When you compare two things (such as two photos), use linking words and expressions to make the comparison clear: *In contrast*, *In comparison*, *On the other hand*, *However*, ...

UNIT 10: KEEP IT LEGAL

LESSON A		LESSON B	
Vocabulary		Vocabulary	
crime		court	inside job
hacking		prison	fine
robbery		judge	lenient
forgery		jury	punishment
mugging		law	severe
shoplifting		prosecute	
smuggling		defendant	
vandalism		lawyer	
accuse		sue	
charge		case	
guilty			
thief			
victim			

Speaking Strategy
Speculating
When you speculate, use modal verbs such as *must / can / could / may / might* to show you are either very certain or less certain:
I think it **must** be a neighbor. (= very certain)
I'm not sure. It **might** be a burglar. (= less certain)

UNIT 11: HUNGRY CONSUMERS

LESSON A	LESSON B
Vocabulary	Vocabulary
get a bargain	selling like hot cakes
consumable goods	take that with a grain of salt
vendors make deals	you can't have your cake and eat it, too
brands	butter up
manufacture	smart cookie
mass-produce	couch potato
shipped	bread and butter
retailers	there's no use crying over spilled milk
customer	piece of cake
consumer	hot potato
haggle	food for thought
hagglers	etiquette
persistent	

Speaking Strategy
Hedging
When discussing prices and trying to get a bargain, we often **hedge** in English. We avoid answering a question, and use vague language:
It's **around** fifty dollars.   That **seems a bit** high.   I can **probably** pay . . . .   **What if I** pay you . . .

UNIT 12: POINTS OF VIEW

LESSON A	LESSON B
Vocabulary	Vocabulary
stunning	(be) in favor of
picturesque	have doubts about
breathtaking	object to
exhilarating	sympathize with
unique	make a strong case for
unbelievable	(be) right behind (you)
exceptional	believe in
one-of-a-kind	side with
unspoiled	approve of
luxurious	(be) opposed to
	(be) critical of

Speaking Strategy
Showing amazement
To show even more amazement, stress certain words in the phrases.
You'll **NEVER** guess what I did. / No **WAY**! / I am **SO** jealous! / You'll have **SUCH** a good time!

1 COMMUNITY

LESSON A

DEFINING RELATIVE CLAUSES

We use defining relative clauses to give essential information to identify a person, object, place, or time. You can also use *that* for people or things instead of *who* or *which*:
*This is the book **that** I told you about.*

*Let me introduce you to my sister **that** lives in Japan.*

	Main clause		**Relative clause**
For things:	This is the book	**that / which**	I told you about.
For people:	Let me introduce you to my sister	**that / who**	lives in Japan.
For possession: (people or things)	I have a friend	**whose**	father is an artist.
For places:	This is the language school	**where**	I studied English.
For time:	There was a time	**when**	we didn't have the internet!

Omitting the Relative Pronoun in Object Relative Clauses

You can omit the relative pronoun (***which***, ***who***, and ***that***) when it is the object of the verb in the relative clause:

This is the book ~~which / that~~ I told you about. / I'm the person ~~who / that~~ you spoke to on the phone.

You cannot omit the relative pronoun when it is the subject of the relative clause:

*It's a useful app **that** / **which** tells you how many steps you walk per day.*
*This is my brother **that** / **who** lives in Peru.*

NON-DEFINING RELATIVE CLAUSES

We use non-defining relative clauses to give extra, non-essential information. Notice the difference:
Defining: *My sister **who lives in Japan** is staying with us.* (I have more than one sister.)
Non-defining: *My sister, **who lives in Japan**, is staying with us.* (It's clear I have only one sister.)

*My best friend, **whose house is over there**, owns six cars!* (It's clear I have only one best friend.)
*This phone is brand new, but it doesn't work properly, **which is really annoying!*** (It's clear the phone doesn't work.)

Always separate a non-defining clause from the main clause with commas. In non-defining clauses, you cannot replace *which* or *who* with *that* and you can never omit the relative pronoun.

Spoken or written?

Overall, defining relative clauses are more common in everyday spoken English and non-defining relative clauses are more common in written English. However, note that we often use non-defining relative clauses to give an opinion or make a comment when speaking: "This phone doesn't work properly, which is really annoying!"

A Join the sentences using a defining relative clause. Use *which* or *who* instead of *that*.

1. Mrs. Brown is the teacher. She taught me to speak English.

   _____

2. This is the office building. I have a job interview.

   _____

3. I have a friend. His twin brother is a musician.

   _____

4. These are the keys. They lock that suitcase.

   _____

5. There was a period of history. The clothes looked so cool!

   _____

6. She's the person. You need to talk to her.

   _____

B Study the answers in **A** and answer the questions.

1. In which sentences can you replace one word with the word *that*?

   _____

   _____

   _____

2. In which sentence can you leave out the relative pronoun?

   _____

C Combine these pieces of information into one sentence using a non-defining relative clause.

1. My aunt and uncle / live in Australia / are coming to visit the family next week.

   _____

2. My local town / was built in the eleventh century / is celebrating its one thousandth anniversary soon.

   _____

3. Sally and Chen / only got engaged last month / are getting married next month!

   _____

4. The Eiffel Tower / is the symbol of France / was built in 1889.

   _____

5. I became a US Citizen in 1999 / is so long ago!

   _____

LESSON B

SUBJECT-VERB AGREEMENT

Normally, sentences with a singular subject have a singular verb, and a plural subject has a plural verb: **My best friend lives** in Paraguay. | **My other friends live** in Mexico.

However, there are some exceptions:

Subject + singular verb

We normally use singular verbs with these types of plural nouns in these cases:

Everyone / anyone / someone / nobody: *Everyone agrees with me.*
Every / Each: *Each student has their own book.*
Expressions with one: *One of my friends isn't coming. | More than one of us has failed the exam.*
None: *None of our community uses a cell phone.*
Quantities and amount: *Thirty dollars is expensive for a bus ride! | Three quarters (of my pizza) has no cheese on it.*
Calculations: *Nine minus three is six.*
Plural countries and organizations: *The United States has 50 states.*

Subject + plural verb
We use plural verbs with *a lot of / none of / some of / both . . . and . . .* + plural noun:
None of *my friends* **live** *in the same town as me.*
Some of *my classmates* **are** *from Brazil.*
Both *Mike* **and** *Laura* **like** *that café.* (But Mike, not Laura, **wants** to go there tonight.)

Subject + singular verb or plural verbs
We normally use singular verbs with these nouns, but sometimes it is also possible to use plural verbs to emphasize certain meanings:

Groups of people
My family lives *in Mexico City.* (emphasizing the collective group)
My family live *all over the world.* (emphasizing that the group are doing different things)
The team isn't *playing well.* (Everyone is playing badly.)
The team aren't *all here yet.* (Two members of the team haven't arrived.)

Structures with *of*
One half of the land is *for farming.* (fraction + singular noun)
Two thirds of the students go *to the university.* (fraction + plural noun)
The majority of *my friends* **spend** *time on social media.* (*majority of* + plural noun)
The majority of *our time* **is** *wasted on social media.* (*majority of* + singular noun)

A   Circle the correct verb.

1. I think nine hundred dollars (are / is) a lot of money to pay for a bicycle.

2. One of my work colleagues (are / is) out sick today.

3. Some of the students (is / are) from Vietnam.

4. The majority of people (don't / doesn't) speak English here.

5. Everyone (think / thinks) I'm correct.

6. None of my family (like / likes) eating fish.

7. More than 3.5 million people (visit / visits) the Statue of Liberty every year.

8. The United Nations (have / has) 193 members.

B   Complete the sentences with the correct form of the verb. If both a singular and plural form are possible, write both.

1. My family ___is / are___ (be) coming for the holidays.

2. Nobody _____ (like) missing out on a party.

3. The majority of the information _____ (be) false.

4. In my circle of friends, everyone _____ (enjoy) the same kinds of films.

5. My favorite baseball team _____ (have) been having problems this season.

6. Every member of my family _____ (love) pizza!

2 THE WORKING WEEK

LESSON A

SIMPLE PRESENT AND PRESENT CONTINUOUS	
Simple present	**Present continuous**
Facts / things that are generally true: *My company employs 250 people.*	Happening now: *My company is recruiting more staff.*
Routines: *I start work at nine.*	Regularly repeated events over a period of time: *This week, I'm starting early at eight.*
Regular change: *The cost of my bus tickets goes up every year.*	Changing situation: *Public transportation is getting more expensive.*
With *always* meaning "every time": *He always arrives on time.*	With *always* meaning "all the time": *He's always complaining about his work-life balance.*
For scheduled events: *Our team meets on Mondays at noon.*	For future plans and arrangements. *I'm meeting a client at noon.*
Dynamic verbs	**Stative verbs**
Dynamic verbs talk about actions and events. We often use them to talk about facts / routines with the simple present and actions in progress with the present continuous: **I work** long hours. (always) *Today,* **I'm working** late. (something temporary)	Stative verbs such as *be, exist, have, know, like, love, think,* and *understand,* talk about states. Some stative verbs are only used with the simple present and never with the present continuous: I **understand** what you mean. / ~~I'm understanding what you mean.~~ We use some stative verbs with both tenses with a change in meaning: **I love** my job. (A general comment about my job.) **I'm loving** my new job. (So far, my new job is great.)
Frequency and time expressions	
We often use the simple present with frequency expressions, (see statives above) such as *frequently, regularly, once a week, every Monday.*	We often use the present continuous with time expressions, (see statives above) such as *now, at the moment, currently, today, this week, nowadays.*

A Make sentences with the words. Use the simple present or the present continuous.

1. We / currently / develop / a new product.

   _____

2. Once a day, / my department / meet / for ten minutes.

   _____

3. The management / always / change / how we work.

   _____

4. Sorry, I / not / understand / the question.

   _____

5. At the moment, / I / feel / great about my new promotion.

   _____

6. I haven't made a final decision yet. I / still / think / about the problem.

   _____

7. He / speak / to someone. Can he call you back?

   _____

8. What's the matter with Gill? She / seem / distracted.

   _____

B Decide which sentences are incorrect and write the correction. Check (✓) the correct sentences.

1. Can you help me? ~~I'm not knowing~~ how to work this photocopier.
   Can you help me? I don't know how to work this photocopier.
   _____

2. They are always arguing with me over the prices. It's so annoying!
   _____

3. I know exactly what you are meaning.
   _____

4. What do you think about the situation?
   _____

5. Unemployment is going up every year.
   _____

6. This desk is belonging to the manager. Don't sit here!
   _____

7. We deliver their packages to a different address for one week only.
   _____

8. He's being very enthusiastic today. I wonder why.
   _____

LESSON B

GET / HAVE / NEED + SOMEONE / SOMETHING
GET SOMEONE TO DO SOMETHING / *HAVE* SOMEONE DO SOMETHING

Use *get someone to do something* / *have someone do something* to explain that you have asked someone to do something for you:

get	someone	infinitive
I get / got	my assistant	to call the customer.

have	someone	bare infinitive
I have / had	my assistant	call the customer.

You can use *get / have something done* to say that you have asked someone to do something for you, but without saying who:

get / have	object	past participle
I got	my car	fixed.

You can also use *get / have something done* to talk about something unexpected (or unwelcome) that happened to you:

get / have	object	past participle
I had	my car	stolen.

Use *need* + *-ing* to say something needs doing (by someone):

something	needs	-ing
My office	needs	cleaning.

A Put the words in the correct order.

1. my / solve / son / I got / to / the computer problem

   _____

2. the shower / had / a plumber / I / fix

   _____

3. got / she / suit / repaired / her

   _____

4. data / he / had / all his / stolen

   _____

5. cleaning / the windows / need / in my office

   _____

B Complete the conversation using the pairs of verbs in the box. Change the form of the verb where necessary.

have + bring   get + come   have + look at   need + fix   have + steal

A: Hello, is this IT? This is Nick in Sales. I (1) _____ my laptop _____.

B: Really? You (2) _____ us _____ it only a month ago.

A: I know, but this time I think I've (3) _____ my identity _____. When I try to log on, it won't open.

B: Are you sure you haven't forgotten your password?

A: Of course I'm sure!

B: OK. I'm busy at the moment, but I'll (4) _____ my assistant to _____ to your office and take a look.

A: Good. And can you (5) _____ her _____ me a replacement laptop?

 CREATIVITY

LESSON A

SUGGESTING, EXPRESSING OPINION, AND GIVING ADVICE
You can use modals and phrasal modals to make suggestions and express opinions.

Suggesting: *should, could, let's, shall*
Use *should, could, let's,* and *shall* + bare infinitive to make suggestions:
We **should** *generate some ideas.*
I **could** *try it a different way.*
Let's *discuss this idea in more detail.*
Shall I / we *start discussing these ideas?*
With the modal verbs *should* and *could*, we often add *maybe* or *perhaps*:
Maybe / Perhaps we **should** *look at this idea more closely.*

Suggesting: *How about . . . ? What about . . . ? Why don't we . . . ? Why not . . . ?*
You can also use questions to make suggestions. Use *How / What about + -ing . . . ?* or *Why don't we / Why not* + bare infinitive?
How / What about *asking everyone's ideas on this?*
Why don't we *ask everyone for their ideas?*
Why not *ask everyone for their ideas?*

Expressing opinions: *should, ought to, had better*

You can also use *should*, *ought to*, and *had better* to express opinions and give advice:

should and *ought to*

Use *should* and *ought to* to give advice in general and specific situations:

*You **should** always ask the staff for their opinions.* (general)

*We **should / ought to** work on this idea in more detail.* (specific)

Note that *ought to* is less commonly used than *should*, especially in negative and question forms.

had / 'd better

Use *had / 'd better* to give strong opinions or advice in specific situations:

*We**'d better** come up with some ideas or we won't find a solution.*

Note that with *had better*, we often say or imply the consequence. (e.g., *or we won't find a solution.*)

In the negative sentence, *not* comes after *better*, not after *had*:

*We**'d better not** forget to have a meeting.*

hadn't you better . . . ? / had you better . . . ?

Use the negative form of the question to give advice. The negative question form is more common than the affirmative question:

***Hadn't we better** ask the staff what they think?*

***Had we better** ask the staff what they think?*

Note that we form the question by inverting *have* with the subject.

A   Put the words into the correct order.

1. ideas / we / get / more / should

   _____

2. ought / for / ideas / to / ask / you

   _____

3. shall / this / spend / some / we / more / time / on / ?

   _____

4. could / discuss / maybe / we / tomorrow / this / again / ?

   _____

5. drawing / about / your / what / idea / ?

   _____

6. why / ask / don't / everyone / we / ?

   _____

7. better / arrive / they'd / time / on

   _____

8. hadn't / finish / we / now / better?

   _____

B   Write the missing words in the conversation. More than one answer is possible in some places.

A: We (1) _____ to make a start. So, we're here to discuss plans for the school's anniversary celebrations. (2) _____ we begin by asking everyone for their ideas?

B: Yes, I think we (3) _____ have a party in the evening.

C: Good idea. (4) _____ have some live music.

A: Sounds good. And what (5) _____ asking everyone to bring food?

B: Is that a good idea? (6) _____ we better get a caterer to make the food? After all, there will be hundreds of people.

A: True. (7) _____ we should contact some companies for their prices.

C: I agree. Also, we'd (8) _____ find out the cost of live music.

LESSON B

ABILITY IN THE PAST
General ability in the past
Use *could* / *couldn't* + bare infinitive or *was* / *were able to* + bare infinitive to talk about a general ability in the past:
Drivers **could** *see in bad weather.*
Drivers **were able to** *see in bad weather.*

Success and failure in a specific task in the past
Use *was* / *were able to* to talk about success in a particular situation, task, or achievement in the past:
People **were able to** *buy her invention in 1904.*
Mary **wasn't able to** *sell her idea in 1903.*

Use *couldn't* to describe failure in a specific task in the past:
Melitta Bentz **couldn't** *find coffee that didn't taste bitter.*

Don't use *could* to talk about success in a particular task or situation in the past. Use *was* / *were able to*:
~~They could find a solution in their meeting last week.~~
They **were able to** *find a solution in their meeting last week.*

Use *managed to* + bare infinitive or *succeed in* + *-ing* to talk about a task that you found difficult but were able to complete.
Bentz **managed to** *find a solution by making holes.*
She **succeeded in** *creating the first-ever coffee filter.*

Possibility and opportunity in the past
Use *could* or *was* / *were able to* to describe a possibility or opportunity in the past:
In my last job, we **could** / **were able to** *try out any of our ideas—no matter how crazy they were.*

A Circle the correct verb form. Both answers are possible in two sentences.

1. It was raining so much I (couldn't / didn't manage to) see out of the car.

2. The weather was terrible, but the climber (succeeded in / managed to) reach the top of the mountain.

3. Even though there were no buses last night, we (could / were able to) get home in time.

4. Despite strong competition, she (was able to / succeeded in) winning the race.

5. My parents (couldn't / weren't able to) find a job in their hometown, so they moved south.

6. When I was young, people (didn't manage to / weren't able to) travel as easily as they do nowadays.

7. Usain Bolt (managed to run / succeeded in running) the 100 meters in record time.

8. When we climbed to the top of the tower, we (could see / succeeded in seeing) for miles.

THE SECOND SELF

LESSON A

WISH / IF ONLY (PRESENT AND PAST)

Use *wish* and *if only* to talk about a regret or an imaginary situation that is the opposite of the real situation. There is very little difference in meaning, though we sometimes use *if only* to add emphasis to our regret:

I **wish** I'd gone to the party.
If only I'd gone to the party.

Use the simple past or past form of the modal (e.g., *will* ➔ *would*, *can* ➔ *could*) with *wish* or *if only* to talk about situations that are not true now.

Present situation	*Wish* statement + past
I'm bored. My pen won't work. My friend isn't coming.	I **wish** I **wasn't / weren't** bored. (but I am) **If only** my pen **would** work. (but it won't) I **wish** my friend **was / were*** coming. * You can use *was* or *were* after *wish / If only* + past form. *Were* is older and more formal.

To talk about situations in the past, use *wish* or *if only* with the past perfect or *could have*.

Past situation	*Wish* statement + past perfect
I shared an old photo. I forgot to bring my phone. I couldn't afford a new tablet.	I **wish** I **hadn't shared** an old photo. (but I did) **If only** I **hadn't forgotten** my phone. (but I did) I **wish** I **could have afforded** a new tablet. (but I couldn't)

Was or *were*?

We often replace the verb *was* with *were* in *wish* sentences:
I **wish** I *was* richer. ➔ I **wish** I **were** richer.

A Underline the correct form in the sentences. Is the sentence about a present situation or a past situation?

1. I wish I (can / could) swim. __*present situation*__

2. I wish I (could go / could have gone) with them last night. __*past situation*__

3. If only I (didn't send / hadn't sent) that email to my boss! _____

4. If only they (live / lived) nearer to our house. _____

5. I'm lost. I wish I (knew / had known) the way. _____

6. It was expensive. I wish I (didn't buy / hadn't bought) it. _____

7. She wishes she (studied / had studied) harder when she was a child. _____

8. If only the app (didn't cost / doesn't cost) so much money. _____

B Read three situations from the world of computers and media. Imagine you are the person who missed the business opportunity and complete the *wish / If only* sentences.

1. In the 1970s, Steve Wozniak had a new idea called a "personal computer." He offered his idea to Hewlett-Packard, but the company didn't think people wanted home computers. Wozniak and his friend Steve Jobs built their first home computer and started their own company called Apple.

   I wish _____

2. In 1999, a company called Excite had the opportunity to buy a new company called Google for one million dollars. Excite thought the price was too high. In 2001, Excite went bankrupt.

   If only _____

3. The company Blockbuster used to rent DVDs. In 2000, the company had the opportunity to take over a small company called Netflix. Blockbuster went bankrupt in 2010. Nowadays, the video streaming company Netflix is worth around $150 billion.

I wish _____

LESSON B

CONDITIONAL FORMS

Conditional forms contain an *if* clause and a result clause. Either clause can come first, but when the *if* clause comes first, put a comma before the result clause.

FUTURE REAL CONDITIONALS

Future real conditionals are used to talk about possibilities or to make predictions. The *if* clause states a possible situation and uses the simple present. The result clause uses a future form (e.g., *will*).

If clause	Result clause
If you change the settings,	you will get automatic notifications.
If we don't have a company profile page,	we won't get any customers.

Result clause	If clause
The computer will update automatically	if you click here.

PRESENT UNREAL CONDITIONALS

Present unreal conditionals are used to talk about imagined or unreal events. The *if* clause states an imagined condition *that* is not true at the moment of speaking and uses the simple past. The result clause uses *would* / *might* / *could* + bare infinitive.

If clause	Result clause
If I knew my password,	I would be able to read my emails.
If you found money in the street,	would you keep it?

Result clause	If clause
We would go out tonight	if we had any money!

PAST UNREAL CONDITIONALS

Past unreal conditionals are used to talk about imaginary situations that did not happen in the past. The *if* clause describes a situation that is often the opposite of what happened and uses the past perfect (*had* + past participle). The result clause presents a hypothetical past consequence of the situation and uses *would have* + past participle.

If clause	Result clause
If they had known the call was fake,	they wouldn't have given their bank details.
If she hadn't woken up,	she would have missed the train.

Result clause	If clause
The company would have gotten a virus	if they hadn't installed the proper software.

A Match the two halves of the sentences and write the name of the conditional form.

_____ 1. If they leave late, _____
_____ 2. If they left late, _____
_____ 3. If they had left late, _____

a. they would have missed the movie.
b. they will miss the movie.
c. they would miss the movie.

_____ **4.** I wouldn't have failed _____ **a.** if I study hard.

_____ **5.** I won't fail _____ **b.** if I'd studied hard.

_____ **6.** I wouldn't fail _____ **c.** if I studied hard.

B These sentences use the past unreal conditional form. Circle the correct option.

1. If I'd (knew / known), I'd (have / had) answered the question.

2. If my computer (hadn't / wouldn't) crashed, I'd (finish / have finished) all my work.

3. I (hadn't / wouldn't have) checked my account if I (hadn't / wouldn't have) received a notification.

4. If the train (would have been / had been) delayed, I (would have / had) missed the job interview.

5. They (had gotten / would have gotten) sick if they ('d eaten / would have eaten) this.

6. Bill (wouldn't have / hadn't) deleted the file if he (would have / had realized) it was important.

⬡5 BRAINPOWER

LESSON A

PAST HABITS: *USED TO* AND *WOULD*

Use *used to* to talk about past:

habits: We **used to go** out every Friday evening.

situations: My family **used to live** in the city.

states: He **used to be** heavier.

I	used to	have	a motorcycle.
They didn't	use to	have	their own house.
Did you	use to	have	a dog?
Notice the spelling difference in *use* and *used*: I used to . . . ✓ ~~I use to . . .~~ ✗ I didn't use to . . . ✓ ~~I didn't used to . . .~~ ✗			

Use *would* / *wouldn't* to talk about past habits: *We **would go out** every Friday evening.*

Do not use *would* to talk about past situations and states: ~~My family would live in the city.~~

Do not use *used to* or *would* to talk about a single past action or an action over a period of time. Use the simple past instead: *We went out last Friday evening. | My family lived in the city for ten years.*

You can also use the simple past to talk about past habits: *I used to go | would go | went to the movies every weekend.*

A Complete the sentences with the correct verb form.

didn't use to   see   used to   use to   used to visit   was   worked   would spend

1. Fritz _____ live in China.

2. Did you _____ read this book when you were a child?

3. Everyone _____ at the party last night.

4. As students, we _____ all our money by the end of the year.

5. The children _____ eat salad. They hated it.

6. We _____ my aunt and uncle in the afternoons.

7. I _____ for this company for three years.

8. Did you _____ Mike last night?

B Rewrite the statements using *used to* where possible. Then look at the statements again. Which can you rewrite using *would* or *wouldn't*?

1. My parents met here when they were young.

My parents used to meet here when they were young. / My parents would meet here when they were young.

2. Were you a student at this university?

_____

3. I saw a fantastic movie over the weekend.

_____

4. They didn't travel by car.

_____

5. As a child, I spent all day in the fields.

LESSON B

VERBS + *-ING* OR INFINITIVE

Verb + infinitive
Some verbs are always followed by the verb in the infinitive form, including *afford, agree, aim, appear, arrange, attempt, choose, decide, demand, expect, hope, intend, learn, manage, need, offer, plan, prepare, pretend, promise, refuse, seem, want,* and *wish.*
We **promise to help** you.   We ~~promise helping~~ you. X

Verb + *-ing*
Some verbs are always followed by the verb in the *-ing* form, including *avoid, can't help, consider, dislike, enjoy, finish, give up, imagine, involve, keep, mention, mind, don't mind, miss, postpone, practice, report, risk,* and *suggest.*
We **avoid going** to the city on the weekend.   We ~~avoid to go to the city on the weekend~~. X

Verb + object + *-ing*
Some verbs can be followed by an object and a verb in the *-ing* form, including *hate, like, dislike, keep, love, prevent, remember, risk, see, stop,* and *mind.*
I **hate other people telling** me what to do!   This helmet **stops the cyclist from getting** hurt.

Verb + preposition + *-ing*
When a preposition follows the first verb, the next verb is in the *-ing* form.
Let me **apologize for being** late. Children **learn by doing**. Don't **worry about making** dinner for me.

Verbs + *-ing* or infinitive with little or no change in meaning
Some verbs can be followed by the verb in either form with little or no change in meaning: *hate, like, love, prefer, begin, start, try,* and *continue.*
The team **starts to play** at three. = The team **starts playing** at three.

With verbs of liking (e.g., *like, love, prefer, hate*), there can be a slight change in meaning:
I **like eating** Italian food. (to emphasize the action in general)
I **like to eat** Italian food when I'm in Rome. (to emphasize an action in specific circumstances)

Verbs + *-ing* or infinitive with change of meaning

Some verbs can be followed by either the infinitive form or the *-ing* form and the meaning changes.

	+ *-ing*	+ infinitive
remember / forget	To talk about memories: My grandfather **remembers writing** letters. He'll never **forget seeing** a computer for the first time.	To talk about necessary actions: I must **remember to call** my friend back. To say if something happened or not: Sorry, I **forgot to call** you back.
go on	To talk about a continuing action already in progress: The film star **went on making** films for the rest of his life.	To talk about a change of situation or sequence of events: After college, he **went on to run** his own company.
stop	To talk about an action that has ended: They **stopped talking** to each other.	To talk about a reason for stopping: They **stopped to talk** to each other.
mean	To talk about the result of an action: Learning a language **means having** to study for many hours.	To talk about something you intend to do: I **meant to learn** a new language this year.
regret	To say you are sorry for something you did: We **regret not giving** her the job.	To say sorry for something you are about to say (often used in writing and very formal): I **regret to inform** you that we are unable to offer you the job.

A Answer the questions with the verbs in the box. You can use some verbs more than once.

> apologize for   dislike   finish   keep   learn by   love   plan   practice   start   want

1. Which are followed only by a verb in the *-ing* form? *keep, practice, dislike, learn by, apologize for, finish*

2. Which are followed only by the infinitive? _____

3. Which can be followed by an object and then the *-ing* form? _____

4. Which can be followed by the verb in either form with little or no change in meaning?

_____

B Circle the correct verb form. In some sentences, both answers are correct.

1. I attempted (to learn / learning) 10 new words a day.

2. We don't mind (to miss / missing) the party.

3. They keep (to tell / telling) everyone the answers.

4. Ray loves (to show / showing) photographs from his vacations.

5. Let me begin by (to talk / talking) about my company.

6. Can you remind the children (to clean / cleaning) their rooms?

7. We didn't manage (to finish / finishing) the race.

8. The student continued (to interrupt / interrupting) the teacher.

C Complete the sentences with the pairs of verbs in the correct form.

> apologize + be   ask + help   avoid + drive   enjoy + do   hate + watch   risk + make

1. Neither of us knows the answers, so we should _____ the teacher _____ us.

2. Isn't there something better on TV? I _____ _____ soccer.

3. I _____ for _____ late. It won't happen again.

4. Let's _____ through the city center. The traffic is terrible in the evening.

5. It's good to _____ mistakes. You can learn from them.

6. My grandmother _____ quizzes and crosswords.

6 STORYTELLING

LESSON A

ADVERBS

-ly adverbs

You can make some adjectives into adverbs using *-ly*: *bad* ➔ *badly*; *terrible* ➔ *terribly*

Sometimes you also need to change the spelling: *true* ➔ *truly*; *happy* ➔ *happily*

We often use *-ly* adverbs in one of two ways:

- **Adverbs of manner** describe how something happens or is done. They can be used in three positions: *She picked up the book **slowly**. | He **awkwardly** looked away. | **Calmly**, they drove off in the car.*

- **Adverbs of comment** comment on an adjective, another adverb, or the whole clause: *He was **surprisingly tall**. | It moved **surprisingly quickly**. | **Fortunately**, she'd left a forwarding address. | She'd left a forwarding address, **fortunately**.*

Adverbs of place and time

These adverbs (and adverbial phrases) tell us where and when something happens:

- **Adverbs of place** usually come after the verb (and the object if there is one): *He was going **back**. | They used to live **here**. | I would like to go **somewhere** this evening.*

- **Adverbs of time** can come in three positions: ***Later**, the young man took a photo of himself. | We **often** saw him. | We saw him **last week**.*

When a sentence contains an adverb of time and place, the adverb of place usually comes first: *They were **here** (place) **last night** (time).*

Adverbs of focus

These adverbs emphasize a particular piece of information: ***Only the grandmother** knew the secret.* (= emphasizing the fact that no one else knew)

- ***alone, only, just:*** to focus on one thing, to the exclusion of all others: *She **alone** knew the password. | He could **only** play one tune on the guitar. | Most people **just** know the classic film version. | **Just** the twins understand the joke.*

- ***also, as well, too:*** to emphasize an additional thing: ***Also**, she plays the flute. | She **also** plays the flute. | She's seen the film, **as well**. | You'll recognize lots of the cast, **too**. (As well and too always come at the end of the sentence.)*

- ***even:*** to show you think something is unusual or surprising: *She **even** speaks Swahili. | Some Star Trek fans have **even** tried to learn Klingon.*

Word order with auxiliary verbs

Adverbs in the middle of a sentence come after the subject and auxiliary verb and before the main verb: *They **didn't even say** goodbye to us! | We**'ve just seen** a great movie.*

A Put these words in the correct order and add punctuation where necessary. Sometimes there is more than one correct answer.

1. the / extremely / quiet / street / was _____

2. show / I don't like / personally / this _____

3. she / plays / the flute / too _____

4. short / the / surprisingly / actor / was _____

5. try calling / don't / even / help line / the _____

6. fortunately / flashlight / with me / I had a _____

7. he / knew / alone / out of the tunnels / the way _____

8. police / arrived / here / the / five minutes ago _____

B Underline the correct words to complete the sentences. In two sentences, both answers are correct.

1. Sorry, she's (just / too) left the building.

2. He works in this building (even / , as well).

3. They (angrily / suddenly) stormed out of the house.

4. We (don't often go / don't go often) to the movies.

5. (Only / Also) my sister could tell a story like that. No one else could.

6. (Calmly, he / He calmly) pulled out the bag.

C Rewrite the first sentence using the adverb in parentheses.

1. Shelley also studies film at the university.

   (as well) Shelley _____.

2. Just my parents are coming.

   (only) _____ coming.

3. I alone know the answer!

   (only) _____ the answer!

4. The children want a drink, that's all.

   (just) The children _____.

5. The price includes delivery, and it has a three-year guarantee.

   (even) The price includes delivery, and _____.

LESSON B

NARRATIVE TENSES

Simple past

Use the simple past to talk about:

single past actions or a sequence of actions: *They opened the box and looked inside.*

past states: *The old couple lived in that house all their life.*

Past continuous

Use the past continuous (*was / were* + verb + *-ing*):

to describe past actions in progress at a certain time or period in the past: *They **were working** here during the nineties.*

at the beginning of a narrative to set the scene: *The rain **was pouring** down the windows, and the wind **was blowing** against the doors.*

to show one action in progress when another action happened (often in the simple past): *We **were watching** TV when the electricity **went off**.*

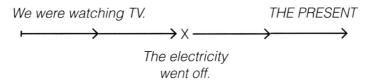

We were watching TV.   THE PRESENT

The electricity
went off.

to show two actions in progress at the same time: *While we **were watching** TV downstairs in the living room, the robbers **were stealing** all our jewelry from upstairs!*

Past perfect

Use the past perfect (*had* + past participle) to show how one action happened earlier in a sequence than another action: *By the time the police **arrived**, the robbers **had gone**.*

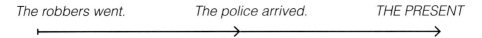

The robbers went.   The police arrived.   THE PRESENT

Past perfect continuous

Use the past perfect continuous (*had* + *been* + verb + *-ing*) to talk about an action in progress before a given point in time: *The old couple **had been living** in the house all their life when they **had to move**.*

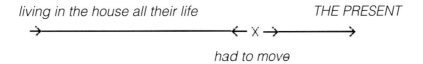

living in the house all their life   THE PRESENT

had to move

A   Underline the correct tense to complete the sentences.

1. The rain (poured / was pouring) when they left the house. It had started the night before.

2. None of the actors (arrived / had arrived), so the director was very worried.

3. She (made / was making) her first film in 1966 and won an Oscar.

4. The police (were looking / had looked) for the robber, but they never found him.

5. While I (was driving / had driven) home, there was an earthquake!

6. Bill and Rosaria (were knowing / had known) each other for five years before they got married.

7. When (did you finish / were you finishing) college?

8. As soon as Huraki arrived home in the morning, he went straight to bed because he (was working / had been working) all through the night.

B   Complete the text with the correct verb forms.

In 1982, the writer Gabriel García Márquez (1) _____ the Nobel Prize for Literature. Internationally, he was probably best known as a novelist for his book *One Hundred Years of Solitude*, which he (2) _____ 15 years earlier. Born in Colombia, Márquez (3) _____ most of his childhood growing up in the city of Barranquilla. Before that, he (4) _____ with his grandparents for eight years in the small town of Aracataca, where—notably—his grandfather had told him many stories. Márquez had studied law, but he (5) _____ as a journalist when he published his first novel in 1955. In the final years of his life, while Márquez (6) _____ with cancer, he completed a book focusing on the first 30 years of his life. He (7) _____ in Mexico City in 2014.

1. a. won   b. was winning   c. had been winning

2. a. was completing   b. had completed   c. had been completing

3. a. spends   b. spent   c. was spending

4. a. is living   b. was living   c. had been living

5. a. worked   b. was working   c. had worked

6. a. was suffering   b. had suffered   c. had been suffering

7. a. died   b. was dying   c. had died

LESSON A

THE PASSIVE 1 (TENSES AND MODALS)

Use the passive form of the verb when you want to focus on the object affected by the action of the verb:

Active: *Humans **use** 100 million straws per day.*

Passive: *100 million straws **are used** per day (by humans).*

The passive form is often used when the person who did the action:

is unknown: *The straws **were thrown away**.*

is not important: *The bridge **is being built** by someone.*

is obvious or already mentioned: *Engineers are building the bridge. It**'s being built** with bamboo by the engineers.*

You only need to include the name of the person who did the action when it is important or especially relevant: *Large amounts of bamboo **are consumed** by pandas.*

	Active	Passive
Simple present	Humans **use** 100 million straws per day.	100 million straws **are used** per day.
Present continuous	Engineers **are constructing** modern bridges with it.	Modern bridges **are being constructed** with it.
Present perfect	People **have used** paper drinking straws since the late 1800s.	Paper drinking straws **have been used** since the late 1800s.
Simple past	Traditionally, people **built** houses with bamboo.	Traditionally, houses **were built** with bamboo.
Past continuous	People **were not replanting** trees.	Trees **were not being replanted**.
Past perfect	Where people **had replanted** forests . . .	Where forests **had been replanted** . . .
Modal verbs	Designers **can make** glass straws in attractive shapes and colors.	Glass straws **can be made** in attractive shapes and colors.

A Rewrite the active sentence in the passive form. Decide if you need to say who did the action (using *by . . .*).

1. People make glass from sand at high temperatures.

   Glass _____ at high temperatures.

2. The average family uses 350 glass bottles and jars each year.

   350 glass bottles and jars _____ each year.

3. Archaeologists found glass beads from 12,000 BC in Egypt.

   Glass beads from 12,000 BC _____ .

4. People have used glass in windows since the 17th century.

   Glass _____ in windows since the 17th century.

5. Designers can change the color of glass by adding minerals.

   The color of glass _____ by adding minerals.

6. Before humans had created glass, they used a natural glass called obsidian.

Before glass _____, humans used a natural glass called obsidian.

7. The heat of a volcano can turn rock and sand into obsidian.

Rock and sand _____ into obsidian _____.

8. People are using glass containers again to replace plastic.

Glass containers _____ to replace plastic.

LESSON B

THE PASSIVE 2 (REPORTING, INFINITIVE, -*ING*)

Passive reporting

Passive reporting structures are used with reporting verbs. These verbs include *say*, *know*, *report*, *believe*, *expect*, *suggest*, and *think*. Form passive reporting structures as follows: *It* + *be* + past participle + *that*:

It is known that *many people still don't recycle plastic.*
It has been said many times before that *the Earth's climate is getting warmer.*
Passive reporting structures are used when the person is unknown, unimportant, or doesn't want to be named.

Passive infinitive

The passive infinitive is used after verbs that are followed by the infinitive. These verbs include *agree*, *aim*, *appear*, *decide*, *hope*, *intend*, *manage*, *need*, *plan*, *prepare*, *seem*, and *want*.
Form the passive infinitive with *to be* + past participle:
My friend ***hopes to be promoted*** *at work.*
No one ***wants to be given*** *a parking ticket.*

Passive -*ing* forms

The passive -*ing* form is used after verbs that are followed by the -*ing* form, such as *consider*, *dislike*, *enjoy*, *finish*, *keep*, *miss*, *practice*, and *risk*. The form is also used after a verb + preposition.
Form the passive -*ing* form with *being* + past participle:
Most people ***dislike being told*** *what to do.*
He ***agreed to being interviewed*** *by a journalist.*

A Write the verbs in the passive form. Remember to use the correct tense.

1. In the past, it _____ (think) that the earth was flat.

2. Nowadays, it _____ (know) that single-use plastic is bad for the environment.

3. It _____ (predict) by some scientists that the world temperature will rise by over two degrees by the year 2100.

4. The problem of parking _____ (report) in our local newspaper many times in recent months.

5. A new plan for bike paths _____ (suggest) at the next meeting.

B Underline the correct passive form.

1. I hope (to be given / being given) a pay raise next month.

2. Charles really dislikes (to be asked / being asked) to tidy his room.

3. These clothes need (to be washed / being washed).

4. Solar panels appear (to be / being) in use more and more around the world.

5. We risked (to be stopped / being stopped) for driving too fast!

6. Instead of plastic, we keep (to be told / being told) to use alternative materials.

⑧ SCIENCE FACT AND FICTION

LESSON A

FUTURE FORMS WITH *WILL*
Future simple
Use *will* / *won't* + verb to make predictions about the future.
You'll drive an electric car in the future. / You **won't drive** a car with a gas engine anymore.
We often use adverbs of certainty with *will* to talk about how certain we are about our prediction:
The Earth will **certainly / definitely** *get warmer in the future.* (very certain)
Most people will **probably** *work from home.* (fairly certain)
I'll **possibly** *move to another country when I'm older.* (less certain)

When you use *will*, the adverb comes between *will* and the main verb. When you use *won't*, the adverb comes before *won't*: I **will definitely** buy an electric car. / I **definitely won't** buy an electric car.

We often use *I think* / *I don't think* . . . with the future simple: **I think it'll** snow tomorrow. **I don't think it'll** be sunny.

Future continuous
Use *will be* + verb + *-ing* to talk about an action that you know or think will be in progress at a certain point in time, or during a certain period of time, in the future:
This time tomorrow, I'll be flying to the Maldives! (at a point in time)
Next year, I'll be studying English at college. (over a period of time)

Future perfect
Use *will have* + past participle to talk about an action that is going to be completed at or before a certain time in the future:
By 2050, the global population **will have increased** *by 2 billion to 9 billion people in total.*
We're so late for the party! By the time we arrive, everyone else **will have gone** *home!*

Future perfect continuous
Use *will have been* + verb + *-ing* to talk about an action that is going to be in progress at some time in the future. It emphasizes that the action will take place over a period of time:
By 2040, I'll have been working here for thirty years.
At the end of this journey, we'll have been driving for more than 12 hours!

A Put the words in the correct order and identify the future form.

1. it / evening / will / definitely / rain / this _____

2. she'll / day / been / have / studying / all _____

3. I / go / out tonight / won't / probably _____

4. flying / for / be / six hours / we'll _____

5. by 2100, / the / have / by two degrees / increased / temperature / will _____
_____

6. won't / tomorrow / it / changed / by / have _____

7. I don't / he'll / think / come _____

8. arriving / at / be / the train / won't / noon _____

B Underline the correct words to complete the sentences.

1. I don't think I (will be / will have been) at work tomorrow.

2. By 2030, they'll (have landed / have been landing) an astronaut on Mars.

3. Rio is 500 kilometers away, so we'll (be driving / have been driving) for most of the day.

4. If we're still here at noon, we'll (be waiting / have been waiting) for three hours.

5. (Will you eat / Will you have eaten) by the time you get here?

6. In the future, more people (will probably become / will have been becoming) vegan.

7. Your parents are coming this weekend! How long (will they be staying / will they have stayed)?

8. After tonight's show, (I'll see / I'll have seen) this band five times!

LESSON B

CONNECTORS: REASON, RESULT, AND PURPOSE

Use *due to / because of / owing to / as a result of / because (of) / as / seeing as / given that* to explain why someones does something or why something happens.
Note that you can structure the sentence in two ways:

1. result + connector + reason: *The city is polluted **due to** the amount of traffic.*

2. connector + reason, + result: ***Due to** the amount of traffic, the city is polluted.*

Result	+ connector	+ reason (noun phrase)
The city is polluted	due to / because of / owing to / as a result of	the amount of traffic.

Result	+ connector	+ reason (subject + verb)
A lot of people drive to work	because / as / seeing as / given that	the public transportation system isn't very good.

Use *As a result, / Therefore, / That's why . . . / so / and so / and as a result (of this) / and therefore / and that's why* to introduce why someone does something or why something happens.

Reason	+ connector	+ result (subject + verb)
Citizen scientists take photos.	As a result, / Therefore, / That's why	we know more about climate change.
Citizen scientists take photos	, so / , and so / and as a result (of this), / and therefore, / , and that's why	

Use *in order to / so as to / in order that / so (that)* to explain the purpose of an action.
Note that you can structure the sentence in two ways:

3. action + connector + purpose: *Take a photo **in order to** share it.*

4. purpose + connector, + action: ***In order to** share it, take a photo.*

Action	+ connector	+ purpose (infinitive)
Citizen scientists take photos	in order to / so as to	help other scientists.

Action	+ connector	+ purpose (subject + verb)
Citizen scientists take photos	in order that / so (that)	we know more about climate change.

Register

In everyday English, we use connectors such *as because*, as, *so (that)* to talk about reasons, results and purposes. These types of connectors are less formal, and common in general communication:
*I need to leave work early **because** I'm going to the doctor.*
*Send me a message, **so** I know where to meet you.*

Other connectors such as *due to*, *because of*, *owing to*, *as a result*, *and therefore*, *in order to*, and *so as to* are more formal. They are more common when people give presentations or write formally about results, reasons, and purposes:

*Consumers are spending more money **as a result** of a growing economy.*

*The government is reducing taxes **in order to** encourage more public spending.*

A Underline the correct connector in these sentences.

1. We stayed at home today (because / because of) the rain.

2. People stopped using horses in the 19th century (owing to / given that) the invention of the engine.

3. We tested the water (in order to / in order that) look for pollution.

4. Can you help me today, (seeing as / due to) I helped you last week?

5. The feedback on our customer service was poor. (As a result, / As a result of) we've improved it.

6. I have an exam tomorrow morning. (So that / That's why) I'm not going out tonight.

7. There's no point in meeting, (owing to / given that) everyone else is away.

8. We're doing this exercise (so as to / so that) we can use connectors correctly.

B Make the two sentences into one sentence using the connector in parentheses.

1. I've started learning Chinese. I want to live in Beijing. (in order to)

2. All the shops are closed. It's a holiday. (as)

3. There's a strike by drivers. The buses aren't running. (due to)

4. Please send that package today. It's so urgent. (given that)

5. It was raining. We decided to stay home. (seeing as)

6. The students are studying their mistakes. They can learn from them. (so that)

 BODY MATTERS

LESSON A

COMPARATIVE FORMS WITH ADJECTIVES AND ADVERBS
Comparatives

Use comparative adjectives and adverbs to compare two things or people. Use them to say:

one has more or less quality than the other: *Your house is **bigger** than mine.* (adjective)

how a situation has changed: *The weather is getting **worse**.* (irregular adjective)

that a change is in progress: *Unemployment is growing **more quickly** this year.* (adverb)

Short adjectives (one syllable, or two syllables ending in -*y*): *old → older*, *big → bigger* / *happy → happier*	Long adjectives (two syllables or more): *beautiful → more / less beautiful*	Irregular adjectives: *good → better* *bad → worse* *far → further*
Short adverbs (one syllable): *fast → faster*, *hard → harder*	Long adverbs (two syllables or more): *happily → more / less happily*	Irregular adverbs: *well → better* *badly → worse*

Superlatives

Use superlative adjectives and adverbs to say that one thing or person has more or less of a certain quality than all others in the same group:

*Mount Everest is **the highest** mountain in the world.* (adjective)

*Who can run **the fastest** in your class?* (adverb)

Common expressions with superlative adjectives include:
one of the green**est** cities, **some of the** wor**st** traffic
the second / third bigg**est** city in the country
the most exciting thing **I've ever** done

Short adjectives (one syllable, or two syllables ending in -*y*): old → oldest, big → biggest	Long adjectives (two syllables or more): *beautiful → most / least beautiful*	Irregular adjectives: *good → best* *bad → worst* *far → furthest*
Short adverbs (one syllable): *fast → fastest, hard → hardest*	Long adverbs (two syllables or more): *happily → most / least happily*	Irregular adverbs: *well → best* *badly → worst*

As . . . as
Use *as* + adjective / adverb + *as* to compare two things and say that they are similar:
We are **as old as** *each other.* (adjective)
The two students work **as hard as** *each other.* (adverb)

Use *not as . . . as* to compare two things and say they are different:
My guitar **isn't as expensive as** *yours.* (adjective)
We both play the guitar, but I **don't play as well as** *you.* (irregular adverb)

A Find the mistake in each sentence and correct it.

1. Your car looks ~~more~~ newer than mine. _Your car looks newer than mine._

2. Martin can run the furthest than everyone else. _____

3. I think we work as harder as each other. _____

4. Singapore is one of most modern cities in Asia _____

5. I want to live in a biger house. _____

6. My hearing isn't as good than it used to be. _____

B Complete the second sentence so that it has the same meaning as the first. Use the word in parentheses and no more than four other words in each blank.

1. My new car is more expensive than my last one.

   (cheap) My new car _____ my last one.

2. Health is more important than things like money and fame.

   (most) Health is _____ in life.

3. The weather isn't any better today.

   (bad) The weather is _____ it was yesterday.

4. Can you play more quietly?

   (noisily) Can you play _____?

5. In my opinion, Peruvian food is the most delicious!

   (than) In my opinion, Peruvian food is _____ any other.

LESSON B

MODIFYING COMPARATIVE FORMS
Use modifiers (e.g., **a bit** *more*, **even** *more*, **by far** *the most*, **nearly** *as . . . as*) with comparative forms to show the degree of difference.

Comparatives

Use these modifiers to:

show small differences: *It's **a bit / a little / slightly** warmer today than yesterday.*
show big differences: *Shopping is **much / a lot / far** more convenient online than in stores.*
add emphasis: *I did **even** worse on the exam than I expected!*

Superlatives

Use the modifiers *easily* and *by far* with superlatives to say that something has much more of a particular quality than all the others:

*This is **easily** the best holiday I've ever had.*
*The blue whale is **by far** the biggest animal on Earth.*

As . . . as

Use these modifiers to show the degree of similarity or difference:

small differences: *A giraffe is **almost / nearly / not quite** as tall as a two-story house.*
big differences: *I think cats are **twice / three times** as smart as dogs. Dogs are**n't nearly** as intelligent (as cats).*
no difference, but to add emphasis: *I think dogs are **equally / just** as clever as cats.*

A   Replace the word in bold with one of the words in parentheses with the same meaning.

1. After taking some medicine, I feel **a little** better this morning. (slightly / even)

2. The traffic was bad, so it took me **much** longer to get here than normal. (easily / a lot)

3. We'd be **a lot** more effective if we worked together as a team. (by far / far)

4. This was **by far** the best party I've ever been to. (easily / almost)

5. A lion is **not quite** as fast as a cheetah. (nearly / not nearly)

6. I did **almost** as well as you on my test. (nearly / twice)

7. My brother is tall, but I'm **equally** as tall as him. If not taller! (almost / just)

B   Put these words in the correct order.

1. nearly / I used to be / as fit / as / I'm / not _____

2. here / the ice cream / far / is / better _____

3. times / we'll arrive / as / three / fast / on this route _____

4. this coat / bit / more / feels / a / comfortable _____

5. tall / as / not / I remember / quite / you're / as _____

6. elephants / are / the / far / cleverest / by / animals _____

 **10 KEEP IT LEGAL**

LESSON A

MODAL VERBS FOR CERTAINTY AND POSSIBILITY

Use the modal verbs *can, could, may, might,* and *must* to speculate about certainty and possibility in the present, future, and past:

must ➜ you are very certain that something is true
may, might, could ➜ it's possible something is true
may not, might not ➜ it's possible something is not true
can't, couldn't ➜ you are certain something is not true

Speculate about present events								
modal + bare infinitive				modal + *be* + verb + *-ing*				
He She	must can't	be be	the thief. at school.	They She	might could	be be	visiting meeting	friends. colleagues.
Speculate about future events and plans								
modal + bare infinitive				modal + *be* + verb + *-ing*				
It It	could might	rain get cold	tonight. this weekend.	They He	might not must	be be	coming planning	tomorrow. to come back.
Speculate about past events (often based on evidence)								
modal + *have* + past participle								
He She They	can't might must	have have have	gotten lost. (The route is easy.) broken down. (Her car is very old.) stolen the money. (No one else had the key to the safe.)					

A Rewrite the first sentence using the modal verb in parentheses to talk about present and future events.

1. It's possible that we'll go to court.

   (might) We _____ to court.

2. He isn't here, so he's definitely having lunch.

   (must) He isn't here, so he _____ lunch.

3. There's a chance the law will change next year.

   (could) The law _____ next year.

4. There's no way she's guilty of the crime.

   (can't) She _____ guilty of the crime.

5. The mugger and the victim live on the same street. Maybe they know each other.

   (might) The mugger and the victim live on the same street. They _____ each other.

B Complete these sentences about past events using the verbs in parentheses.

1. There's a mess in the kitchen again! My roommate _____ (must / have) another party.

2. She _____ (might / got lost). I wonder if I gave her the right address.

3. The building is surrounded by police, so the burglars _____ (can / not / escape).

4. The hacker _____ (may / stole) everyone's passwords and personal details.

5. Do you think they _____ (could / forgot) to lock the safe?

6. The security guards _____ (must / not / see) the thieves climb in through the skylight.

LESSON B

REPORTED SPEECH

Use reported speech to report someone's words. When you report someone's words, you often move the tenses "backwards." The reporting verb can be followed by *that*, but it is not necessary.

Direct speech	Reported speech
*The witness said, "I **know** the accused."* (simple present)	*The witness said (that) she **knew** the accused.* (simple past)
*The police officer said, "We'**re looking** into the case."* (present continuous)	*The police officer said (that) they **were looking** into the case."* (past continuous)
*The accused said, "I'**ve never been** to that bank in my life."* (present perfect)	*The accused said (that) she **had never been** to that bank in her life."* (past perfect)
*The leader of the gang said, "We **won't / can't** get caught."* (will / can)	*The leader of the gang said that they **wouldn't / couldn't** get caught.* (would / could)

No verb change in reported speech
You do not have to change the verb tense in reported speech:

if the information refers to facts that are still true, or in progress: "The speed limit is 90 kilometers per hour." ➜ She said that the speed limit is 90 kilometers per hour. / "We are changing the law." ➜ They said that they are changing the law.

when the reporting verb is in the simple present (*says / tells*): "I'm angry!" ➜ He **says** he'**s** angry.

when the spoken verb is in the past perfect or the past perfect continuous: "I **had been** there." ➜ He said he'**d been** there.

when the spoken modal verb is used: "You **must** follow the rules." ➜ I said you **must** follow the rules.

Change in pronouns, place, and time
When reporting, you might need to change other words:

Pronouns: "**I**'m feeling sick." ➜ The child said **she** was feeling sick.

Place: "Sit **over here**." ➜ The teacher told the student to sit **over there**.

Time: "I'm not at work **this week**." ➜ My friend said he wasn't at work **last week**.

Reported questions
To report *wh-* questions, the word order is the same as in affirmative sentences. For *yes / no* questions, use *if* or *whether* and do not use the auxiliary verb *do*.

"What are you doing here?" (*Wh-* question)	*The police officer asked the man **what he was doing there**.*
"Do you need any help?" (*Yes / No* question)	*He asked him **if / whether he needed any help**.*

Commands and requests

The police officer said, "Slow down."	*The police officer **told me to slow down**.*
The judge asked the jury, "Can you give your verdict?"	*The judge asked the jury **to give their verdict**.*

Reporting verbs
The most commonly used reporting verbs are *say / said* and *tell / told*:
The witness **said** that she knew the accused.
The witness **told the court** that she knew the accused.

You can also use other reporting verbs to summarize the meaning of the direct speech; for example:
"We all agree with the decision." ➜ Everyone **agreed** with the decision.
"I'm so sorry for being late." ➜ The student **apologized** for being late.

A Rewrite the direct speech as reported speech.

1. "I'm very angry with you!"   My mother said that _____.

2. "Gill is calling the police."   He said that Gill _____.

3. "We've found the stolen money."   The police said that they _____.

4. "I can't come this week."	Brian said that he _____ last week.	
5. "How much does it cost?"	She asked how much _____.	
6. "Do you know my brother?"	He asked if she _____.	
7. "Stop at the traffic lights."	The driving instructor told me _____.	
8. "Can you work late?"	My boss _____.	
9. "Mount Everest is the highest mountain."	The teacher _____.	
10. "I've been there twice before."	Ahmed _____.	

 **11 HUNGRY CONSUMERS**

LESSON A

NEGATIVE AND EMBEDDED QUESTIONS
Negative questions
You can ask questions using the negative form of the verb instead of the positive form:
Would you like to buy it? ➔ *Would**n't** you like to buy it?*
You often ask questions in the negative form in order to:

check something is correct or true: *Isn't this jacket on sale? Shouldn't the price be lower?*
show surprise or annoyance: *Haven't you eaten it yet? Don't you like my cooking?*
request something (and expect a negative answer): *Can't I take it now and pay later? Don't you give discounts?*

When you use negative questions in spoken English, you normally use the contracted form only:
Don't . . . ? / Do you not . . . ?

Embedded questions
Embedded questions make a question less direct and more polite or tentative:
Do you give a discount? (direct)   ➔ *Can I ask if you give a discount?* (less direct)

Common phrases to use in embedded questions include: *Can / Could I ask you if . . . / Do you know . . . ? / Do you have any idea . . . ? / I'd like to know . . . * / I was wondering *
(*These phrases introduce a statement, not a question, so do not use a question mark at the end.)

After these expressions, the word order is the same as for an affirmative sentence (with the subject before the verb):
Have they finished yet? ➔ *Do you know if **they have finished** yet?*

With *yes / no* questions, use *if / whether*:
Is this on sale? ➔ *I'd like to know **if / whether** this is on sale.*

With object questions, do not use the auxiliary verb *do / does / did* in the embedded question:
What did it cost to ship it? ➔ *I was wondering **what it cost** to ship it.*

Note: We often start a conversation with an embedded question and then continue with a more direct question:
A: *Excuse me, can I ask how much this is?* (embedded)
B: *Fifty dollars.*
A: *Really? Do you give discounts?* (direct)

A Put the words in the correct order to make negative and embedded questions.

1. phone / isn't / in your / your / bag / ? _____

2. you / I / can / it's / on sale / ask / if / ? _____

3. already / haven't / had / lunch / they / ? _____

4. I / you / was / knew / wondering / if / each other / . _____

5. shouldn't / vacation / on / you / be / ? _____

6. you / they / do / take / if / credit cards / know / ? _____

7. delivery price / isn't / included / the / ? _____

8. know / to / I'd / like / supermarket / where / the / is / . _____

B Write the questions as negative questions.

1. Has she sold any today? Hasn't she sold any today? _____

2. Can I order it online? _____

3. Have they come home yet? _____

4. Is this your lowest price? _____

5. Do you work long hours? _____

6. Are you buying a new pair of socks? _____

7. Did you get a lower price than that? _____

8. Could I have it delivered to my house? _____

LESSON B

QUESTION TAGS

Use question tags in informal speech to:

confirm something is true (and you already think it is): *It's twenty dollars, isn't it?*
check and clarify (if there is a misunderstanding): *It isn't twenty dollars, is it?*

When the main verb is affirmative, the question tag is negative: It**'s** *twenty dollars,* **isn't** *it?*
When the main verb is negative, the question tag is affirmative: *It* **isn't** *twenty dollars,* **is** *it?*
When the subject is a pronoun, repeat it: **You** *cooked this, didn't* **you**?
When the subject is a noun, use the appropriate pronoun: **Sally** *cooked this, didn't* **she**?
Note: Always use a comma before the question tag.

For the following verb forms, use the auxiliary or modal in the question tag.

be (*is, are, was, were*)	It's Bruno, **isn't** it? You're hungry, **aren't** you? He was at the party, **wasn't** he? They weren't happy with the food, **were** they?
Simple present (*do / does*)	You work in a restaurant, **don't** you? He doesn't like broccoli, **does** he?
Simple past (*did*)	She passed her exams, **didn't** she? He didn't get the job, **did** he?
Perfect and perfect continuous (*has / have*)	We've met before, **haven't** we? He's been cooking since six, **hasn't** he?
Modal verbs	I should go now, **shouldn't** I? I couldn't have another serving, **could** I?
Imperative (with imperative forms, use *will*)	Wash up your plates, **will** you? Don't forget to call me, **will** you?

A Match the sentence to the question tag.

1. It's Peter, _____   **a.** will you?

2. You didn't eat your burger, _____   **b.** do you?

3. We haven't shopped here before, _____   c. isn't it?

4. Those two people were in that movie, _____   d. weren't they?

5. You don't like soup, _____   e. did you?

6. Clean your room, _____   f. could you?

7. She works for my company, _____   g. doesn't she?

8. You couldn't go, _____   h. have we?

B Three sentences are correct (✓) and five sentences have a mistake (✗). Cross out the mistake and write the correct words.

1. You're late, aren't you? ✓ _____

2. She didn't finish her dinner, ~~didn't she~~? ✗ _did she?_ _____

3. We should have reserved a table, don't we? _____

4. They worked here, don't they? _____

5. Pass me a pen, will you? _____

6. She hasn't forgotten, forgot she? _____

7. Richard passed his test, has he? _____

8. You can come, too, can't you? _____

 POINTS OF VIEW

LESSON A

DETERMINERS

Determiners come before nouns and include articles, possessive adjectives, demonstratives, and quantifiers. Learners often make these common mistakes with determiners.

Type of determiner	Common mistakes	Explanation
Indefinite article (a / an)	~~I'm tour guide in Toronto. It's city in Canada.~~ ✗ I'm **a** tour guide in Toronto. It's **a** city in Canada. ✓	Use the indefinite article with everyday jobs, with one person or thing, with one of many, and to talk about things in a general way.
Definite article (the)	~~Himalayas have most stunning views in world.~~ ✗ **The** Himalayas have **the** most stunning views in the world. ✓	Use the definite article with superlatives, deserts, rivers, oceans, mountain ranges, groups of islands, geographical regions, unique and specific things.
No article	~~Go to the Cape Town in the South Africa.~~ ✗ Go to Cape Town in South Africa. ✓	Don't use an article with most countries, cities, lakes, mountains, languages, and school subjects.
Demonstratives (this, that, these, those, here, there)	~~Is these your luggage?~~ ✗ Is **this** your luggage? ✓ ~~Is this your car over there?~~ ✗ Is **that** your car over there? ✓	Use this / that with singular and non-count nouns. Use these / those with plural count nouns. Use this / these and here for objects near to you. Use that / those and there for objects further away.
Possessive adjectives (my, your, his, her, its, our, their)	~~Egypt is famous for it's pyramids.~~ ✗ Egypt is famous for **its** pyramids. ✓	Don't confuse its with it's (it is) or their with they're (they are).

Type of determiner	Common mistakes	Explanation
some, any	~~We have any water.~~ ✗ We have **some** water. ✓ ~~We don't have some water.~~ ✗ We don't have **any** water. ✓	Usually, use *some* in affirmative sentences and *any* in negative sentences and questions. We use *some* in questions such as offers.
less, fewer	~~You have less clothes.~~ ✗ You have **fewer** clothes. ✓	Use *less* with non-count nouns and *fewer* with plural count nouns.
little / a little, few / a few	~~A little tourists visit every year.~~ ✗ A few tourists visit every year. ✓ ~~Don't spend any more money. We have a little left!~~ ✗ Don't spend any more money. We have so **little** left! ✓	Use *few / a few* with plural count nouns. Use *little / a little* with non-count nouns. *A little / a few* has a positive meaning. *Little / few* has a negative meaning.
each, every	~~Give every of the people a T-shirt.~~ ✗ Give **each** of the people a T-shirt. ✓ Give **each** person a T-shirt. ✓ Give **every** person in the group a T-shirt. ✓	There is little change in meaning with *each* and *every*, but use *each* for one of two or more individual things, and *every* for all things in a group.

A Underline the correct word to complete each sentence. Underline X if no word is needed.

1. My father is (a / the) teacher in a large school.

2. Rio de Janeiro has (the / X) most visitors all year round.

3. (X / the) Mount Kilimanjaro is in (X / the) Tanzania.

4. (This / That) passport over there belongs to me.

5. There aren't (some / any) cafes near here.

6. (Every / Each) of the students needs his or her own pen.

7. (Less / Fewer) tourists visit this city every year.

8. I wish you'd bring (less / fewer) stuff with you on these trips.

9. (A few / Few) people visit this museum anymore. It's very sad.

10. I have (a little / little) money left, so we can afford lunch.

B Two sentences are correct and eight have a mistake. Correct the mistakes.

1. Mount Everest is the highest mountain ~~in world~~. in the world _____

2. J. K. Rowling is an author of the Harry Potter books. _____

3. I can't meet on weekend, but I can meet next Tuesday. _____

4. There's a plate in a kitchen. I'll get it for you. _____

5. The center of our city is always full of the tourists. _____

6. The coldest region is in north of the country. _____

7. Would you like some sugar with that? _____

8. You need to bring less bags with you. _____

9. Every major city has a tourist information center. _____

10. There are few buses to the airport. About three an hour. _____

LESSON B

CLEFT SENTENCES

We use cleft sentences to emphasize important information or our opinion. A cleft sentence is divided into two parts. The first part often uses the words *it + (be) / what . . . (be) / the thing . . . (be)*:

Normal sentence: *I like the pizza at this restaurant.*

Cleft sentences: ***What I like is*** *the pizza at this restaurant.*

It's *the pizza I like at this restaurant.*

The thing I like *(at this restaurant)* ***is*** *the pizza.*

Cleft sentences with *what*	
What I like is . . .	a good meal with lots of friends.
What surprises me is . . .	your opinion!
What you need to do is . . .	write your name here.
What happened was . . .	they gave me the wrong dish.
Cleft sentences with *it + is / was*	
It's your attitude (that) . . .	I don't like.
It's the manager (who / that) . . .	you need to speak to.
Cleft sentences with *thing / place / person / reason*	
The thing I like is . . .	a vacation on a sunny beach.
The best thing to do is . . .	talk to the manager.
The place (where) we always go is . . .	a quiet village in the mountains.
The person (who is) in charge is . . .	not here today.
The reason (why) I disagree is . . .	because / that you have no evidence!

A Match the two halves of the sentences.

1. What I love is _____

2. What happened was _____

3. The thing I like to eat most _____

4. It's the teacher _____

5. What you do is _____

6. It's his views on politics that _____

7. The reason why I agree _____

8. The continent I love to travel around _____

a. is pasta.

b. I disagree with.

c. a stunning view!

d. who you need to ask, not me!

e. press this button here.

f. we took the wrong train.

g. is Asia.

h. is because of the evidence.

B Rewrite the first sentence as a cleft sentence.

1. I like going to the movies on weekends.

What I like about weekends is _____*going to the movies*_____.

2. Switch the laptop on here.

What you need _____ the laptop on here.

3. I object to his impolite manners.

It's _____ to.

4. They have doubts about your idea.

The thing _____ your idea.

5. We oppose your plans because they are too expensive.

The reason why _____ too expensive.

6. Martin is in charge of customer service.

The person _____ Martin.

UNIT 2: LESSON B, VOCABULARY

D Work in pairs. You each have a different crossword with adjectives describing personal qualities.

   1. Prepare your clues to define your words (without using the word). For example: *willing—always wanting to help and do one's best.*

   2. Take turns asking for and giving a definition. When you guess a word, write it in your crossword.

STUDENT A

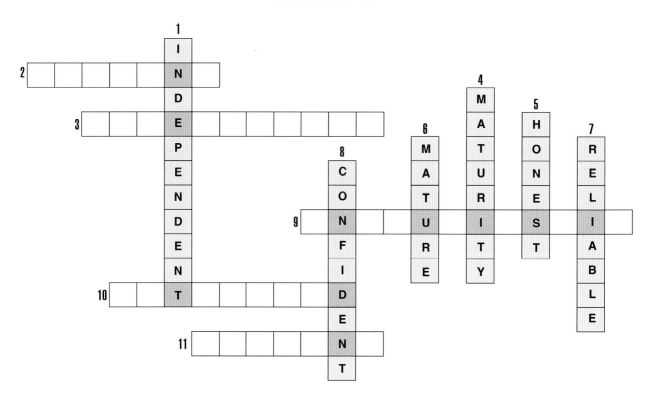

Down

1. independent

4. maturity

5. honest

6. mature

7. reliable

8. confident

UNIT 5: LESSON A, ACTIVE ENGLISH

B You are going to try to remember 15 words. You have 15 seconds to remember all the words. When your teacher says "GO," turn to page 214. When your teacher says "STOP," close your book and write the 15 words. Use one of the memory techniques in **A** or your own technique.

vision	majority	community
third	willing	mind
box	mute	flexible
week	truth	second
identity	alien	create

UNIT 2: LESSON B, VOCABULARY

D Work in pairs. You each have a different crossword with adjectives describing personal qualities.

1. Prepare your clues to define your words (without using the word). For example: *willing—always wanting to help and do one's best.*

2. Take turns asking for and giving a definition. When you guess a word, write it in your crossword.

STUDENT B

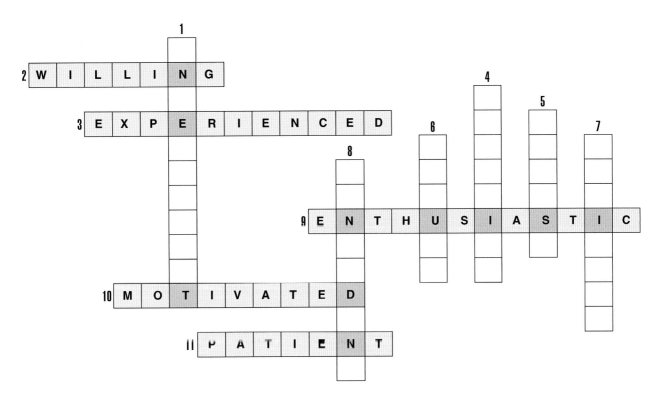

Across

2. willing

3. experienced

9. enthusiastic

10. motivated

11. patient

UNIT 6: LESSON A, SPEAKING

C Practice a similar conversation in pairs. You both watched the first episode of a new TV series shown in the pictures below. Student A describes the first episode. Student B has also seen the next episode of the series. (Student B turn to page 215.) Start the conversation when you are ready.

A Work in groups of three or four students and sit in a circle with one dice. You are going to tell some stories using the images below.

1. Roll the dice to see who goes first (highest goes first).

2. The first player rolls the dice and looks at the image that corresponds to the number they rolled on the dice. Use an idea from the image to tell the first sentence of a story.

3. The next player rolls the dice and continues the story with the next sentence.

4. Player three rolls the dice. Continue the story in this way until you have 12 sentences in total (using some images more than once). Try to use some storytelling adverbs.

Game 2

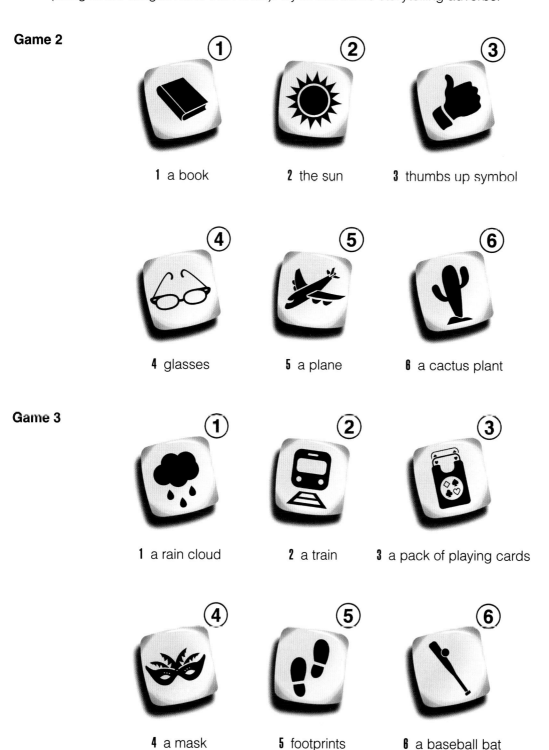

1 a book

2 the sun

3 thumbs up symbol

4 glasses

5 a plane

6 a cactus plant

Game 3

1 a rain cloud

2 a train

3 a pack of playing cards

4 a mask

5 footprints

6 a baseball bat

UNIT 8: LESSON A, ACTIVE ENGLISH

Student B

Picture 1 shows a street in the future. Describe it to your partner using future forms and find seven differences.

Picture 2 shows a home today. Describe it to your partner using present forms and find seven difforencoc.

UNIT 9: LESSON A, SPEAKING

D Now describe and compare the following:

UNIT 1 AN OPINION PARAGRAPH

[1]There are different arguments for and against digital communities and social media in our lives. Overall,[2] I feel they are a negative part of modern life. First,[3] we are always worried about having hundreds of online friends and so-called "followers," but most of them are not part of our actual circle of close friends. In addition,[3] many teenagers have anxiety about their online profile, and there is an increase in cyber bullying. Finally,[3] we spend so much of our time taking photos and looking at screens that we have forgotten how to have meaningful relationships. So, to sum up,[4] twenty-first century humans need to spend less time online and more time meeting face-to-face with people that they have something in common with.

[1]Use a topic sentence to introduce the subject of the paragraph.
[2]Explain which side of the argument you believe.
[3]Use sequence words such as *First* or *Second* to structure your arguments.
[4]Write a concluding sentence to sum up your overall opinion.

USEFUL EXPRESSIONS

There are different arguments for and against . . .
Overall / On the whole . . .
In my opinion / I feel / I think / I believe . . .
First / Second / Finally
In addition / Also / Not to mention . . .
So, to sum up / conclude

UNIT 2 A COVER LETTER

[1]Dear Ms. Rogers,

[2]I am writing in response to your advertisement for the position of Call Center Operator. Currently, I am completing my degree in Business Studies, and I will graduate at the end of this month.

[3]I believe that I am a confident and highly motivated person. Although I have not worked in insurance before, I did complete an internship last summer with a promotions company. During this time, I gained valuable office experience and worked as a reliable member of a team.

[4]I am available to interview in the next two weeks and would be able to start work in July. I live locally, but would be able to move if necessary.

[5]I'm attaching a copy of my resume, which gives details of my qualifications, skills, and experience. It also has the contact details of two people who are willing to provide references.

[6]I look forward to hearing from you.

Yours sincerely,

Ryan Kleon

[1]A formal beginning
[2]Where you saw the job advertisement, and your current situation
[3]A personal description suggesting why you are suitable
[4]Availability
[5]Attachments, resume, and references
[6]A formal ending

USEFUL EXPRESSIONS

Dear Sir or Madam / Dear Mr. / Mrs. / Ms.
I am writing to . . . / in response to . . . / with reference to . . .

I am attaching / enclosing . . .
Please find attached / enclosed . . .

I'm attaching my resume, which includes details of . . .
As you can see from the enclosed resume, . . .

I look forward to hearing from you.
If you have any further questions, do not hesitate to contact me.

Yours sincerely,
Best regards,

UNIT 3 A BIOGRAPHY

[1]Yayoi Kusama is a Japanese artist whose paintings are famous for their colorful dots. She is sometimes jokingly referred to as "the princess of polka dots," but her work is taken very seriously and sells for millions of dollars around the world.

[2]Kusama was born in 1929 into a very traditional Japanese family. She was the youngest of four children, and at that time a girl wasn't able to study art. However, at the age of ten, she had hallucinations in which flowers looked like dots, and they spoke to her. Privately, she started to draw these visions and developed a love of art.

[3]When she was 13, World War II began, and Kusama had to work in a military factory sewing parachutes. She remembers the darkness of the factory and the horror of war. Despite this period of her life, she learned to sew and work with fabric. These skills—along with the themes of war—can be seen in much of her later art.

[4]After the war, Kusama was able to go to art school, and she managed to sell some of her paintings. Later, she moved to the United States and became influenced by the pop-art movement of the sixties. She enjoyed great success, but eventually she returned to Japan in the seventies, in poor physical and mental health.

[5]For many years after, Kusama avoided publicity, but in 1993, she showed her paintings at an exhibition in Venice and she became globally famous once more. Nowadays, art critics love her work, and artists including Andy Warhol, Yoko Ono, and Damien Hirst have all said she has influenced them.

[1]A general introduction to the person
[2]A historical description of childhood
[3]The next period and difficulties in life
[4]How early success began
[5]The impact of this person in the present day

USEFUL PHRASES	
was born in (year)	the oldest / youngest of four children
at this / that time	was able to / wasn't able to
At the age of . . .	. . . managed to / succeeded in . . .
Despite this period of her life . . .	. . . influenced by . . .
After the war . . .	. . . enjoyed great success . . .
Later, she moved to . . .	
For many years after,	
Nowadays, . . .	

UNIT 4 A NEWS ARTICLE

> [1]**UNIVERSITY STUDENTS RAISE MONEY TO SEND JANITOR ON VACATION**
>
> [2]A janitor at the University of Bristol in the UK has been given £1,500 by the students.
>
> [3]Herman Gordon and his wife had wished they could see their family back in Jamaica, but as a part-time cleaner, Herman couldn't afford the plane ticket. So, he was amazed when students at Bristol University gave him the ticket with a note that said, [4]"You have brightened many of our days and we want you to know that we love and appreciate you."
>
> [5]Hadi Al-Zubaidi, a 20-year-old medicine student, set up an online funding page and invited other students to donate money because Herman "spends his whole time being nice to everybody. It's about time we were nice to him." Within 5 days, over 230 students had donated money.
>
> [6]When Herman received the money, he was overcome with emotion and started to cry with happiness.

[1]Include a headline.
[2]Introduce the main story with a statement of fact.
[3]Give background information on who, what, where, and when.
[4]Include quotes.
[5]Include numbers and statistics.
[6]Add details, especially about human emotions.

UNIT 5 REFLECTIVE LEARNING JOURNAL

Writing a learning journal is a good way to reflect on your own progress as a language learner and think about how you can improve. Reflective writing is also important at school or in the workplace when you have to evaluate a project or reflect on your own performance.

> March 19th
>
> [1]What did I learn today?
>
> I had my third lesson in Chinese today. [2]The teacher introduced the numbers one to ten and we tried writing in Chinese for the first time. She showed us cards with the number on one side and the Chinese character on the other. She said the word and we repeated it.
>
> [1]What went well?
>
> At first, learning to say the numbers was difficult because they don't sound anything like numbers in my native language. But slowly I picked them up, and learning by repetition really helped. We also enjoyed working in pairs and testing each other.
>
> What did I want more of?
>
> I found writing the Chinese characters for numbers really hard. The first three numbers are just one, two, or three lines, so they're easy, but the rest are more complicated. I wanted more time to practice these.
>
> What do I need to work on next?
>
> - [3]I need to review the numbers and become more confident with the pronunciation.
> - Learning how to write in Chinese needs a lot of work. [4]I plan to try writing a few every night before bed.

There are no strict rules on writing a journal.

[1]Using questions is one useful way to structure your writing.
[2]Try to include real examples from the lesson.
[3]Bullet points are a good way to list your main ideas.
[4]Include practical ideas.

UNIT 6 A SHORT STORY

> ### [1]A Modern-day Cinderella
>
> [2]Everyone was gorging themselves at the party when a poor-looking man rushed through the door. He [3]was gasping for breath and holding his stomach. Awkwardly, the chatter stopped, and the guests stared.
>
> The silence was broken by Chia—the host of our gathering—who stepped forward and whispered in the man's ear. The man replied, "Water."
>
> [4]Gradually, the party resumed, and Chia encouraged the man to stay. At first, he seemed like he wanted to leave, but Chia stayed by his side, and the two of them continued to chat. From time to time, people [5]glanced across at the couple but left them alone.
>
> [4]Suddenly, it was five minutes to midnight. The man jumped to his feet, thanked everyone, and hurried to the front door. Chia followed him, but he left without a word of goodbye.
>
> Everyone crowded around Chia: Who was he? Where did he come from? She [5]sighed and said she knew none of the answers. Then one of the guests picked up a scribbled note from the floor with Chia's name. The man [3]had left a number.

[1]Give your story an interesting title.
[2]Begin with a descriptive opening sentence.
[3]Use a variety of narrative tenses.
[4]Use a variety of adverbs.
[5]Use descriptive language.

UNIT 7 A REPORT

> ### [1]Proposals for Sustainability in the Town
>
> [2]Following the council's recent meeting to discuss sustainability, three proposals have been made:
>
> [3]Recycling bins
>
> Members of the public have reported that there are not enough recycling bins in the town center. So, it is proposed that new, colorful bins should be placed around the town with signs for plastic, paper, or metal.
>
> [3]Electric buses
>
> Diesel buses [4]are currently being replaced with electric buses. [4]This project began last year, but the change is taking longer than expected. It is now hoped that all buses will be electric in two years' time.
>
> [3]Cycling days
>
> It is also suggested that we introduce cycling days to the town. These are special days when adults and children are encouraged to bike to work and school. Cars and private vehicles will be banned on these days.
>
> [5]Before these proposals are finally agreed on, the council invites people in the town to email their views to feedback@council.org.

[1]Give your report a title.
[2]Introduce the report.
[3]Use clear subheadings.
[4]Reports are usually impersonal. Use passive and active forms.
[5]Include a conclusion with an action plan.

UNIT 8 A "FOR AND AGAINST" ESSAY

---

[1]The Impact of Space Tourism

[2]We are in the early stages of space tourism, where people will pay large sums of money in order to orbit the Earth. There are different arguments for and against this new kind of tourism.

[3]Some people believe it will have a positive impact on the future. First, [4]it will lead to new scientific discoveries and the possibility of living in space. Second, it is a new industry, so it will bring new jobs. Third, it will be enjoyable and exciting, which has a positive impact of people's health.

[5]However, other people are less optimistic. They forecast that space tourism will [6]result in faster global warming [6]due to the rockets burning fossil fuels. There will also be a social impact because only rich people will be able to afford it; most people will never have the opportunity to enjoy such tourism.

[7]Overall, I feel that space tourism will have a positive impact on our lives and, given that we are in the early stages, I think the cost will decrease, so more people will eventually have the opportunity to visit space.

---

[1]Give your essay a clear title.
[2]Introduce the main topic.
[3]Paragraph 2 gives the arguments *for*.
[4]Because this is about the future, the writer uses *will*.
[5]Paragraph 3 introduces the arguments *against*.
[6]Use vocabulary and connectors for describing causes, reasons, and results.
[7]End with your overall view.

UNIT 9 A SUMMARY OF DATA

---

[1]Pet Ownership Survey

[1]Survey method
[2]A survey into pet ownership was carried out with more than 27,000 consumers aged 15 and older, from 22 different countries. They were interviewed online.

[1]Results
[3]There were a number of key results showing similarities and differences, both globally and between countries.

[1]Internationally
Globally, over half of people [5](57%) have at least one pet. Out of these, dogs and cats are [4]by far the most popular types of pet. People are three times more likely to own a dog (33%) or twice more likely to own a cat (23%) than any other pet. Next, fish (12%) are twice as popular as birds or other pets. Globally, other pets, such as rabbits, are just as popular as birds (both 6%).

[1]By gender
[6]Compared to the international results, the results by gender are very similar, with only a few small differences. Dogs and cats are slightly more popular with women, whereas fish are a little more popular with men. Overall, however, there is very little difference between them.

[1]By top three countries
A comparison of the results by country shows a few greater differences. For example, pet fish are the most popular in China (17%). [6]In contrast, cats are much more popular than dogs in Russia. Cats are also popular in the US (39%), but they aren't nearly as popular as dogs in Argentina (66%).

---

[1]When you summarize key results and data, use clear titles and subheadings.
[2]Explain how the survey was done and who took part.
[3]Sum up key similarities and differences.
[4]Use modifiers and comparative forms.
[5]Sometimes, add the actual result in parentheses for clarification.
[6]Use connectors for comparing.

UNIT 10 AN ANNOUNCEMENT

[1]Dear all,

[2]As many of you will know, a recent incident of theft was reported by a member of staff. Money and personal items were taken from this person's bag on her desk. On the same day, an unknown person was seen walking around the building. One member of staff asked him if he needed help, but he left quickly afterwards. We assume he must have been the person responsible.

[3]The police were informed the same day, and they have advised us to review our security policies. As a result, please note the following:

- [4]Staff are reminded to wear their identity badges at all times. If you forget to carry one, security will not let you in the building.
- We have asked a security firm to install more cameras, so movement in every part of the building can be monitored.
- Any visitors to the building must be accompanied at all times. Anyone who is alone and not wearing a badge should be reported to security.
- Some staff [5]have also asked if security in the garage can be improved, so we are installing further lighting and cameras in this area.

[6]The safety and security of everyone who works in this building is our top priority. In addition to the procedures above, we would like to remind everyone to keep their personal belongings with them at all times and report any suspicious behavior to security immediately.

[7]If you have any further questions about this issue, feel free to email me at any time.

[1]With formal writing, use *Dear* instead of *Hi*.
[2]Give background and reasons.
[3]Introduce the main points.
[4]You can use bullet points for lists of items.
[5]Report what people have said.
[6]Conclude.
[7]Invite further contact if necessary.

UNIT 11 A COMPLAINT

[1]Dear Sir or Madam,

[2]I am writing to complain about my recent meal at your restaurant. I visited on July 21st with my family to celebrate my daughter's graduation.

We ordered drinks and garlic bread as starters. [3]First, the waiter got our drinks order wrong—twice. And then we had a very long wait for the garlic bread, which also turned out to be stale. When we complained, the waiter seemed unsurprised.

[3]Next came the main course—again, after an extremely long time—and my fish was cold. But much worse was that my daughter, who is a vegetarian, found pieces of chicken in her salad. I asked to speak to the manager, but was told she wasn't available and that I would have to contact her in writing.

In the end, I paid for what we had eaten and left. I now regret this decision, and I'd be grateful if you would reimburse the full cost of our meal. [4]I've enclosed a copy of the receipt. [5]I'd also like to know what action you will take to improve your levels of customer service in the future.

[6]I look forward to hearing from you.

[6]Sincerely,
P. J. Rosling

[1]Use *Dear Sir or Madam* if you don't know the name of the person.
[2]State the reason for writing.
[3]Describe in detail what happened.
[4]Say if you have enclosed anything with the letter (or attached it to an email).
[5]You can use embedded questions in formal letters or emails.
[6]End the letter formally and politely.

USEFUL PHRASES FOR FORMAL LETTERS

Dear Mr. / Mrs. / Ms. / Dear Sir or Madam,
I am writing to . . . / With reference to . . .
I have enclosed a copy of . . . / Please find attached a copy of . . .
I'd be grateful if you would . . . / I'd like to know if . . .
I look forward to hearing from you.
If you have any further questions, please do not hesitate to ask.
Sincerely, / Yours sincerely,

UNIT 12 A SPEECH

[1]I'm here today to talk to you about something that I strongly believe in. I'd like to make the case for paying students to attend high school. [2]You might think this sounds like an extreme idea, but let me tell you the reasons why I'm in favor of this.

[3]First, I'm seventeen years old, and I attend school. I live with my parents, and they feed me. Without them, I couldn't get an education. But not every seventeen-year-old is as lucky as me. Some students have to work, and [4]it's the reason why they don't get a good education.

Here's another argument. [5]Did you know that in this country, the overall school absence rate is nearly [6]5%? One in every twenty students misses school regularly. How can we change this [7]unbelievable figure? Well, one way would be to pay students, or, as one school has done successfully, have schools pay students a cash bonus at the end of every term for 100% attendance.

My final point is that paying students to attend school would teach kids about earning money and how to manage money from a young age. It's a benefit that they will need later in life.

[8]So, to sum up, I'd like to propose we start paying students when they start high school, which would make a better education available to all. Thank you for listening. Are there any questions?

[1]Introduce your talk.
[2]Give your reasons.
[3]Make your speech personal.
[4]Use cleft sentences to add emphasis.
[5]Use rhetorical questions.
[6]Quote figures and data.
[7]Use emotive words.
[8]Conclude and ask for questions.

CREDITS